SOCIAL POLICY AND SOCIAL WORK
Critical Essays on the Welfare State

MODERN APPLICATIONS OF SOCIAL WORK

An Aldine de Gruyter Series of Texts and Monographs

SERIES EDITOR

James K. Whittaker

Ralph E. Anderson and Irl Carter, **Human Behavior in the Social Environment: A Social Systems Approach** (fourth edition)

Richard P. Barth and Marianne Berry, **Adoption and Disruption: Rates, Risks, and Responses**

Larry K. Brendtro and Arlin E. Ness, **Re-Educating Troubled Youth: Environments for Teaching and Treatment**

Kathleen Ell and Helen Northen, **Families and Health Care: Psychosocial Practice**

Marian Fatout, **Models for Change in Social Group Work**

Mark Fraser, Peter J. Pecora, and David Haapala (eds.), **Families in Crisis: The Impact of Intensive Family Preservation**

James Garbarino, **Children and Families in the Social Environment**

James Garbarino, Patrick E. Brookhouser, Karen J. Authier, and Associates, **Special Children—Special Risks: The Maltreatment of Children with Disabilities**

James Garbarino, Cynthia J. Schellenbach, Janet Sebes, and Associates, **Troubled Youth, Troubled Families: Understanding Families At-Risk for Adolescent Maltreatment**

Roberta Greene, **Social Work with the Aged and Their Families**

Roberta R. Greene and Paul H. Ephross, **Human Behavior Theory and Social Work Practice**

Roberta Greene and Betsy Vourlekis (eds.), **Social Work Case Management**

Jill Kinney, David Haapala, and Charlotte Booth, **Keeping Families Together: The Homebuilders Model**

Paul K.H. Kim (ed.), **Serving the Elderly: Skills for Practice**

Robert M. Moroney, **Shared Responsibility: Families and Social Policy**

Robert M. Moroney, **Social Policy and Social Work**

Peter J. Pecora and Mark Fraser, **A Practical Guide to Evaluating Family Preservation Services**

Peter J. Pecora, James K. Whittaker, Anthony N. Maluccio, Richard P. Barth, and Robert D. Plotnick, **The Child Welfare Challenge: Policy, Practice, and Research**

Steven P. Schinke (ed.), **Behavioral Methods in Social Welfare**

Albert E. Trieschman, James K. Whittaker, and Larry K. Brendtro, **The Other 23 Hours: Child-Care Work with Emotionally Disturbed Children in a Therapeutic Milieu**

Deborah Valentine and Patricia G. Conway, **Guide for Helping the Natural Healer**

Harry H. Vorrath and Larry K. Brendtro, **Positive Peer Culture** (second edition)

Heather B. Weiss and Francine H. Jacobs (eds.), **Evaluating Family Programs**

James K. Whittaker and James Garbarino, **Social Support Networks: Informal Helping in the Human Services**

James K. Whittaker, Jill Kinney, Elizabeth M. Tracy, and Charlotte Booth (eds.), **Reaching High-Risk Families: Intensive Family Preservation in Human Services**

James K. Whittaker and Elizabeth M. Tracy, **Social Treatment, 2nd Edition: An Introduction to Interpersonal Helping in Social Work Practice**

Hide Yamatani, **Applied Social Work Research: An Explanatory Framework**

SOCIAL POLICY AND SOCIAL WORK
Critical Essays on the Welfare State

ROBERT M. MORONEY

ALDINE DE GRUYTER
New York

ABOUT THE AUTHOR

Robert M. Moroney is Professor of Social Policy and Planning, School of Social Work, Arizona State University. Dr. Moroney has been a major contributor to numerous journals and is the author of several books (including *Shared Responsibility* published by Aldine de Gruyter, 1986). He currently serves as a board member of the Rosalyn Carter Institute for Human Development.

ALDINE DE GRUYTER
A division of Walter de Gruyter, Inc.
200 Saw Mill River Road
Hawthorne, New York 10532

The paper used in this publication meets the minimum requirements of American National Standards for Information Sciences—Permanence of Paper for Printed Library Materials, ANSI Z39.48-1984.

Library of Congress Cataloging-in-Publication Data
Moroney, Robert, 1936-
    Social policy and social work : critical essays on the welfare
state / Robert M. Moroney.
        p.   cm. — (Modern applications of social work)
    Includes bibliographical references (p.) and indexes.
    ISBN 0-202-36061-X (cloth). — ISBN 0-202-36062-8 (paper)
    1. Public welfare—United States.   2. Social service—United
States.   3. United States—Social policy.   I. Title.   II. Series.
HV95.M66 1991
861.973—dc20   90-49124
                                                                              CIP

Manufactured in the United States of America
10 9 8 7 6 5 4 3 2 1

*To Monica, Micheen,
and Jeanine*

CONTENTS

PREFACE

Taken separately, the ideas expressed in this book are not new. Other analysts have used concepts associated with political economy; still others have introduced normative frameworks. This book attempts to integrate both.

Throughout this book, we argue that it is only possible to understand our system of social policies by understanding our particular political economy. The term *political economy* itself is not familiar to most people, and yet, until this century, political economy was a subject taught at most universities. Political economists were those who studied the relationship between the economic and political systems of a particular country, a relationship characterized as one in which the primary goal of the state was to further the goals of the prevailing economic system. Social policies were instruments used by the state to achieve these ends. It has only been in this century that, in an attempt to remove the social sciences from any hint of being normative, the economic and political systems have been split into two distinct disciplines: economics and political science.

What I find troublesome, however, is that, when asked if they have heard the term *political economy,* most students I have taught over the past 20 years, associate it with socialism and communism. They seem to be unaware that our capitalist society, with its assumptions of free enterprise, is a type of political economy that needs to be studied if we are to understand why we have the social policies we have. They are there for a reason.

Our purpose is not to suggest that capitalism is the "enemy" and that the solution requires finding an alternative. While we do suggest that some forms of capitalism, such as those found in a number of European countries, offer a more balanced perspective on the relationship between economic and social objectives and define the functions of the state, industry, and the workforce in less hostile and competitive terms, our major concern in this book is to identify where and under what conditions social policies intersect with economic policies. As we point out, capitalism is a system that inevitably produces cycles of growth followed by cycles of recession—cycles of inflation and cycles of high unemployment. A primary task of the welfare state, then, becomes one of humanizing these cycles, of buffering the periodic hardships suffered by some people, and of providing an infrastructure for those who seem to be rejected by the economic system. It is a system in which there are winners and losers, and more often than not we can predict who the winners and losers will be. This becomes critical when our beliefs about the free-enterprise system are not supported by empirical data, e.g., economic growth does not benefit all—the benefits only trickle down so far.

A second framework used in the analysis is one that attempts to tease out the underlying assumptions of our political economy as they relate to our understanding of human relationships and to balance these assumptions with alternative perspectives. We argue that an emphasis on individualism and freedom runs counter to notions of community and interdependence and that the trade-offs need to be exposed. Furthermore, we suggest that this belief in freedom and individualism has produced a somewhat divided society in which people with needs in common are unwittingly pitted against each other as they compete for scarce resources.

Third, we develop the analysis by choosing six policy areas. Three of these deal with substantive areas: (1) income maintenance, (2) housing, and (3) the personal social services. Three others deal with population groups: (1) families and children, (2) the elderly, and 3) the poor. The reader will quickly see the many overlaps between the chapters. This was done purposely. Our choice of these six areas is not offered as an exhaustive list of the major policy issues. While we deal with Medicare and Medicaid in some depth in the chapter focusing on the elderly, the issue of health care could have been treated more comprehensively in a separate chapter. We chose those six to demonstrate that the frameworks used have relevance in analyzing either substantive areas or target populations.

One additional comment needs to be made. In dealing with each example of policy, we have taken time to trace its history. We recognize that many students today either believe that history has nothing to offer or that history began the day they were born. Furthermore, they argue, history is not exciting. We cannot argue that history is exciting (excitement is in the eye of the beholder) but we can argue that to ignore history is to arrive at an incomplete and at times an inaccurate understanding of that policy area.

Finally a few words on the subtitle of this book: *Critical Essays on the Welfare State*. There are two parts to this: (1) critical essays, and (2) essays on the welfare state. These two phrases are used in acknowledgement of the contributions of two theorists, Jürgen Habermas and Richard Titmuss.

Habermas, the current leader of the Frankfurt School of Critical Theory, has forcefully argued the need to integrate empirical analysis with a concern for normative questions. For Habermas, analysis needs to be grounded in acceptable methodological rigor, but it also must go beyond the limits imposed by logical positivists. The analyst cannot be "detached" and value free when he or she deals with policy issues. Rather, it is appropriate for the analyst to go beyond description and explanation and to provide insight or understanding into the "why" of policies, especially if those policies strengthen or maintain inequalities in that society. He urges the analyst to probe and uncover contradictions so that corrective action might become part of the decision-making discussion.

Titmuss, on the other hand, is more widely known and has long been an advocate for universal services and the building of communities through social policies. Many of the seminal ideas he introduced in his 1958 publication, *Essays on the Welfare State,* are found throughout this analysis and are as useful today as they were then.

CHAPTER 1

THE FIELD OF POLICY

The purpose of this chapter is to introduce and then explore the concept of policy as a process of decision-making. Rather than attempting to offer a precise definition of policy at the outset, we begin instead with the concept of decision-making and then describe policy analysis in terms of four significant "decision" questions:

- What *should* be done when confronted with a situation that has been labeled a problem?
- What *can* be done?
- What *must* be done?
- *By whom* should it be done?

The relevance of these four questions as a general guide to policy formulation and analysis is discussed in the context of the Social Security Act.

We then examine a number of key issues—always found in policy debates in this country—which are concerned with rationales for government intervention: under what conditions and for what purposes should government become involved in the lives of its citizens? Explicit in our treatment of social policy is the importance of political economy as it shapes social policy. We argue that it is impossible to analyze policy without (1) acknowledging the interrelationship between political and economic processes, and (2) recognizing that the political economy of a society, whether it be some form of capitalism or socialism, will determine that society's social policies. Political economy, as used in this book, recognizes that the primary role of the state is to support the existing economic system and that social policies are instruments used by the state to achieve economic objectives. We will argue throughout our analysis that unless this notion of interrelationship is under-

1

stood, it is not possible to understand our existing policies, e.g., income maintenance, housing, personal service, and mental health.

Decision Making and Choice

Policy is primarily concerned with decision making and choosing among alternative courses of action. Choices have to be made among competing claims for resources, each of which may be reasonable or at least be perceived as reasonable by some group. Policy might involve the question of allocating resources between, e.g., defense, transportation, and social programs. It might be concerned with choosing between specific military systems or choosing between health programs for children or for the aged. To complicate this decision-making or choice process even further, we are also faced with issues involving the future. Shall we continue to consume existing natural resources at a rate that will leave little for future generations or shall we ration their use now so that adequate resources will be available for our children and grandchildren? Shall we continue to allow the national debt to increase (with its impact on the federal deficit) so that our children's and their children's future is heavily mortgaged before they are even born? An overriding concern in all of these situations is a term used by economists—*opportunity costs*. Simply stated, this means that once a decision is made to support one goal or claim, e.g., health programs for the aged, we have, de facto, made a decision to forgo supporting other valued goals or claims.

Choices also have to be made between proposed implementation strategies once a goal has been established. These would include:

- issues of financing and reimbursement, e.g., sources of revenue and formulas for sharing costs;
- whether to use market mechanisms or public provision, or some combination of both;
- the appropriateness of administrative mechanisms for a particular policy; and
- level(s) of government involvement and appropriateness of roles.

Policy formulation, then, involves a *process* of decision-making that results in selecting a course of action. It is a dynamic activity that is open to modification when conditions change. The products of policy (e.g., a law, a set of regulations, or a judicial statement) are also subject to modification over time for the same reasons. Policy, therefore, is a fairly stable but potentially changeable statement of a desired *end* or goal. The development of policy involves the identification of alternative strategies or *means* to achieve these goals, and the identification and application of criteria judged useful in choosing among the strategies. Policy is also concerned with the *implementation* of the chosen strategy and, finally, the *evaluation* of its impact. Because policy contains statements of goals and values, depends on procedures to analyze alternatives, and is concerned with implementation strategies and evaluation of results, it consequently includes both normative and technical aspects.

Policy formulation begins with the following:

- the definition of the problem;
- the presentation of relevant information;
- a critical appraisal of the dynamics of the underlying issue, and
- working through the implications of various courses of action.

Analysis, the cornerstone of the policy process, begins with description. This descriptive function raises a variety of questions from a range of sources and, to the extent possible, ensures a balanced perspective. Analysis clarifies and sharpens the discussion. This does not mean, however, that the analysis is value neutral or value free.

Policymakers *label* a condition or situation a "problem" to be corrected or, in some instances, a source of future problems. We are using the term *problem* in a specific way: as a condition that needs addressing, one on which action will be taken. This labeling is based in part on the analysis and in part on the beliefs and values of the policymaker. At this point in the process we have shifted from a purely descriptive/analytic set of activities to one that integrates both descriptive and normative aspects or dimensions— one that addresses the question of *what should be done*.

When sufficient consensus is reached by the policymakers and political preferences have emerged, short- and long-range strategies need to be developed. These are often shaped by the existing state of knowledge and technology, the availability of resources, and political feasibility. The question now shifts from what should be done to *what can be done*.

Since many so-called experts disagree on ways to solve complex social problems, we are usually faced with choosing among alternative solutions. Procedures are required to weigh carefully each proposal—procedures that are grounded in competing and often contradictory values, emphasizing for example:

- individual freedom
- efficiency
- effectiveness
- equality
- equity
- comparative justice.

As will be argued throughout this book, these and other values cannot be simultaneously *maximized*—a concept used by economists, which in essence means you can only realize one value at the expense of the others.

Finally, policy is concerned with implementation issues. These include questions of coverage, financing, administrative structures, personnel requirements, and the roles of the public and private sectors.

The policy process, then, is a blend of fact and preference. The participants in this process include policymakers, policy analysts, policy implementers, and policy influencers or special-interest groups advocating specific policies. While roles often become merged, or at least blurred, these are the actors (Rein 1970; Moroney 1976, 1986; Baumheimer and Schorr 1977).

The above description of the general policy process can be thought of as a response to four fundamental questions: What should be done? What can be done? What must be done? By whom should it be done? The following example takes this framework and applies it the the Social Security Act of 1935.

The Social Security Act of 1935: An Example

What Should Be Done?

This question is normative in that it seeks to identify the goal we hope to achieve. We often assume that the (elected) policymaker has the responsibility to answer the question in that he or she, having been elected, is seen as the person who in theory has offered his or her ideas, proposals, or even vision to an electorate, and in being elected has had these affirmed by "the people." The policymaker is given a mandate and is held accountable through an elaborate system of political checks and balances, the ultimate being the reelection process. In turn, elected officials appoint administrators who not only have the responsibility to implement policies, but in reality will also make policies.

For example, in 1935, Congress passed the Social Security Act, legislation emphasizing that the economic security of the people of the United States was an important national goal. No comparable public statement had existed before. Historically, American social policy was shaped by a belief in laissez-faire economics. Initially this position assumed that the positive force of the free-enterprise system far outweighed the potential negative impact of government intervention in the economy or in the lives of people. In fact, state intervention was thought to be legitimate only if its purpose was to strengthen and support the free market's continuing operation.

In time, society began to recognize the need to humanize the economic system—to develop a buffer by providing corrective measures for individuals who were shunted aside by the market system. These attempts to balance individual and collective welfare with the free-enterprise system were grounded in the long-standing poor law tradition. People were divided into two groups: (1) a minority, or residual group, who needed assistance to survive, and (2) the majority, who could take care of their own needs without government intervention.

Almost all social policy prior to the Social Security Act purposely ignored the well-being of this majority in the belief that they would always be self-sufficient. When these individuals did experience difficulty, the cause of their problems was believed to be either a moral flaw in their character or some other personal deficit (Wilensky and Lebeaux 1965).

The Social Security Act was a departure from this view insofar as we eventually recognized that modernization and industrialization had created risks and consequences that potentially affected *all people* and not just a small percentage of the population (Wilensky and Lebeaux 1965; Hobbs et al. 1984). When we believed that only small numbers of people were involved, we could and did, in Ryan's (1976) term, "blame the victim." However, when these numbers increased (as they did during the depression), this belief became untenable. Not only did the numbers of unemployed people increase dramatically—4 million in 1930, 8 million in 1931, 12 million in 1932, 18 million in 1933—but these people had formerly been productive and still wanted to work. To argue that they were the cause of their own unemployment was not only irrational but was politically untenable.

Beginning with the Social Security Act, enacted over fifty years ago, we have responded to the question What should be done? by identifying basic goods and services citizens should have as rights:

- economic security;
- employment (the Federal Employment Act of 1946 expressed the goal of full employment for everyone able to work);
- housing (the Housing Act of 1949 stated that all Americans have "the right to decent housing, in decent surroundings of their choosing");
- health (the Comprehensive Health Planning Act of 1967 stated that Americans have the right to the highest quality of health care services available);
- education for handicapped children (P.L. 94-142 of 1975 insured the provision of a free, appropriate public education for all).

What Can Be Done?

The translation of these broad goals into actual programs proved to be much more elusive. While politically tenable, goals are stated in so general a fashion they cannot become working objectives (Baumheimer and Schorr 1977). Specific proposals are shaped by the availability of resources and competing demands for those resources, knowledge and technology, political acceptability, and administrative capability. Concern about a situation is, of course, a necessary prerequisite, but unless viable strategies are available, this concern has limited value.

Today, social welfare analysts have identified a number of mechanisms that government might use to achieve the economic security of its citizens. The government can, for example,

- act as employer, e.g., through public works projects;
- stimulate the development of jobs through the tax system;
- subsidize jobs for the hard-core unemployed as it did in the automobile industry during the 1960s;
- stimulate economic growth at the national and state levels under the assumption that such growth would eventually "trickle down" to all people; and
- transfer funds directly to those who are "economically insecure," e.g., social insurance, unemployment insurance, family allowances, public assistance, or negative income tax programs.

It is important to note, however, that each of the strategies emerges from a different set of assumptions about the nature of the problem. Moreover, proponents of one solution argue that certain strategies are counterproductive to other strategies, e.g., economic growth is negatively affected when direct transfers are substantial or when expenditures for social programs reach a certain level.

While our "knowledge" today has produced a range of possible theories leading to multiple proposals, such was not the case during the depression. By 1932 the economy was paralyzed, public confidence was shaken, and the clamor for increased governmental action was growing. One problem facing the policy analysts and decision-makers of the day was that there were few precedents on which to fall back. Furthermore, the number and types of alternatives were limited to those that emphasized the need to strengthen the existing free-enterprise system.

Two major strategies were eventually employed: (1) social insurance, and (2) social assistance. Social insurance provided benefits to the aged who could not work (a federally administered plan of compulsory old-age annuities; OASI, old-age social insurance) and to those who were temporarily unemployed (a federal-state program of unemployment insurance, UI).

Social insurance was viable for two reasons: (1) It was *politically acceptable* because, in theory, benefits were given to people who had made prior payments. Given this, it was argued, the program was built on sound actuarial principles. Recipients did not feel stigmatized since they were entitled to the benefits. (2) The policy formulators had a number of existing social insurance models to draw upon. *They were not creating a new, untested system*. In the 1880s Bismarck had initiated a set of social insurance programs in the newly unified Germany, and early in the twentieth century Lloyd George, the prime minister of England, developed an insurance system in England.

The second major strategy—social assistance—was, in effect, an extension of the poor law with its emphasis on the dole and "work relief," although great pains were taken to argue that the poor law was being replaced. The English poor laws (often referred to as the "Elizabethan Poor Laws") had been brought to the American colonies by the early settlers and became the basis for the modern public assistance programs. The poor laws established public responsibility for the care of the "worthy" poor. Under these laws, responsibility was placed on local communities to care for those residents who were aged, sick, handicapped, or the children of widows and orphans. They were labeled "worthy" in the sense they were not held accountable for their poverty.

The Social Security Act of 1935, recognizing that some persons would not be covered by social insurance, established three categories of social assistance: Old Age Assistance (OAA), Aid to the Blind (AB), and Aid to Dependent Children (ADC). Unlike the social insurance programs under which people received benefits as their right, beneficiaries under the social assistance programs were required to pass a means test proving that they were old, blind, or a dependent child *and* poor, i.e., their income was below some predetermined level.

Work relief was another poor law program with deep historical roots. After 200 years of trying to deter vagrancy and indiscriminate giving alms through harsh measures (e.g., imprisonment, flogging, maiming, or even death for the "incorrigibles"), Parliament, over a 100-year period, (1495–1597) passed a series of new poor law statutes that clearly delineated between the "impotent" or "worthy poor" and the "sturdy beggar" or "able-bodied" poor. This latter group was forced to work on local government projects—forced in the sense that if they refused to work, they were "remanded to local houses of Correction." Throughout the seventeenth and eighteenth centuries these "work fare" programs were modified, culminating in the watershed reform of 1834, known as the Victorian Poor Laws.

Whereas the social assistance income maintenance programs focused on the worthy poor, the employment programs targeted the able-bodied poor, who could and should work. Work, it was believed, not only provided the individual with the means to buy needed goods and services and thus stimulate economic growth, it not only supported and maintained the economy by guaranteeing a viable work force, it also had spiritual and psychological value for the individual. Therefore, people who could work, should work. While the particular forms of work relief changed in the thirties from coercive to voluntary, and while the work itself became more meaningful, the basic assumptions remained the same. The Roosevelt administration decided early in 1933 to create jobs for the able-bodied. Through programs such as the Federal Emergency Relief Act (FERA), the Civilian Conservation Corps (CCC), the Public Works Administration (PWA), and the Civil Works Administration (CWA), the federal government created millions of jobs.

While radical in terms of national government involvement, both the income support program (social assistance) and employment programs had an historical basis. While certain demeaning aspects of the poor law were replaced with a more humane system, this country's response to the depression was not a rejection of that poor law. The earlier laissez-faire system was humanized through significant modifications, but the philosophy of that system was incorporated into the New Deal. This was a political necessity at that time and these century-old underpinnings provides us with insights into current income maintenance programs.

The stated national goal of economic security for all was translated into income support for the aged, the blind, and fatherless children, and jobs for the able-bodied. If an individual was in economic need but did not fall into one of these categories, that individual received no assistance. Decisions were made as to which portion of the population would be covered and which would be excluded. The specific strategies chosen were, moreover, shaped by political and ideological factors. The approach continued to emphasize the value of (1) independent, strong, competitive individuals and families, and (2) a state concerned primarily with economic principles.

When the state did intervene, it did so reluctantly and minimally, consistent with the well-being of the economy and only secondarily with humanitarian concerns. Social policy in the 1930s continued to emphasize the provision of a minimum standard of living and (with the exception of the social insurance program) a reactive, crisis-oriented provision of goods and services. It was guided by economic concepts, with social services functioning as "the ambulance at the bottom of the cliff, rather than the fence at the top that prevented people from falling over" (Marsh 1970:13). For example, unemployment insurance does not prevent unemployment, health insurance does not prevent illness, and social assistance does not maintain independence and self-reliance. In previous times we spoke of subsistence levels and a basic minimum. Today, we speak of a safety net—one whose holes expand and contract not in response to shifting human need but to the needs of the economy at that time. Unfortunately, there tends to be an inverse relationship between the two sets of needs, i.e., when the economy contracts or stagnates, human needs increase; when the economy heats up and expands, more people are able to care for themselves. When growing numbers of people need assistance we say we cannot afford to provide that assistance; when fewer people need help we say we can expand our efforts.

What Must Be Done?

The decision that something must be done provides a stimulus for action. During 1931–32, for example, talk of revolution and civil unrest was widespread. Hunger riots were common, and many unemployed and homeless persons were being arrested, some by their own choice. The Soviet Union advertised for skilled workers to construct their dams, and over 100,000 Americans applied. Perhaps the single most important event was the Bonus March of 1932 when veterans came to Washington demanding the bonus they had been promised by a grateful Congress after World War I was won. President Hoover's response was to call in the army under General Douglas MacArthur, which burned the veterans' tent encampments and physically forced the veterans to leave the city. The image of mounted soldiers riding through scores of veterans wearing their uniforms and medals horrified the nation.

The Hoover administration experienced a number of equally devastating public relations fiascoes. States, having exhausted their own resources, requested the federal government to become more directly involved in supporting their "public relief" efforts. In some instances this meant direct financial support to the unemployed; in other cases, low-interest loans; and in a small number of instances, money to buy seed for farmers who otherwise would not be able to plant their crops.

President Hoover refused their requests, arguing that such involvement was unconstitutional. His position was that similar federal involvement had been tested earlier when President Pierce vetoed a bill to establish federally supported institutions for the mentally ill. In his veto Pierce stated:

> If Congress is to make such provision for such objects, the fountains of charity will be dried up at home, and several states instead of bestowing their own means in the social wants of their own people, may themselves through strong temptation, which appeals to the States as individuals, become humble supplicants for the bounty of the federal government, reversing their true relation to the Union. (Trattner 1974:62)

During this same period, the president approved the awarding of millions of dollars to a small number of banks experiencing financial difficulties. President Hoover publicly argued that, while direct aid to individuals was not constitutional, the direct support of banks was. These actions, and many others, were instrumental in his losing the election in 1932. As a result of that election, Roosevelt perceived that he had been given a mandate to deal with these problems. Even the Supreme Court supported the administration's becoming directly involved in assisting people, by declaring in 1937 that the

Social Security Act was constitutional. Reacting to President Pierce's earlier veto, the Court concluded:

> [N]eeds that were narrow or parochial a century ago may be interwoven in our day with the well-being of the nation. (Helvering v. Davis 301 U.S. 619)

Another aspect of the question of what must be done concerned the level of effort to be implemented. As discussed above, not all people would be covered. Benefits would be given primarily to the elderly, the blind, children without fathers, and those who were temporarily unemployed. This, however, is only part of the issue. The other decision concerned the amount they would receive. Table 1.1 shows the average monthly benefit under each program in 1940, and the percentage of the median income that the benefit constituted.

All grants were well below the average monthly income for an employed worker ($102.42). Economic security, by definition, involved the provision of benefits to achieve and maintain subsistence, i.e., the minimum necessary to meet basic needs, and not wage replacement.

Who Should Do It?

The fourth question—Who should do it?—deals specifically with the appropriate roles of government and the private sector. Should responsibility for meeting the basic needs of people reside in the private or the public sector and, if the latter, at which level of government? Should needs be met directly by providing goods and services, or indirectly through market mechanisms? The Social Security Act is an excellent example of a mixed strategy:

- The compulsory retirement program (OASI) was financed through payroll taxes contributed to by both employer and employee and administered by the federal government.
- Under the employment insurance (UI) program, employers were taxed by the federal government, which then channels these funds to states to administer.
- The social assistance programs (OAA, AB, ADC) were to be financed by both the federal and state governments and administered by the state.
- The service components of the act (public health, child welfare, etc.) were also financed by both levels of governments and administered by the state.

In some instances, services were provided by government (e.g., medical-care services for children, adoption services, and surplus food), but in the income programs, which assumed that recipients were capable of purchas-

Table 1.1.   Average Monthly Benefits: Social
             Security [a,b]

Program	Benefit ($)	Percentage of median family income
OASI	22.60	22
UI	42.24	41
OAA	20.25	19
AB	25.35	25
ADC	32.40	32

[a] With the exception of ADC, all beneficiaries are individuals. ADC beneficiaries are families.
[b] Median monthly income at the time was $102.42.

ing what they needed in the market, individuals received money. To understand this mixed strategy, we now need to examine our views toward government and identify those preconditions necessary for intervention.

Rationales for Government Intervention

Assumptions

All of the rationales on which the government might justify its intervention
in social and economic life are based on three general assumptions:

The first assumption states that an economic system characterized by
perfectly competitive markets provides socially optimal results, i.e., products of the highest quality will be provided at reasonable prices when people
(consumers) want them. A market may be defined as a group of people who
are in contact with one another for the purpose of buying and selling some
commodity. Given this, the appropriate role of government is to refrain from
entering those markets. The one exception is when a market does not yield
those optimal results predicted by the model of perfect competition (Adam
Smith's "invisible hand").

The second assumption suggests that certain goods and services are the
rights of all people by virtue of their citizenship. Such goods and services,
called *merit wants,* are usually specified in basic social documents, such as
the Constitution, or may be legislatively mandated. An example would be
trial by a jury of one's peers.

The third assumption rests on the concept of *public goods.* At the heart of
this concept is the distinction between collective and individual action and
between public and private action. But what persuades members of a society that values individualism to seek a collective solution to a problem rather
than to rely on their own individual actions?

The need for collective action arises when individuals believe that they cannot achieve their objectives individually—that problems transcend individual solutions. Collective action is justified when some segment of the public wants and is prepared to pay for goods and services other than what the unhampered market will produce. Collective goods, however, need not be public goods, e.g., a voluntary church-sponsored day care program.

In its purest form, the public-goods rationale for government intervention is invoked when the consumption of particular goods and services by a substantial proportion of the population does not prevent or preclude their consumption by the rest of the population. For example, when the government allocates resources for national defense, each citizen (in theory) can consume all of the security obtained from the expenditures without preventing others also from consuming the same amount of security. Local police and fire departments as well as governmental support of an art gallery can be similarly justified. One person's use and enjoyment of the facility does not use it up; others can use and enjoy it equally. The only constraint is the timing of consumption by each person, i.e., everyone cannot use the art gallery or the fire and police services at the same time.

Beyond these three arguments, two other rationales are often introduced: (1) externalities, and (2) market imperfections.

1. Externalities and the Public Interest. The externality rationale is used when, in forcing individuals either to do something or to stop doing what they are doing, society as a whole benefits. Government is justified in intervening in the market even if individual members of the society may receive different benefits and even if some individuals may feel that the intervention is not warranted from their perspective.

It is assumed in these instances that the private-market system will not produce the optimal quantity of the particular good because markets reflect the private benefits that accrue to each individual. Since "rational" individuals seek to maximize their own personal utility (well-being), they may not consider the utility of society or may believe that actions to improve the well-being of society may be at too great a personal expense.

Historically, services such as education and public health immunizations are justified on externality grounds. In both instances, individuals and society benefit from individual consumption of the services. In the first case, society as a whole achieves a general level of literacy; in the second, target diseases are eradicated, thereby improving the general health and productivity of the population. Moreover, all citizens pay for these services even if they are not using them, e.g., adults without children are taxed for schools:

> If the community, or at any rate, a sizable part of it has an interest in a
> particular utility accruing to an individual, then it would clearly be unreason-
> able to allow the creation of the more general utility to depend solely on that

individual; he might not value the state activity highly enough to make the sacrifice of paying the required fee or charge, or else ignorance may cause him or poverty force him to do without the service. Herein lies the chief justification of the modern demands for free or very cheap processes of law, education, medical care, certain public health measures, etc. (Wicksell 1958:15)

The above are examples of "positive" externalities: many people will benefit if actions are taken, even if coercion is used. Parents have to demonstrate that their children have received the required immunizations before they are allowed to begin school; children are required to attend school for so many years or until they reach the prescribed age; all working people are required to participate in the Social Security system whether they have alternative pension plans or not.

We also find "negative" externality arguments used to justify government intervention. While positive externalities force people to take action, the negative externality argument is used to force people to stop doing what they are doing. For example, a steel mill is forced to stop polluting the air because the pollution is negatively affecting residents of neighboring towns. This would be justified even if the residents of the town where the plant is located were to vote to maintain the existing system, arguing that pollution is a reasonable price to pay for guaranteed jobs. We often see negative externalities referred to as "neighborhood effects" in the literature.

2. Market Imperfections. Efficient (i.e., perfect) markets presuppose adequate information so that consumers can make informed decisions, timely adjustments (when a need arises, providers will respond quickly), sufficient competition, and modest transaction costs. The absence of any of these may legitimize government intervention in these imperfect markets. Governmental intervention may take a number of forms, some of which are preferable to others under our specific political economy. If government is to become involved at all, that involvement should be as unintrusive as possible. The following interventions are listed in hierarchal order, from most to least preferred:

- The provision of an extensive information and referral service so that people needing or wanting a service can find that service (e.g., a long-term care clearinghouse that would inform families of available private nursing homes in a community). This assumes that adequate resources exist.
- Furthermore, if there are time lags in the private sector (i.e., there is a private market but it is incapable of meeting existing need because of a shortage of facilities or skilled personnel), government can intervene by stimulating supply side factors (e.g., low-cost construction loans and/or financial assistance for training programs).

- Regulations and licensing (e.g., a state might set standards, license, and monitor nursing homes).
- Contract with private providers to pay for low-income patients.
- The actual provision of a service (e.g., a county might administer its own system of public nursing homes).

As discussed earlier, the 1935 Social Security Act was a major departure from earlier social welfare measures in that it resulted in a much broader role for government. Moreover, each of the major provisions of the act was justified by one or more of the above rationales.

The income programs, i.e., social insurance (OASI), unemployment insurance (UI) and social assistance (OAA, AB, ADC), were seen as necessary governmental responses in that the economic system was not providing the socially optimal results predicted by the market. The benefits cannot, however, be defined as merit wants within a strict definition of the term, i.e., benefits provided as right of citizenship; nor do they meet the strict criterion of public goods in the sense that one person's consumption does not lessen the quantity of the good. They have been justified with an externality rationale: that it is in the public interest to provide these benefits. Moreover, by providing income benefits rather than goods and services, governmental preference was clearly for the least intrusive intervention: the giving of money so that individual recipients could enter existing markets to obtain desired or wanted goods.

The service programs under the act incorporated a similar justification. Public health and child welfare services were seen as necessary because of a nonresponsive market and also were justified under the externality rationale. These programs provided benefits not only to the individuals and families receiving them, but also to society as a whole. The decision was also made to provide services and goods (unlike the income programs that provided the means to purchase goods and services) and thus directly to influence patterns of consumption.

Roles of Government

The issue of governmental involvement goes beyond the issues discussed in the previous section. Once a decision has been made that government will become involved, the next concern to be addressed is which level of government. America's political tradition historically has stressed decentralized decision-making, with wide discretion left to the states by constitutional reservation and political inclination.

The federal government has utilized the politically expedient grants-in-aid approach—one that is less intrusive than others—resulting in the states being given a significant role. This supports the strong historical preference

for state and local administration of domestic programs. While some benefits such as Social Security and other income transfer programs are provided
by the federal government directly, the great bulk of public services in
health, education, housing, highway construction, public protection, parks
and recreation, and social services are provided by state and local government, although all of these areas are partially funded by the federal government. As Heller has suggested:

> A very large part of what we do through Government is done through state and
> local units. They are the ones to whom we usually turn as we seek to maintain
> or upgrade our educational efforts, improve our physical and mental health,
> redevelop our decaying urban areas, build better and safer highways, over-
> come air and water pollution and equip our suburbs with water systems,
> sewers, roads, parks, schools and the like. The list is striking partly because
> each item on it represents either an essential function or a reasonable aspira-
> tion of a great and growing society; partly because each item falls squarely
> within the traditional sphere of state-local operations; and partly because so
> many items on the list are suffused with a national interest that transcends state
> and local lives and demands Federal action and support. (1967:121–22.)

This pattern is deeply rooted in the historical development of this country.
In the colonial period, before the advent of state and national governments,
public services were the responsibility of local government, i.e., the township in New England, the county in the southern colonies, and a mixture of
both patterns in New York and Pennsylvania. Throughout the nineteenth
century, federal involvement was virtually nonexistent. Major exceptions at
the federal level included medical care for merchant seamen, lepers, and
Native Americans. The rationale for these three groups differed somewhat:

1. Merchant seamen did not meet local residency requirements (did not
pay local taxes) and therefore were not eligible for medical care (the existing
market was imperfect). The nation needed a strong merchant navy for protection from external powers and to establish international trade relationships (the externality argument). Given this, the federal government was
justified in establishing a network of hospitals from Boston to New Orleans
to serve this population group. Eventually, this network became the foundation of the U.S. Public Health Service.
2. Leprosy was such a low-incidence condition requiring costly and
highly specialized medical services that local and even state markets were
not efficient providers (the existing market was imperfect). Leprosy was also
an infectious disease, and therefore the public interest required lepers to be
quarantined (the externality argument). Based on these rationales, the
federal government established a specialized hospital for the treatment of
leprosy at Carville, Louisiana.
3. Medical-care markets were nonexistent on reservations established

by the federal government and market forces were not likely to respond (the existing market was imperfect and unintrusive measures were unlikely to prove effective). By law, Native Americans in the eighteenth century were not citizens of the state in which their reservation was located and therefore were not the responsibility of the state. This argument parallels that used in the case of the merchant seamen. Given this, the federal government was justified in establishing the Indian Health Service.

State involvement was equally small. The major exceptions were in the areas of mental illness and certain communicable diseases such as tuberculosis. The rationale used was similar to that used at the federal level in the case of lepers—low incidences and protection of the public interest.

Federal participation did, of course, increase significantly in the twentieth century. In the 1920s, federal grants-in-aid were available for vocational education, vocational rehabilitation, and maternal and child health programs. During the depression, a dozen major grant programs were enacted. These were justified with the argument that the resources of state and local governments were inadequate to provide necessary public services since they were unable to raise sufficient revenue. Furthermore, it was argued that state and local taxes were not only inflexible and regressive, but also that citizens would not receive equal treatment since some states were poorer than others.

By 1985, the role of government in general and that of the federal government in particular had grown considerably. Social-welfare expenditures as a percentage of the gross national product (GNP) have more than doubled since 1950. Or, to put it another way, whereas the GNP increased by almost 1,300% between 1950 and 1985, social welfare expenditures grew by 3,000%.

Whereas Table 1.2 identifies increased public expenditures (at all levels of

Table 1.2.   Public Social Welfare Expenditures as a Percentage of the GNP

	1950	1960	1970	1980	1985	1987
Social insurance	1.9	3.9	5.7	8.4	9.4	9.3
Public aid	0.9	0.8	1.7	2.8	2.3	2.5
Health and medical	0.8	0.9	1.0	1.1	1.0	1.0
Education	2.5	3.5	5.3	4.7	4.2	4.6
Other	0.2	0.2	0.4	0.4	0.3	0.3
Total [a]	8.9	10.5	15.2	18.7	18.4	18.8

[a] Total includes other categories such as housing, veterans, etc., so that the above listed do not add up to the total.
Source: Adapted from *Social Security Bulletin,* Table 1, pp. 10–11 (January 1988); and Table 1, pp. 12–13 (February 1990).

Table 1.3. Federal Expenditures as a Percentage of Public Expenditures in Social Welfare

	1950	1960	1970	1980	1985	1987
Social insurance	42.5	74.1	82.7	83.2	84.0	83.1
Public aid	44.2	51.6	58.5	67.8	63.8	62.5
Health and medical	29.2	38.9	48.2	46.6	46.1	46.7
Education	2.3	4.9	11.6	11.1	8.3	7.8
Other	38.9	36.6	54.5	64.6	54.1	55.7
Total	44.8	47.7	53.0	61.6	62.0	59.9

Source: Adapted from *Social Security Bulletin,* Table 1, pp. 10–11 (January 1988); and Table 1, pp. 12–13 (February 1990).

government) for social welfare from 1950 to 1985, Table 1.3 provides insight into the increased rate of involvement by the federal government in particular. We see that the largest increases occurred from 1950 to 1970.

In terms of federal vs. state expenditures, the former's share of *all* public expenditures for social welfare reached 62%; with a low of 8% for educational programs and a high of 84% for income transfer programs.

Given these increases, in conjunction with the federal deficit and the rising national debt, the mood in the country now seems to question seriously whether we should continue the federal government's functions as defined over the past 50 years, functions that include the establishment of broad national goals and the targeting of "at-risk" recipient groups for specific health and social services.

In 1987, the federal government spent $195.4 billion to pay interest on the national debt (see Table 1.4). This represented almost 20% of the federal budget for that year. Whereas this interest accounted for 10% of the budget throughout the 1970s, it averaged 18% in the 1980s (U.S. Bureau of the Census 1988).

This mood seems to support the more historical position (i.e., predepression) of supporting state and local governments' responsibilities to meet the health and social needs of their citizens.

The "new" role of the federal government emphasizes less federal re-

Table 1.4. Increases in the National Debt (1980–1987)

	Federal deficit	National debt
1980	$56 billion	$800 billion
1985	$200 billion	$2 trillion
1987	$210 billion	$3 trillion

strictions, cutbacks on categorical programs that restrict the use of federal funds, and an increase in the number and amount of less-restrictive block grants. These shifts, however, raise a number of critical questions:

- Why would states expand their efforts and be willing to spend more on social programs when previously they were unwilling to do so?
- Are we retreating to the position that the federal government's responsibility should be restricted to national defense and other international issues?
- Are we arguing that *all,* or at least most, social and economic problems can be more effectively dealt with at the state and/or local level and that regional and national solutions are neither needed nor relevant?

Most proposals, moreover, in offering more autonomy and more responsibility to the states (a "positive outcome") are also capping the amounts of federal funds that will be available for these programs—caps that could be used to eliminate the use of federal funds for these purposes as a means to solve the federal deficit problem.

Summary

This chapter has defined public policy as a process of making choices among competing demands, especially when there are scarce resources. In making these choices, decisionmakers either implicitly or explicitly rely on values. The policy process has been identified as a set of activities addressing four basic questions. While the first question (What should be done?) is clearly normative, the other three also have value dimensions. Rationales for government interventions were then introduced, followed by a discussion of the locus of authority and responsibility. These issues are key to the understanding of the specific social policies analyzed in later chapters. The next chapter continues to develop the overall conceptual framework to be used in analyzing specific policies. It begins with a discussion of the major and conflicting functions carried out by the dominant schools of policy analysis and concludes with the identification of fundamental concepts analysts and policymakers must deal with.

CHAPTER 2

POLICY ANALYSIS

The purpose of this chapter is to explore, in some detail, the professional activity referred to as policy analysis. While the discussion in the preceding chapter dealt with the umbrella concept *policy* and a number of significant issues related to it, here we emphasize analysis. Our concern is the activity itself, with specific attention given to the role of the analyst. Two competing approaches are introduced. The first approach is grounded in and limited to technical analysis, while the second assumes a much broader perspective— one that systematically incorporates values into the analysis. Following this, the implications of a value-analytic approach, including the generation of first principles and criteria that eventually set the stage for choosing among alternatives, are explored. While theoretical and somewhat abstract, the chapter does provide the foundation and the glue for later chapters, which deal with specific substantive issues.

Policy Analysis and Research

Rein (1970) argues that no single academic or professional discipline can be expected to provide the insight necessary for developing the most appropriate framework for analyzing social problems and identifying effective policies and programs. The analyst, in fact, must "trespass on academic and professional domains in which he may have no special competence" (1970:xii). The analyst's unique contribution, then, becomes one of identifying and understanding approaches used in the different disciplines (e.g., economics, political science, history, philosophy) and professional fields (e.g., public health, social work, education, law) and then synthesizing them into a meaningful whole.

More often than not, the analyst relies on available data and existing research rather than the collection of new data. What tends to distinguish policy analysis from traditional research is the way the question is formulated and the specific purposes of the analysis. Policy analysis sets out to produce something that legislators or administrators can easily translate into action, while traditional research attempts to provide a better understanding of social phenomena. Policy analysis, then, relies heavily on research, while research can stand by itself, although Bronfenbrenner (1974) has suggested that social science should rely on social policy for both its vitality and validity.

Policy analysis, to be useful, must be responsive to the needs of policymakers, who are often operating under considerable time constraints. Researchers who inform a decisionmaker that the specific information requested will not be available for several years soon lose their audience. Similarly, researchers who inform policymakers that research findings must be treated as tentative and in need of further verification contribute little to the policy process. For example, at a small invitational conference attended by child development specialists and government program and legislative staff members, the major question to be addressed was What should the federal government's policy be toward child care outside the home? The researchers were uncomfortable with the question and responded by reviewing the findings of various research projects. They expressed the belief that questions like What should be done? were outside the purview and competency of social and behavioral scientists. And yet, this is the question policymakers are faced with. While the best possible information may not exist, the analyst must reexamine what is available and, through a synthesizing process, generate reasonable policy options and recommendations. Available information is superior to one person's intuitive judgment.

This perceived nonresponsive attitude on the part of traditional behavioral and social scientists is probably the major reason that policy analysis has become a new and somewhat parallel activity. It has filled a vacuum. Over the past ten years, significant numbers of public policy curricula have come into existence and have attracted large numbers of undergraduate and graduate students. Today, policy centers draw considerable support from governmental agencies and private foundations and are found in most major universities.

In the remainder of the chapter, a range of frameworks for policy analysis will be discussed. Two distinct approaches to policy analysis will be explored in some detail. One approach emphasizes the process of policy analysis by focusing on the technical aspects of decision-making, while the other emphasizes the purpose or end to be achieved by the policy.

Approach 1: Emphasis on Process

Policy has been defined as a "study plan," the product of a rational exercise involving the determination of goals, the examination of alternatives, and the selection of a strategy (Kahn 1967). Within this framework, policy formulation assumes that decisions are made rationally, with the analyst functioning in a technical capacity. Analysis is introduced only when the general goal has been worked out. The analyst accepts the "goodness" of the general policy statement, implicitly saying to the decisionmaker, "Tell me what you want and I'll tell you how it can be achieved." The analyst does not determine the goals nor does he or she have responsibility for selecting among alternatives. Rather, analytic activity is limited to the generation of alternatives and the application of various criteria to those alternatives.

Traditionally, these criteria have tended to be grounded in economic analysis, with specific emphasis on efficiency and cost-effectiveness. An example of this approach was the analysts' role in the welfare reform proposal introduced in Congress in 1969 (commonly known as the Family Assistance Plan). This proposal embodied the administration's basic incentive mechanism for shifting recipient families from a welfare program to a workfare program. To support the workfare program and to facilitate the employment of AFDC (aid to families with dependent children) mothers, day-care would be expanded and supported with up to 90% federal reimbursement. The analyst, as technician, approached this issue with day-care as a given (rather than one strategy/alternative among many) and identified alternative ways to deliver the service to the target population. Variables such as size of day-care programs, types of services, and staffing ratios became the basis for a modified benefit-cost analysis. The results of the analysis were then given to a decisionmaker who would make a choice(s) among the alternative day-care strategies. This approach has strong support in the literature. Dror (1970, 1971), for example, describes the basic function of policy analysis as "identifying and documenting various alternatives within a range of decision possibilities" (1970:136). His seminal work is still one of the major influences on the practice of policy analysis.

Dror suggests that the policy sciences "constitute a new and additional approach to the uses of systematic knowledge and structured rationality for the conscious shaping of society" (1970:137) and represent an integration of pure and applied research. Within the policy sciences, policy analysis provides "heuristic methods for the identification of preferable policy alternatives" (1970:139). Dror's approach builds on three fundamental components:

- a systems view, i.e., examining problems and alternatives in such a way that all relevant variables and probable results are taken into account;

- searching for an optimal (single best) solution within a "broad benefit-cost frame without being limited to environmental changes" (1970:141);
- identification of the preferable alternative "with the help of a large set of techniques ranging from mathematical models to human gaming and from canvassing of expert's opinion to sensitivity testing" (1970:141).

In sum, Dror argues that policy analysis, based in the management sciences and systems analysis, can provide the decisionmaker with the means to choose among proposed courses of action once a goal has been articulated. He suggests that such analysis can be helpful in the identification and evaluation of alternatives. He assumes furthermore that "rationality and intellectualism" are the only appropriate foundations for policy analysis. Even more important is his belief that knowledge provides the authority to plan and act. Finally, the role of the analyst is that of a technician.

Lasswell (1970), who first proposed the concept of policy sciences, offers a similar perspective. For him, the purpose of the policy sciences is to augment, by scientific methods of decision-making and data from the behavioral sciences, the process that humans use in making judgments and decisions. Where Dror argues for systems analysis, Lasswell sees the distinguishing characteristic of policy analysis as "tending toward contextuality in place of fragmentation and toward a problem-oriented, not a problem blind orientation" (1970:6). Lasswell further suggests that this perspective forces the analyst to become less and less "method bound," that the multidisciplinary approach both reflects and contributes to contextuality and problem orientation, and that this is achieved through a synthesis of technique. Lasswell thus agrees with Rein's position in this respect. Whereas Dror's approach is based on three fundamental tenets, Lasswell's approach emphasizes five components of analysis:

- goal clarification
- trend analysis
- theory formation
- projection of future possibilities
- invention, evaluation, and selection of alternative strategies.

Unlike Dror, Lasswell does not see policy analysis as a linear process. Rather, he describes the activity more in terms of iterations, a moving "back and forth between images of the whole and particular details of time, place, and figure" (1970:13). Finally, though both Dror and Lasswell tend to view the analyst as technician, Dror allows for "organized day dreaming" and Lasswell speaks of "creative flash," i.e., the examination of factual data in a way that leads to creative rearrangements of the data and eventually to novel solutions. This creativity, however, only deals with generating means and not ends. Furthermore, while the various phases of analysis are rational and scientific, this creative process is seen by these policy scientists as "irrational" and prescientific in nature. Dror and Lasswell are grounded in logical positivism and scientism, which recognizes only two models for legitimate knowledge: the empirical or natural sciences, and the formal disciplines such as logic and mathematics. As Popper argued:

> There is no such thing as a logical method of having new ideas or a logical reconstruction of the process. My view may be expressed by saying that every discovery contains an "irrational element" or a "creative intuition." (1968:32)

Structured rationality in the decision-making process is not, however, the invention of policy scientists. It has a long-standing tradition in the field of planning. As John Freidmann and Barclay Hudson state:

> For most people, including planners, planning is identified with advanced decision-making. Planning in this view is a set of methods designed to prepare information in such a way that decisions can be made more rationally. The continuing attractiveness of this approach to planning is made evident in a recent compendium edited by Ira M. Robinson (1972). In his forward to the volume, Britton Harris refers to it as "a well-established paradigm of the planning process." According to Harris, this paradigm requires the setting of goals, the formulation of alternatives, the prediction of outcomes, and the evaluation of the alternatives in relation to the goals and the outcomes. (1974:6)

Freidman and Hudson contend that the policy sciences were derived from a tradition of empiricism within a framework of logical positivism—the dominant emphasis of planning practice since the 1950s. Planning and the policy sciences have both emerged from the same theoretical foundation, with planning serving as the parent for the policy sciences. For example, Dror, a major figure in the policy sciences, was an earlier contributor to the planning literature.

It is interesting to note that Dror, in 1967, defined planning as "the process of preparing a set of decisions for action in the future directed at achieving goals by optimal means" (1967:9). In elaborating this definition, he identifies the planning phase as:

- translating planning objectives into weighted operational goals
- collection of data to construct a model of the subject matter
- the search for main alternatives
- relative evaluation of the main alternatives and identification of the optimal strategy.

Dror then concludes that these phases "are identical with the phases of rational decision-making. Progress in the selection of data and quantification or semi-quantification of data on the one hand, and progress in the theories and methods of statistical decision-making in all its branches on the other hand are, therefore, essential prerequisites for more rational planning" (1967:34).

Policy analysis and planning are both concerned with rational decision-making, and the function of the analyst or planner is to support this process through technical activities. Moreover, Dror argues that the planner/analyst must submerge his or her values—must remain objective or neutral. Values are an important part of the policy process, but not the analyst's values. Dror points out that the translation of planning objectives with weighted operational goals is closely involved with the value judgments of the decision-makers. Therefore, most of the "contacts and collisions between planning, the political units, and the political environment occur in this phase" (1967:31).

Dror's position on the role of the planner/analyst and values is consistent with the dominant view expressed in the planning literature over the past 80 years. As early as 1910 we find that reformers concerned with the inefficiency and corruption of existing political mechanisms were agitating for new processes of decision-making, processes that would facilitate representation of "the community as a whole" or "interests at large and not specific interests" (Banfield and Wilson 1963). These new processes would produce a more democratic government capable of utilizing scientific or rational techniques of management. The key element in this movement was the notion of the public interest:

> There is a public interest that can be applied to all issues of local government. The public interest is that course of action which best serves the public as a whole. Private interests . . . must take a back seat to the public interest . . . "politics" involves the serving of private interests and, therefore, should be kept out of government. (Ranney 1969:46)

This new paradigm of rationality, grounded in science and technology, introduced before World War I, was more fully developed during the early 1950s by Banfield:

> 1.   The decision-maker considers all of the alternatives (courses of action) open to him; i.e., he considers what courses of action are possible within the conditions of the situation and in light of the ends he seeks to attain.
> 2.   He identifies and evaluates all of the consequences which would follow from the adoption of each alternative, i.e., he predicts how the total situation would be changed by each course of action he might adopt.
> 3.   He selects that alternative the probable consequences of which would be preferable in terms of his most valued ends. (1955:314)

This model of rational decision-making begins with the concerns of the decisionmaker. Meyerson, a colleague of Banfield, identified these decisionmakers in a later work:

> They are the mayors, the city managers, the heads of operating municipal departments, the home builders, the merchants and industrialists, the civic leaders. Their decisions are the decisions that set the stage for the decisions of the everyday citizens (1956:1379)

The model seeks to provide those who are influential in the political system the kind of information they need in order to make decisions more rationally with respect to their "most valued ends." Implicitly, these valued ends are seen to be in the public interest. The role of the planner/analyst is limited to analysis that will aid the decisionmaker to choose among alternatives, and to do so the planner must suppress personal values.

Criticism of the Process Approach

Despite its great intellectual appeal, rational decision theory has not been able to resolve a number of problems. Freidmann and Hudson (1974) identify difficulties with this approach. The first is the problem of knowledge and information. Rational decision-making, as noted earlier, requires a consideration of all the alternatives and an evaluation of all of the consequences that would follow from the adoption of each alternative. This is to be achieved by applying various techniques such as operations research, decision theory, cost-benefit analysis, input-output studies, information theory, and simulation models. However, most decision analysis in the public policy arena involves nonrepetitive situations, which in turn affects our capability to predict consequences. Moreover, such analysis requires an information system with accurate, relevant, and comprehensive data. Such a system, however, has not been realized to date. Freidmann and Hudson also point out that human intelligence is such that only a limited number of variables can be taken into account, that continuous social change is the norm and not the exception, and that this turbulent environment only allows for the development of partial and limited social models for estimating the impact of decisions.

A second limitation or obstacle is our inability to derive a community welfare function, i.e., "a collection of tradeoffs among a community's preference for different objectives" (p. 11). Without this function, the analyst has no independent and objective basis for evaluating alternatives. The notion of a community welfare function was derived from the works of Jeremy Bentham and J. S. Mill and has its roots in utilitarianism. "Good" decisions were those that maximized the utility (well-being) for the greatest number. If we aggregate individual and group preferences, we should be able to derive the community welfare function and thus choose the alternative that is in the public interest. While the concept is reasonable, the technical means to do this have not been found (Arrow 1951).

The third problem raised by Freidmann and Hudson is concerned with implementation:

> Decision theorists work on the assumption that once a decision is made, it will be carried out with a minimum of friction. Again, this belief stems from the notion that within bureaucratic organizations decisions are, in effect, commands and that commands are invariably obeyed. But empirical studies of organizational behavior have concluded that coordination not only may be difficult to achieve but may in some cases be altogether impossible. (1974:11)

A fourth criticism was raised by Mannheim (1940) over 50 years ago. He argued that planners were preoccupied with "functional rationality" at the expense of "substantial rationality." Functional rationality is concerned with relating means to given ends, while substantial rationality deals with the appropriateness of the ends themselves. The analyst who operates within the process approach to policy formulation assumes that his or her role is purely technical and that questions of substantial rationality belong only to the decisionmakers. Mannheim used Germany of the 1930s as an example of functional rationality in its extreme. The analyst's function was not to question the decisions of those in power: it was solely one of implementation of the "final solution."

The process approach is not only limiting but in many ways dysfunctional in that it emphasizes means and tends to bypass the issue of ends. Because it is convenient to do so, we assume that a fundamental consensus on societal goals exists. Policy analysis within this framework is primarily concerned with technical or administrative issues of social engineering. In reality, this fundamental consensus does not exist and the tendency to sidestep the existing ideological conflict has resulted in formulating policies that are at cross-purposes with other policies. Policy design has come to be viewed as a choice among neutral alternatives, and analysis an activity that helps decisionmakers achieve an optimal solution for some predetermined goal. Analysis tends to be concentrated on how services will be financed, organized, and administered and all too rarely on the nature, aims, and value of the services.

A number of committees, commissions, and individual scholars in recent years have stressed procedure and have not attempted to relate these procedures to a set of desired outcomes. Arguments are made in terms of who has what responsibility: Does the public or private sector? If the public sector, at what level of government? Should needs be met through the direct provision of services or indirectly through market mechanisms? If the latter, should the strategy be focused on income maintenance programs such as the negative income tax, on a family allowance program, on a modified public assistance program, or on vouchers earmarked for certain categories of goods, e.g., housing, food, day-care or education? Whether this growing emphasis on procedures reflects a discouragement with the alleged failure of previous large-scale programs, a distrust of government, or a lack of confidence in being able to deal successfully with complex social problems, it does reflect a reluctance to sort out values, to define relationships between means and ends. This criticism is in no way meant to suggest that procedures are unimportant. The issues related to the financing, organization, and administration of services are critical but they are dependent upon the purpose of the services. They address the issue of what can be accomplished given resources, knowledge, and technology. However, it should be underscored that these administrative and technical issues are, in fact, not neutral or value free. In the absence of an identified purpose or outcome, means are inevitably chosen on efficiency criteria, with primary consideration given to cost-effectiveness in achieving narrowly defined objectives.

These limitations have been addressed from two distinct perspectives. The first can be labeled conservative in that it argues for a more modest and realistic approach to policy analysis. The second suggests that the parameters of policy analysis be enlarged, not in terms of additional techniques, but more in terms of the scope of the analysis process.

Dyckman (1971) recognized the failure of formalistic methods of analysis such as simulation, systems analysis, and program planning and budgeting systems and argues that we reject the notion of comprehensive analysis. He concludes that planning and policy analysis with its rationalistic tradition needs to be replaced by a more pragmatic approach to informing decisionmakers.

Accepting the notion of a turbulent, ever-changing decision-making environment as endemic, Dyckman sees scientific rationality as insufficient and comprehensive analysis impossible. While accepting functional rationality as appropriate, he suggests that analysts be pragmatic, approach problems incrementally, and only analyze conservative rather than reform directed strategies.

Habermas (1971, 1973, 1975) rejects this "solution" and argues for a much broader role for the analyst. Although Habermas is well known in Europe and is the current intellectual leader of the Frankfurt School and its approach to policy analysis (called *critical theory*), it is only recently that his ideas and approach have been introduced into this country.

He accepts Mannheim's position on substantial rationality and extends the argument by asserting that rational decision-making (as defined by Dror and Lasswell), which assumes that analysts function as neutral technocrats and that the purpose of analysis is to identify the single best solution, will eventually result in a form of technical fascism. As discussed earlier, policy analysis within the process approach should produce a "solution" that is in the public interest. In practice, however, this public interest is defined by the decisionmakers—those in power. Earlier, we pointed out that for Dror policy analysis provides "systematic knowledge and structured rationality for the conscious shaping of society" (Dror 1970:137) and that knowledge provides authority to act. Over time, Habermas argues that more and more people will be led to believe that most problems are extremely complex and transcend the human mind's ability to comprehend them; that solutions to these problems require sophisticated information systems and technical analysis; and finally, that such analysis will produce the best solution. Eventually, fewer and fewer topics will become issues for political discourse and individuals will be isolated from social decision-making. Policy analysis in the end becomes a tool for those in power to maintain the existing system. The analyst's role models become Machiavelli and Clausewitz. Whereas the former subjugated his personal interests to those of the prince, the latter viewed war primarily as a technical problem (Mayer, Moroney, and Morris 1974).

Habermas also criticizes those who limit the empirical sciences to a logical positivist formulation and argues that objective knowledge (a prerequisite for rational decision-making in the narrow sense of the term) is an impossibility. Observations are colored by theory. Furthermore, positivists tend to equate the real world only in terms of what they can measure. What cannot be measured, the positivists believe, is not useful and therefore not real. Habermas does not reject empirical concepts. Rather, he suggests a more comprehensive concept of rationality—one that does not artificially separate facts (empirical reality) and values. In Bolan's view, "the professional has to be seen as a moral agent—not a purely instrumental problem solver" (1980:273).

Lindblom and Cohen (1979) in their provocative book *Usable Knowledge* appear to agree with Habermas. Most social scientists, they suggest, are conditioned in their training to assert that social-science methodology can solve social problems, that problem solving is a scientific activity, and that analysis based on social-science methods is superior to other forms of problem solving. They also charge that these "scientists" are "imperialistic and authoritarian" in that they expect the decisionmakers to take action once their analysis is completed. Lindbloom and Cohen also point out that since traditional social science is not useful in dealing with values or normative questions, the analyst invariably ignores them. They then conclude that a more fruitful approach to problem solving and public policy would be one in which the analyst accepts the reality of partisan ends.

The approach discussed in the next section attempts to combine functional and substantial rationality, to systematically integrate facts and values.

This approach, we suggest, needs to begin with a concern for purpose or outcome and not means.

Approach 2: Emphasis on Purpose

Titmuss defines social policy as the "study of the range of social needs and the functions, in conditions of social scarcity, of human organizations traditionally called social service or social welfare systems to meet those needs" (1968:20). He argues that the analyst must be concerned with the ends and not just the means of policy. When we direct our attention toward social-policy objectives, we are usually concerned with their moral justification. To put this another way, how do or might supporters of a social policy aimed at a particular object justify its pursuit? What alternative objectives can be morally justified? For Titmuss, values not only influence policy decisions, but the analyst should make these values clear, expose value choices that confront society, and probe and push the value assumptions underlying the development of policy. Titmuss suggests that:

> Social policy models . . . with all their apparent remoteness from reality, can serve a purpose in providing us with an ideological framework which may stimulate us to ask the significant questions and to expose the significant choices. (1971:136)

Rein agrees with Titmuss' view: that social policy is a concern for choosing among multiple, conflicting, and yet desirable goals, that no scientific rules exist to make these choices, and that values provide the criteria by which we judge the desirability of a course of action. Given the probability of conflicting ideologies, there is never one "true" analysis but potentially a number of different analyses, each one to be judged good or bad within the framework of its value assumptions.

Social policy then is concerned with social need and can be defined in terms of social purposes. It involves societal mechanisms to bring about social change, and values permeate the entire policy process. Values influence the selection of a specific policy issue and how it will be defined. They are the basis for setting policy goals and objectives, for selecting criteria for comparing policy options to achieve these goals and objectives, and for evaluating policies once they are implemented.

Rein (1976) amplifies the point by suggesting that the study of social policy involves the interaction between values (found in statements of purpose/goals), operating principles (means or instruments to achieve these purposes), and outcomes. To put it another way, social policy is an *articulation of the ideology between means and ends.* Values concern both ends and

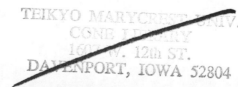

means of public intervention involving normative propositions and assumptions about what public policy is and what it should be. Theory provides insight into factors possibly related to policy issues, assisting us in interpreting how the world operates and how it might work in the future. Finally, research provides factual information relative to values, either repudiating or confirming existing beliefs about how people, institutions, and society function. Insofar as values are central to the policy domain and influence decision-making, they must become central to policy analysis.

Since values have a subjective aspect and are inherently controversial, they cannot be addressed exclusively within a positivistic framework. Purists in the behavioral and social sciences have therefore been reluctant to explore the role of values in policy analysis, since—they argue—values are outside the purview of the scientist unless they are the object of the inquiry, i.e., they are seen as dependent variables (Nagel 1956).

In some respects, their reluctance is warranted in that two extreme but complementary errors have been committed in the intellectual history of value studies (Dewey 1939). One is the value-arbitrary error, which holds that all values are equally good, a view that, says Dewey, "if it were systematically acted upon would produce disordered behavior to the point of complete chaos" (1939:69). The other is the value-absolute error, which asserts that the ultimate standards of valuation are a priori ends-in-themselves: "This theory, in its endeavor to escape from the frying pan of disordered valuations, jumps into the fire of absolutism" (1939:70).

Accepting these caveats, systematic inquiry into the nature of values is a necessary activity. What is needed is an explication of these values and the application of scientific methods in the development of public policy as an articulation of these values. Rein's comments are helpful in resolving the apparent scientific/prescriptive dilemma. He calls for:

> an examination of goal concepts in their own terms but this task is difficult because there are no final solutions and no self-evident criteria against which to judge progress. End values, societal goals, etc., are inherently controversial. They cannot be treated "scientifically" along positivist lines. The value-critical perspective does not make the assumption that there are discoverable causal relationships which are stable over time. . . . Research within the value-critical framework does try to discern patterns; it seeks general principles that take account of the context and commingle facts and values. (1976:74)

Public policy can therefore be seen as the development of fact-value appreciations in order to make appropriate decisions, and policy analysis, at least in part, is an attempt to improve the quality of decision-making by tracing through the fact-value implications of alternative courses of action (Vickers 1968). Analysts using this approach do not suggest, however, that policy analysts can develop an objective-value calculus that rationalizes different value sets and multiple goals.

However, as noted earlier, there can be no single calculus just as there cannot be a single "true" or correct analysis. The values that inform policy analysis are the values that society or groups in that society espouse, and there are inherent conflicts implicit in these. Take, for example, the expressed goals of liberty, equality, and community. While all three may be desirable organizing principles for social-policy formulation, they cannot all be maximized at once. In fact, more of one will inevitably result in less of the others. An emphasis on absolute liberty will lead to an individualistic and competitive society. An emphasis on equality calls for a more just society, a society committed to reducing age-old inequities in the redistribution of resources and in access to opportunity. An emphasis on community underscores the importance of social interaction, interdependency, and exchanges—the existence of common need and risk, the necessity for shared responsibility.

The issue becomes one of determining which value is to be given primacy. If we begin with a communitarian first principle, absolute liberty is not possible in that social responsibilities are a sine qua non. The same happens, of course, if we begin with liberty, with its emphasis on individualism.

Titmuss (1968) argues for the former while Milton Friedman (1962) supports the latter. Friedman is opposed to those who would suggest we begin with a concern for equality or community. In his view, we must start with extending freedom and choice, that anything else is paternalistic and in the long run, counterproductive to the economic and social well-being of a society. This extension of freedom is best achieved through a competitive market, which will not only be responsive but will achieve a proper balance between government, the private sector, and individuals. These competitive mechanisms, in time, will increase national wealth, and in turn provide society with the means to achieve social objectives. Social objectives can only be achieved by first realizing economic objectives. Friedman builds his approach to social policy on an economic definition of the human person, one who interacts with others in bilateral, impersonal transactions:

> Under ordinary circumstances, the exchange is impersonal . . . requiring no special effort or attention from either buyer or seller. Once the exchange has taken place, there is no residual or accumulation of unfulfilled obligations, and thus no inherent dynamic to extend the relationships beyond the time contractually specified. (Pruger 1973:290)

Individuals thus have the responsibility to act only in their own interests, and the idea of collective responsibility or welfare is nonexistent.

Titmuss, on the other hand, can be characterized as a communitarian, i.e., he believes that by nature we are social beings with responsibility for others. In his view, industrialization and modernization, with their emphasis on economic values, have brought about community breakdown and alienation. Specifically, he argues that past and present approaches to social welfare are consistent with Friedman's postulation in that they emphasize a "we-they" relationship that has produced a divided society. "We," the non-poor, provide for a residual proportion of society because "they" are incapable of providing for themselves. This divisiveness is often reflected in separate service delivery systems that involve psychological stigmatization for the poor. Both positions are value laden, and depending on which foundation one accepts, some options will be acceptable and others will be rejected. They involve different views of society, the state, individuals, and families.

Moreover, while their positions may appear to be abstract and philosophical, both have had significant influence in the political arena: Milton Friedman on the conservative wing of the Republican party in the United States and Richard Titmuss on the Labour or Socialist party in the United Kingdom.

Friedman, in beginning with the principle of freedom and the position that the free-enterprise system (competitive capitalism) is the only way to ensure that freedom, argues that government efforts to improve the quality of life of individuals and families are undesirable and inevitably harmful. In essence, he is arguing the position discussed in Chapter 1 under rationales for government intervention, that intervention invariably becomes interference and eventually leads to an ineffective family unit. To put this another way, when you take responsibilities away from people, you make them irresponsible. If government is to intervene, it should do so reactively, i.e., only when there is clearly defined pathology. Furthermore, if government is to have a role, it should be decentralized; local government is preferred over state government and state over national government, in that centralized decision-making leads to coercion and a weakening of individual freedom.

Titmuss, in beginning with the principle of community, on the other hand, argues that families have been weakened and are experiencing stress in an industrialized society characterized by periodic shifts in a less than perfect market economy. He also accepts the notion of pathology, but argues that the basic problems reside in the structures and institutions of society and not in the individual. Therefore, government at the national level (only at this level does the state have the ability to acquire and distribute resources as well as guarantee fairness to all citizens) should proactively work to reduce these risks. This is, of course, the argument used by the Roosevelt administration during the depression of the 1930s.

With this as background, it is understandable that Friedman has actively fought against compulsory social insurance (OASDI), public housing, minimum wages, and national health insurance, while Titmuss has supported these policies. Friedman would have individuals and families develop their own insurance (retirement and health) plans, find the housing they can afford in the marketplace, and be free to choose work at whatever wages are offered. If government is to get involved, it should only do so with the poor and "those whom we designate as not responsible," e.g., children and the mentally ill. Titmuss disagrees and argues that risks should be shared and services available to all citizens because they are bonded by their citizenship. What needs to be stressed is that when we view Friedman and Titmuss in terms of their first principles (freedom or community), both are logical and consistent in their recommendations.

We introduced Titmuss and Friedman to identify polar positions on the role of the state and appropriate social policies. Both are radical in their prescriptions. Both are arguing for a society that does not exist, i.e., Friedman for competitive capitalism and Titmuss for a pure socialist state. With few exceptions, most people find themselves some place in between and probably to the near right or left of center. For example, neoconservatives such as Moynihan (1986, 1988), Glazer (1983, 1987), and Kristol (1978, 1983) argue that many of the human services have created dependency (and thus have reduced individual freedom) and that to continue on our present course would help neither the recipients of the services nor the economic system. However, unlike others who are more conservative, they do not argue for drastic retrenchment of social expenditures as such. Rather, they propose a shifting of these resources from direct services to indirect services, from social services to benefits that permit the recipient to enter the market to purchase services. Theoretically, this would allow families to develop their own capabilities in that it allows for choice. Examples of policies neoconservatives might support would include national health insurance, housing vouchers, and negative–income tax programs. Liberals (i.e., New Deal, Great Society liberals) support these policies but also defend the value of social services and direct governmental provision of these services. What becomes apparent, however, is that, unlike Friedman and Titmuss, neither the neoconservatives nor the liberals have a comprehensive theory underlying their positions—a theory of the state.

Up to this point, the argument is simple enough, i.e., values shape the policy process and the carrying out of policy analysis. The next section extends this discussion and focuses on formulations of social policy. It is influenced by what Boulding (1967) called the search for common threads that unite all social policies and common denominators to evaluate heterogenous policies. In his view, social-policy analysis, unlike economic analysis with its clear structure and relatively simple body of principles, "looks

like a sticky conglomeration of the ad hoc" (1973:5). The purpose of this
section is to explore how one might operationalize an abstract goal and
eventually generate criteria for analyzing alternatives.

Social Policy: Purposes and First Principles

Titmuss (1968) views social policy as concerned with different types of
moral transactions embodying notions of exchange, or reciprocal obligations, which have developed in modern industrial societies in institutional
forms to bring about and maintain social and community relations. Within
this framework, the concerns of social policy are identified as essentially
moral rather than technical. Titmuss is not alone in his definition of social
policy encompassing moral transactions and social relations. Schottland
(cited in Gil 1973) defines social policy as a "statement of social goals and
strategy, a settled course of action dealing with the relations of people with
each other, the mutual relations of people with their government" (1973:5).
Boulding argues that the "objective of social policy is to build the identity of
a person around some community with which he is associated" (1967).
MacBeath suggests that "social policies are concerned with the right order-
ing of the network of relationships between men and women who live
together in societies, or with the principle which should govern the activities
of individuals and groups so far as they affect the lives and interests of other
people" (1957:3). Tawney (1964) in his work on equality identifies fraternity
and fellowship as prime concerns for social policy. Others, such as Gil
(1973) and Ponsioen (1962), view social policy in similar terms, i.e., moral
transactions and social relations.

These ideas also have a foundation in traditional sociology. Nisbet suggests that the "rise of sociology was a direct response to, or reflection of,
new forms of association life in Western Europe, forms that industrialism and
social democracy brought with them" (1967:47). Within this tradition, community was viewed as:

> all forms of relationships which are characterized by a high degree of personal
> intimacy, emotional depth, moral commitment, social cohesion and con-
> tinuity in time. Community is founded on man conceived in his wholeness
> rather than in one or another of the roles, taken separately, that he may hold in
> a social order. (1967:47)

As a social scientist, Nisbet then argues that most of the earlier so-
ciologists were concerned with the idea and reality of a moral community.
These social theorists include Comte, LePlay, Tonnies, de Coulanges,
Weber, Durkheim, Simmel, and—from a radically different perspective—
Marx. While each of these writers indicts the excessive individualism, im-

personality, acquisitiveness, and rational calculating of capitalism, they do not agree with each other. Marx, for example, suggests that the loss of community is a consequence of capitalism, while Tonnies treats capitalism as the consequence of loss of community. Both Marx and Durkheim are critical of societies "in which economic activities and values have become separated from and commanding over all other spheres of collective life. The most intense social activity in modern industrial societies, economic activity, was the least social" (Horton 1964:286). All tend to argue that the notion of a moral community is critical, and that without this we will be faced with high levels of anomie and alienation. Unfortunately, their solutions are not very feasible. The enemies to be dealt with are the extension of bureaucratic forms of domination and their effect upon the quality of social life (Weber), capitalist modes of production (Marx), and the industrialization of society insofar as it has eroded social solidarity and moral relationships (Durkheim).

Kohlberg and Mayer (1972) take a similar position. The purpose of education, in their view, is to stimulate the development of ethical principles in students, i.e., mature stages of reasoning, judgment, and action, ethical patterns of judgment or problem solving, and justice. Basically, they are discussing social relations. Earlier we pointed out that a number of social-policy theorists viewed social relations as the primary object of social policy. Boulding develops this idea more fully when he suggests that social policy should be concerned with building an "integrative system," a system "that includes those aspects of social life that are characterized not so much by exchange in which a quid is got for a quo as by unilateral transfers that are justified by some kind of appeal to a status or legitimacy, identity or community" (1967:5). He suggests that a major purpose of social policy is to assist individuals and families in becoming members of communities. Why? Boulding's argument rests clearly on those concerns raised by earlier theorists. Alienated people cause problems and those integrated into a community solve problems:

> One thing is clear: we must look upon the total dynamic process of society as essentially a process in human learning. . . . It is even clearer that the development of social integration is a learning process. We have to be taught to love just as we have to be taught to hate. Practically nothing in human life comes naturally. It is from vague and formless biological drives and the extraordinary learning potential of the human nervous system that the intricate structure of our personalities, our identities, our values and our communities are molded. (Boulding 1967:9)

In his analysis of the blood transfusion system, Titmuss (1971) argues that such a system "shows that detailed, concrete programs of political change— undramatic and untheatrical as they may often appear to be—can facilitate

pression of man's moral sense. Thus, it serves as an illustration of how
al policy, in one of its potential roles, can help to actualize the social
d moral potentialities of all citizens" (1971:238). Policies not only reflect
values, they can also shape values and enforce behavior. In his examination
of a range of countries, Titmuss concluded that those societies that rely
solely on the voluntary giving of blood foster a sense of altruism, while those
that rely on paid or contract donors foster self-interest and individual gain:

> The role of social policy has thus to be redefined in a broader perspective. In
> the past . . . social policy provisions were economically and politically justi-
> fied as functional necessities. There was really little choice for society. The
> functional necessities of public health, factory and labor legislation, primary
> education and so forth made, in a sense, social policy inevitable. According to
> this interpretation of history, such limited or residual interventions by the state
> were needed to prevent the collapse of a particular kind of society and to
> operate as instruments of social control in relation to those elements in the
> population who threatened or were thought to threaten the established order.
> (1971:241)

Titmuss concludes that such a view of social policy gives rise to determin-
istic welfare theories and the belief that moral problems can be resolved by
technical means and social engineering.

We have, up to this point, assumed that the purpose of social policy is to
enhance community. With this as a first principle, we have presented a
theoretical rationale for this position. Given this, it is necessary to discuss
how this can be used to understand and analyze actual policies. We begin
this discussion by raising the question, Do existing social policies enhance
community? This question is critical in that we agree with Gil (1973) that
social policies are not merely potential solutions of social problems but can
be the underlying cause of existing problems.

First Principles: An Application

R. Friedman (1968) offers a useful framework that begins to operationalize
these concepts. He also begins by suggesting that policies can be classified
by purpose and that, depending on the purpose, specific forms of policy
design are likely to be implemented. While he does not directly deal with
the issue of community, the bridge is easily made.

Social-welfare policies, according to Friedman, can be initially dis-
tinguished into those that are pure welfare and those that are social insurance. The pure-welfare model tends to emphasize a curative function, while
the social-insurance model focuses on prevention. Table 2.1 has been developed from Friedman's analysis and identifies the tensions between the two

Table 2.1. Models of Social Welfare

	Social-insurance model emphasis	Pure-welfare model emphasis
Purpose	Prevention	Cure
Concept of fault	Restoration	Minimum standard
Eligibility	Entitlement	Charity
Eligibility	Earned Benefits	Unearned benefits
Administration	Centralized	Decentralized
Mode of distribution	Cash	In-kind

approaches, tensions that affect how and under what conditions goods and services are provided to different groups of people.

The Concept of Fault

Social policies implicitly divide the population into one of two groups: those who are experiencing problems or deprivation through no fault of their own and those who are to blame for their situation. This division was introduced in Chapter 1 in the discussion of the Social Security Act. This concept of fault has serious consequences related to levels of benefit. In those instances where the condition (problem, need, etc.) is not perceived to be the fault of the individual (e.g., old age and retirement are inevitable, veterans do not start wars, people lose their jobs because of uncontrollable events), benefits tend to be restitutionary. The beneficiaries have fallen from an economic or social position they once had and the program restores them to a previous position. Given this, benefits will vary according to the individual's status. For example, retirement benefits under the Social Security Act are measured by contributions and contributions are a function of wages. The more you earn, the more you contribute, the more you will receive, at least up to a point. The same is true for unemployment insurance. In principle, benefits are wage related, with minimum and maximum benefits set by state law.

Underlying other policies, however, is the concept of personal fault, whereby a person is perceived to be experiencing deprivation by choice— he or she is not blameless. With this as a beginning point, people should not be encouraged to choose deprivation, i.e., if the state provides benefits that are too attractive, adults will quit work. In these instances, benefits are not restitutionary but maintenance, and to provide an incentive to work, the maintenance must be at a bare minimum. Under the AFDC provision of the Social Security Act, each state determines that minimum and, depending on family size, each family will receive the same benefit. Moreover, in practice the benefit levels are only a percentage of what the state has established as necessary to meet basic needs

The Concept of Eligibility as a Right

Programs can be classified by whether eligibility is or is not a matter of right. In Friedman's definition of right, if a beneficiary follows the rules for claiming a benefit and meets the legal definition of a beneficiary, he or she must be given the benefit. He further points out that, in theory, the supply of the benefits must equal the number of beneficiaries. Finally, programs that define eligibility in terms of rights tend to provide goods and services to the middle-class population. Unemployment compensation, old-age pensions, and Medicare, all of which are provisions of the Social Security Act, are examples of benefits as rights. A recipient is required only to demonstrate that he or she is unemployed or elderly and has contributed to the program. No one, in theory, can be turned away because the supply of benefits has been exhausted. Moreover, these programs do not have the appearance of charity.

Other programs target the poor and use some form of means test. Beneficiaries must not only demonstrate need but must also prove that they are poor. Also, officials must investigate and verify eligibility on a case-by-case basis. When provision is based on rights, beneficiaries do not have to prove that they are poor, nor do they have to use their own resources before they receive benefits. In means-tested programs, they do. The means test is associated with programs that benefit people of inferior social position and usually result in stigmatization. This, in turn, serves as a deterrence by making receipt of welfare unpleasant. Furthermore, these beneficiaries are vulnerable—in times of fiscal retrenchment, programs for the poor are the first and simplest to cut.

Whereas programs tend to be universal when benefits are defined as rights, in means-tested programs they are selective in provision. We introduced this concept earlier when discussing the targeting of certain groups for goods and services. In that context, we suggested that many policies are reactive and deal with a residual population. *Selective* can also be used in another sense. Universal programs, by definition, provide benefits to all who meet eligibility requirements. In some selective programs, the eligible recipient is not guaranteed the benefit. Public housing is a good example of this. The supply of housing units is always smaller than the number of eligible families and program administrators must choose among beneficiaries. Furthermore, unlike universal programs, program administrators can deny anyone the power to review their decision.

The Concept of Earned Benefits

Friedman further distinguishes benefits between those that are earned and those that are unearned. Retirement pensions and unemployment insurance under the Social Security Act are earned, in the sense that the worker has paid into the system. AFDC and Supplementary Security Income (SSI), on the other hand, are considered charity, benefits that are not earned. The above earned benefits, however, are not in the strict actuarial sense "earned." It is more a sense of earning in psychological and political terms. People feel they have earned the benefit and there is no social stigma attached to the receipt of the benefit.

Unearned benefits, such as AFDC, carry a stigma, and the process of determining eligibility and monitoring the status of these families is basically to keep them from receiving the benefits. Rather than viewing recipients as people who are entitled to the maximum benefit allowed, AFDC mothers are seen as chiselers attempting to defraud the system. Moreover, Friedman argues that employees, in those programs where the recipient is viewed as having earned the benefit, tend to be helpful and polite while poor people are often kept waiting for service at a clinic or for a social worker's time.

Administration: Centralized versus Decentralized

In Chapter 1, we introduced the concept of federalism and pointed out that social policy involves all three levels of government: federal, state, and local. Prior to the twentieth century, state and local governments carried major responsibility, with the federal government minimally involved. Today, some programs are federal, some state, some local, and still others are a combination of levels. Friedman would place these on a continuum from highly centralized (federal) to highly decentralized (local).

With this as a beginning point, he argues that highly centralized programs tend to target the middle class, are highly bureaucratized with rules and regulation clearly spelled out, and finally that the programs are run by "clerks" who routinely carry out the policy. Decentralized programs, on the other hand, allow for professional discretion in dealing with recipients. Friedman's analysis is intriguing in that the latter approach (professional discretion and flexibility) would on the surface appear more attractive than government by clerks, but his conclusion is just the opposite:

> If government reduces itself to a roomful of clerks with merely ministerial duty, program initiative passes to the beneficiaries themselves. It is they who decide. . . . For those who comply with rigid rules and who can know and master the rules, it is far more manageable than the free discretion of the professional. Hence, the middle class tends to demand, paradoxically, that programs be as bureaucratized as possible. (1968:59)

The federal retirement program (OASDI) is such a program. AFDC, on the other hand, is more decentralized, administered by professionals, and allows for some discretion in application. Friedman concludes, however, that the poor tend to be victimized by such flexibility. An example of this was the refusal by many state welfare departments in the late 1960s to make available to welfare rights organization the manuals that welfare workers used to determine eligibility and benefits. Whereas clerks view beneficiaries as intelligent consumers to be served, professionals tend to be more patronizing and view beneficiaries as unequals.

Mode of Distribution: Cash versus In-Kind

Some programs provide benefits in cash while others provide for benefits in-kind. Cash payments give the beneficiary freedom to choose, to enter the market to purchase goods and services. In theory, cash benefits introduce the least amount of control. It is interesting that both preventive and curative, restitutionary and basic premium programs provide benefits in cash, e.g., OASDI, UI, AFDC, SSI. However, public opinion tends to run counter to cash grants for the poor. We question whether they are capable purchasers and continually experiment with reducing benefits by providing in-kind services such as food (commodity programs) or at least by controlling their purchasing through vouchers such as food stamps and housing allowances. Some welfare departments, moreover, have experimented with direct payments to landlords and utility companies when recipients have fallen behind in their payments.

Programs that define benefits as rights usually provide cash (a major exception is Medicare, but the rationale is to protect a defenseless recipient against an uncontrollable market); those that define benefits as charity usually provide in-kind.

First Principles Revisited

We have introduced Friedman's analysis of social policy to demonstrate the relevancy of the first principles discussed in an earlier section. The column on the left of Table 2.1 describes a system that would strengthen a sense of community—the position of Titmuss. It is not divisive, nor does it polarize the population. It assumes common risk, common need, and citizenship as the basis for eligibility. Wilensky and Lebeaux (1965) would refer to this as the *institutional approach* to social welfare. The column on the right correlates well with Milton Friedman's position—the extension of freedom. Benefits should be made available only when problems have occurred (the *residual approach*) and benefits should be proposed as temporary measures until the individual or family can function independently. Whereas Titmuss argues that "we" are the objects of social policy, Friedman argues that "they" are the object. The five sets of criteria are excellent examples of operationalizing first principles.

Criticism of the Purpose Approach

Bulmer (1981) offers a cogent and provocative analysis of the strengths and limitations of both the process and purpose approaches to policy analysis. He traces our rejection of the purpose approach with its concern for value explication to the rise of the social sciences following the first world war. In the tradition of the logical positivists, Park, a leading exponent of the new sociology "advocated the detached scientific study of social phenomenon untrammelled by political or philosophical ends" (1981:36). He felt that the "world was full of crusaders" and that the role of the social scientist should be that of the "calm, detached scientist." The social scientist did have a contribution to make to policy formulation but this contribution was achieved through the application of theory and methods, not through "moral and prescriptive explorations." These early social scientists believed that to go beyond theory and methods leading to understanding would result in a weakening of the professional status of the social sciences. To maintain their credibility as scientists, the sociologist, economist, and political scientist had to demonstrate that their personal values did not shape their work.

According to Bulmer, proponents of the value-analytic approach as characterized by those in the preceding section are "strong on application, moderate on empirical research and extremely weak on theory" (1981:39). In practice, their approach is less a science and more a "humanistic social science with strong links to history and philosophy and ethics" (1981:39). Bulmer cites Pinker, who argues that this approach "begins with fact finding and ends in moral rhetoric, still lacking those explanatory theories that might show the process as a whole and reveal the relations of the separate problems to one another" (1981:39).

Bulmer concludes his analysis with the recommendation that neither approach is adequate:

> The answer is not to discard a moral dimension altogether, but to combine it with an adequate theoretical and methodological structure. In this respect Gunnar Myrdal's magisterial survey of American race relations more than a generation ago, *An American Dilemma*, remains a model of the fusion between ethics and science that is both compelling and methodologically adequate. (1981:41)

Summary

This chapter has introduced two approaches to policy analysis and argued that the value-analytic approach is more relevant and more useful than the approach emphasizing process. While the latter may be the dominant approach to policy analysis in this country, the former approach is more clearly grounded in practice. The values of the analysts cannot be submerged in the process. Given this, it is only fair that the values that underpin the analysis be raised to the forefront so that the reader can more adequately understand why the analysis took the direction it did.

The remainder of the book attempts to demonstrate the value of this approach. Concepts from this and the previous chapter are applied in a number of policy areas. They include appropriate roles of government, the role of the private sector, our understanding of human behavior as it is shaped by economic rationales, and the critical tensions between first principles such as freedom, equality, and community in attempting to achieve social objectives through social policies. While the above may not be brought together in a tight and synoptic framework in each chapter that follows, the ideas in the first two chapters are the keys to such an understanding.

To make this manageable, we have chosen six applications. Furthermore, we have divided these six into two major sections. The first offers three examples of the application of this approach to substantive areas: income maintenance (Chapter 3), housing (Chapter 4), and the personal social services (Chapter 5). The second section focuses on three target population groups: families and children (Chapter 6), the poor (Chapter 7), and the aged (Chapter 8).

While the choice of these may be criticized as being too limited and other areas should have been included, e.g., mental health and medical care, our rationale is simple. First, we chose these topics because they are critical areas of social policy. Second, we include chapters on housing and the poor because they do not find their way into many social-policy texts and yet they raise issues that are key to most people's quality of life. Finally, the purpose of this monograph is not to offer an exhaustive treatment of all issues. We are more concerned with the application and relevance of the approach outlined in the first two chapters.

Finally, in the last chapter, we offer a review and synthesis of the critical issues we are still faced with in these areas and possible directions we might take.

CHAPTER 3

INCOME MAINTENANCE

In Chapter 1 we suggested that within our capitalist society the roles and functions of the sate are more narrowly prescribed than in other forms of political economy. Three basic arguments for exception to the agreed upon minimalist role were introduced and discussed: (1) the public-goods argument, (2) the externality argument, and (3) specific market imperfections.

Accepting these basic rationales, this nation over the past 50 years has evolved (though some would argue rather reluctantly) into its unique form of a modern welfare state:

> A welfare state is a state in which organized power is deliberately used (through politics and administration) in an effort to modify the play of market forces in at least three directions —first by guaranteeing individuals and families a minimum income, irrespective of the market value of their work or property; second, by narrowing the extent of insecurity by enabling individuals and families to meet "social contingencies" . . . which lead otherwise to individual and family crises; and third, by ensuring that all citizens without distinction of status or class are offered the best standards available in relation to a certain agreed range of social services. (Briggs 1967:29)

While Briggs does not offer a philosophical rationale for this statement, he is clear as to what the intervention involves: First, a welfare state has a responsibility to provide to everyone some agreed upon minimum income regardless of their work status. Second, the state has a responsibility to buffer various risks to economic security in an industrial society. These risks would include sickness, old age, and unemployment. Finally, Briggs would argue for a more egalitarian society, or at least a society that does not establish separate social-service delivery systems for the poor and the nonpoor. This last idea is a clear articulation of the importance of community as discussed in Chapter 2—an issue that is integrated throughout this book and dealt with in some detail in Chapter 5, The Personal Social Services.

The first two dimensions of the modern welfare state are associated with what we have come to label income maintenance or income transfer policies and programs. Income maintenance is a major pillar of the welfare state, a foundation upon which other social policies are built. As Beveridge so eloquently argued, the basic threats to all modern societies are: (1) want, (2) disease, (3) ignorance, (4) squalor, and (5) idleness (1942: para. 8). He continued to say that while health care, education, housing, and employment were essential to achieving and preserving the well-being of individuals and families, these efforts would be dissipated unless they were integrated with an adequate system of income maintenance.

Furthermore, recent national surveys suggest that most Americans believe that these functions are legitimate and worthwhile. The difficulties come when specific policies are evaluated or proposed, since their goals have to be balanced with other equally important goals. As Ozawa points out, we are constantly attempting to develop an income maintenance system that is based on "a coherent incentive system so as to preserve the work incentive, and yet, at the same time, allow the nation to care and provide adequately for vulnerable groups of individuals, i.e., children, the elderly and the disabled" (1982:viii). This is the dilemma we face: How do we create a desirable balance between economic goals and social goals?

This is the age-old issue that continues to shape the welfare debate and to raise that debate to an emotional level that often transcends the reality of available data. In other words, income maintenance is not a technical problem to be solved, though it has technical dimensions. It is, first and foremost, a moral problem that pulls and pushes us between values that cannot be maximized simultaneously—but values that we have been conditioned to believe in and hold dearly since childhood.

Theoretical Considerations

Income Maintenance and Political Economy

The search for such a calculus has become a major issue since many believe that the well-being of all individuals in our complex modern society depends on the economic system, its success in producing wealth, and the ways in which this wealth is shared. In simpler terms, the question can be reduced at the societal level to one that asks, How much income can we afford to transfer so that economic growth will not be adversely affected? At the micro level it becomes even more of an issue in that it begins to question whether the giving of financial support to an individual or family will have negative effects, i.e., will it prove to be a disincentive to work, which in turn would have adverse effects on the economic system?

This is, of course, the overarching question facing all political economies, regardless of ideology. While the language used—"create a balance between and among desirable objectives"—might suggest a sense of equal value or worth between economic and social objectives, such is not the case. Political economy is a term used to underscore the interrelationship between the political and the economic systems of a given country. This interrelationship, however, is not an equal partnership, since the primary purpose of the political system is to further the goals of the existing economic system. Social policies, including income maintenance policies, are created to function as instruments used by the political system to achieve specific economic objectives. In our country, this system is referred to as a market economy that has been shaped to reflect the demands of advanced capitalism. It is only through applying this framework that we are in a position to understand why our social policies are secondary to and dependent upon economic policies. In fact, it is fair to say that our social policies have meaning only within the framework of political economy.

Income Maintenance and the Concept of Citizenship

A second (and related) major framework useful in our understanding of past and existing social policies is the position developed by T. H. Marshall, a leading theorist in the area of British social policy. One of Marshall's many contributions to modern social policy is his work on the meaning of citizenship as a criterion for governments to build on when they develop and modify their policies (Marshall 1965). For Marshall, within our modern societies, the rights of individuals are determined by their ability to claim citizenship. Moreover, citizenship itself is a multifaceted status involving different aspects of rights. Finally, Marshall argues that these rights, involving three major categories of citizenship—(1) civil, (2) political, and (3) social—have evolved sequentially over the past 300 years.

As we moved from a feudal economy to a market economy, our practice of allocating rights (including access to goods and services) on the basis of social class began to be questioned. Pressure from a number of fronts to modify the more glaring inequalities found in such a class-driven society grew. These pressures were related in part to the emergence of a middle class that was concerned with both protecting its newly acquired status (and property) and maintaining a reasonably stable work force.

These concerns became the basis for creating the concept of *civil citizenship* in the eighteenth century and for providing "the rights necessary for individual freedom—liberty of the person, freedom of speech, thought and action, the right to own property and to conclude valid contracts and the right to justice" (1965:71). As Marshall points out, these rights were the domain of the judicial system.

The second component—*political citizenship*—only became a reality in the nineteenth century, when larger numbers of citizens were given the right "to participate in the exercise of political power, as a member of a body invested with political authority or as an elector of the members of such a body" (1965:72). Marshall points out that while political rights were considered unacceptable in the eighteenth century since they were seen as potentially damaging to the emerging capitalist system, they were now seen as necessary for the growth of modern capitalism. However, these new rights were viewed as narrow extensions of civil rights.

The third component—*social citizenship*—has only begun to emerge during the twentieth century. Under this, Marshall includes

> the whole range from the right to a modicum of economic welfare and security to the right to share to the full in the social heritage and to live the life of a civilized being according to the standards prevailing in that society. The institutions most closely connected with it are the educational system and the social services. (1965:72)
>
> Citizenship is a status bestowed on those who are full members of a community. All who possess the status are equal with respect to the right and duties with which the status is endowed. There is no universal principle that determines what those rights and duties shall be. . . . [T]he urge forward along the path thus plotted is an urge towards a fuller measure of equality. . . . Social class, on the other hand is a system of inequality. (1965:84)

Marshall disagrees with those who argue that current income maintenance policies maintain and strengthen existing inequalities since they only guarantee a minimum supply of essential goods and services or a minimum income. While he agrees that this system "raises the floor level at the bottom and does not automatically flatten the superstructure" (1965:101) he argues that "equality of status is more important than equality of income" (1965:103).

What proves problematic, however, is that the process of defining these "social rights" is open-ended and the list of these social rights is susceptible to change when circumstances of living change. As Dahrendorf (1976) suggests, the right to a minimum wage, to old-age pensions, to health care, to adequate housing and education are merely the beginning of a long and endless list.

While Marshall's first two aspects of citizenship—civil and political—are grounded in law and contract theory, the third—social rights—is not. Rather, it is primarily consensual and rests on the concept of social cohesion and shared social purpose. This again brings us back to the arguments proposed in Chapter 2 and the importance of community as a criterion when developing or analyzing social policies. It also helps us understand more fully why we encounter strong disagreement when we attempt to modify, expand, or add to the existing list of social rights. Donnison recognizes this and points out that we need to be actively involved with "creating and recreating an evolving social consensus" about those measures that will "protect the weak and reduce vulnerability and accompanying disadvantages" (1975:6).

Income Maintenance: An Instrument of Economic Policy

In Chapter 1, we introduced the notion that policy is concerned with decision-making and choosing among alternative courses of action. Choices have to be made among competing claims for resources, all of which may be desirable or, at least, desirable to some group. We also introduced into this discussion the reality that we can never maximize these competing claims simultaneously because of insufficient resources. In Chapter 2, we complicated an already complex issue by arguing that, in some instances, we are also faced with making choices between conflicting values or aspirations, e.g., the first principles of liberty, equality, or community, all of which are desirable but incapable of being maximized at the same time.

Earlier in this chapter we introduced Briggs's position that a modern welfare state is one that interacts with or even modifies the economic system so that the basic needs and security of individuals and their families are met. O'Neill agrees with this position:

> It is the duty of the community through the power of the state to modify deliberately the normal play of economic forces in a market economy in order to assist the needs of the underprivileged groups and individuals by providing every citizen with a basic real income adequate for subsistence, irrespective of the market value of his work. (1967:72)

While this view would appear to be reasonable given the unpredictability of modern life, whatever consensus we thought existed usually breaks down when we begin to operationalize the concept into policies and programs.

A major concern is that acceptable options must "create a desirable balance among the goals of high employment and positive economic growth and the broader social goals of choice and equality of opportunity" (Lampman 1984:7). What, then, constitutes "a desirable balance"? What are we capable of introducing into the economy that will moderate cyclical swings of production and employment?

Historically, we have come to accept a certain level of unemployment as inevitable if inflation is to be contained. In fact, full employment has been defined over the past 30 years to mean unemployment rates that ranged from a low of 4 percent in the Johnson administration to a high of almost 10 percent in the Reagan administration.

To put it another way, the two goals of full employment and price stability are in conflict. The more closely we achieve one, the further we move from the other. As inflation increases to an unacceptable level, we allow unemployment to increase as a deflationary strategy. As prices stabilize, we implement strategies to increase employment. This dynamic and cyclical phenomenon was summarized in the now famous "Phillips curve" (Phillips 1958).

Another part of the debate is concerned with both Briggs's and O'Neill's position that individuals and families be provided with an income "adequate for subsistence, irrespective of the market value of [that] work." While today this debate is concerned with minimum-wage policies and their perceived "negative" impacts on the American economy and our ability to remain competitive with other nations, the debate has a number of historical antecedents that have implications of a different kind for today.

Morris (1986) points out that as far back as 594 B.C., the Greek city-states distributed corn at reduced prices from public granaries to supplement low income, a practice continued for centuries in the Roman Empire. Similar policies were enacted in England between 1495 and 1597 through various poor-law statutes when the price of bread and other staples rose sharply. Perhaps the most important (at least in terms of understanding current income maintenance policies) were the reforms that occurred in England toward the end of the eighteenth century, especially those known as the Speenhamland System. This system offered, in effect, both a guaranteed minimum wage and the guarantee of work. In reality, it was a strategy to adjust real income to the needs of the worker and not to the prevailing wage structure. When employers argued that lower profits required their lowering wages (the market value of the work) the state intervened by subsidizing those wages, thus guaranteeing a minimum level determined to be adequate for meeting basic needs. The subsidy, as elaborate as it was, was basically tied to the price of bread.

Shortly after it was introduced, political economists (or perhaps more accurately, philosophers concerned with political economy) such as Smith, Bentham, Malthus, Ricardo, Mill, and Pareto attacked Speenhamland as a system that interfered with the natural workings of the market and those "laws" that determined these workings, e.g.:

- There is a fixed amount of funds available for wages regardless of the number of people who want work (J. S. Mill).
- There exists only a limited amount of money available for wages. When public assistance is subtracted from this pool, there remains that much less for wages (Adam Smith).

- To increase wages you must decrease the number of workers (J. S. Mill).
- Income distribution is determined by natural law, and this distribution will always be uneven (V. Pareto).
- Labor is bound to a wage that can never rise above subsistence (the iron law of wages) (P. Ricardo).
- Subsidized wages or wages above subsistence levels will encourage premature marriage and increase the birth rate to the point that population will outstrip resources (T. Malthus).

All agreed that to provide wages above market value and to guarantee these wages despite market fluctuations (i.e., to remove this issue from concerns about production, exchange, distribution, and price structure) would (1) stimulate employers to reduce wages since the state would make up the difference, (2) remove the from the employee any incentive to work since a living wage was guaranteed and not tied to productivity, and (3) result in dramatically lower levels of production.

These beliefs (there were few empirical studies to test these "laws" and "hypotheses") were accepted and the earlier Elizabethan Poor Law gave way to the Victorian Poor Law enacted in 1834—a law that has had a lasting impact on many aspects of our current income maintenance policies.

The political economists of the nineteenth century were not the "detached" social scientists of the twentieth century. Bentham, for example, treated political economy as a theological phenomenon and held that individual or even community deviations from the accepted economic "laws" were problems of moral turpitude and should be treated as sins.

Bentham's position became the theoretical underpinning for the new poor law since it embodied positive economic functions and negative welfare functions (true welfare was to be found in the economic market). Bentham argued that the "economic virtues of industry, sobriety and thrift were to be accorded a prominent place and raised to the level of spiritual values" (Poynter 1969:320).

Moreover, to stimulate this "industry," Bentham argued that poverty had to be defined as more than a social fact (i.e., the lack of money, etc., necessary to meet basic needs)—it also had to be viewed as a form of spiritual bankruptcy. To put it in simpler terms, if the problem was defined as a lack of resources leading to dependency, the solution was to give the poor person resources. The individual was not blamed for his or her condition because the problem was a structural problem involving economic cycles. But this interpretation leads to Speenhamland-type solutions!

If, however, the problem could be redefined as first and foremost a problem of dependency that led to poverty (over time we shifted the definition of dependency from one involving "moral pathology," to a condition involving "character flaws" or other forms of deficits) the solution would require the

dependent person to change. While the first definition concludes that poverty (a lack of resources) causes dependency, the new definition suggests that
people are poor because they are dependent. Bentham successfully combined the explanation of the problem with the solution or treatment of the
problem.

To complete the transformation, Bentham argued that the term *poverty*
(connoting a condition) should be replaced with the term *pauper* (connoting
a weakness in the individual). A pauper, then, was seen as someone with
serious character flaws or moral deficits, and pauperism was regarded as a
failure of character. In essence, Bentham was stating that God (and a
wrathful God at that) was a capitalist and salvation was to be achieved only
through an acceptance of the new work ethic—one that would transform
farmers into obedient factory workers who would show up on time, work a
full day, and accept without question the mind-dulling routinized tasks of
the new factory system. Finally, Bentham's reformulation of the earlier poor
law included the long-lasting prescription that anyone receiving alms, the
"dole," or "relief" should receive less than the lowest paid worker. Otherwise, there would be no incentive for workers to continue working or for
those receiving support to seek employment. This concept—less eligibility—was also a psychological device in that it reminded people of what they
did *not* want. As a policy, its purpose was to separate the genuinely poor
from those who were lazy.

Spencer took Smith, Bentham, and Ricardo, mixed them with his version
of Darwin's position on the survival of the fittest, and concluded that human
behavior also responds to natural laws and should not be the object of
government intervention. To involve government would impede the evolu-
tionary process and would lead to adverse consequences regardless of inten-
tions. If one group is supported, another is weakened since the first benefits
at the expense of the other. As Coll (1970:62) demonstrates, Spencer's ideas
became the theoretical underpinning for the emerging Charity Organization
Society, which over time emphasized personal failure as the major cause of
poverty and assumed that no one would work unless every aspect of their life
was constantly investigated, that close supervision was required, and that
the lowest level of relief should be given.

The remainder of the chapter will (1) introduce various rationales for
income maintenance programs, (2) describe our existing policies, and (3)
critique them against these different rationales.

Rationales for Income Maintenance Programs

There have been at least three major rationales offered to justify previous,
current, and proposed income maintenance programs:

- to buffer the risks associated with temporary or permanent unemployment;
- to stabilize the labor force and prevent the possibility of civil unrest;
- to promote a more egalitarian society through the redistribution of wealth.

These rationales, however, are neither exclusionary nor contradictory and are often used in some combination to argue for a particular policy.

1.   To Buffer the Risks Associated with Temporary or Permanent Unemployment.   This rationale is the most explicit of the rationales and dominates debates on income maintenance policies. It has been argued that the purpose of income maintenance policies is clearly stated in the words themselves, i.e., the maintenance of income during periods when a person is not working, whether these periods are temporary or permanent. Traditionally, we have identified five major threats to economic security of workers and their families:

- retirement because of age;
- inability to work because of industrial accidents;
- permanent disability or temporary illness;
- death of the breadwinner(s);
- unemployment caused by economic fluctuation.

Other formulations of income maintenance policies include such notions as the provision of economic security when employment is interrupted and the replacement of lost income. Under this rationale, we usually find three distinct formulations of the major purpose of these transfers: (1) to replace wages, (2) to prevent poverty, (3) to meet basic needs. If income maintenance programs are to replace wages, then the amount of income to be transferred to an individual would be equal to the amount earned while he or she worked. If the programs are to prevent poverty, the amount of income to be transferred would be the difference between actual income and the agreed upon poverty level. Finally, if the programs are structured to provide a minimum subsistence level, the task is to document what amount is required to meet basic needs. All of these would, moreover, must have an anti-inflationary mechanism in place that would increase the amount of the transfer as the cost of living increased.

2.   To Stabilize the Labor Force and Prevent the Possibility of Civil Unrest. Earlier in this chapter, we pointed out that in advanced capitalism the two goals of full employment and price stability are in conflict and that the more closely we achieve one, the further we move away from achieving the other. Periodic unemployment for some and more permanent unemployment for others has become a fact of life in our society. Our economy is such that (1) cycles of growth are always followed by cycles of decline, (2) inflation

ty increases as unemployment declines, and (3) structural and fric-
ictors in our economy "cause" higher unemployment rates in certain
markets, regional disparities, and the channeling of women and mi-
.ties into secondary labor markets with low paying, dead-end jobs.
Given this, some analysts argue that income maintenance policies are concerned with labor market effects, and that their primary purpose is to provide
disincentives to welfare when an expanding labor force is needed (i.e.,
eligibility is more difficult to achieve) but income support when the labor
force contracts (i.e, eligibility requirements are loosened).

3. To promote a More Egalitarian Society through the Redistribution of
Wealth. Since the days of the New Deal and the Great Depression, we
have been told that because of changes in fiscal policies, income maintenance policies, and the expansion of the health and social services, our
society is becoming more and more equal. Equality is, however, an extremely elusive term. As mentioned above, Marshall held that equality of
status is more important than equality of income. Others such as Keynes
(1931, 1936), Beveridge (1943, 1944), and Galbraith (1958) have argued
that equality of opportunity should be given the highest priority and that
efforts to produce a more equal society through the redistribution of income
and wealth would be inefficient. On the other hand, the Fabians, including
Titmuss (1958, 1968), Tawney (1931, 1964), and Crosland (1970), define
equality as some combination of opportunity *and* outcome. And finally,
there are those such as Gil (1973) and Harrington (1975) who most emphat-
ically argue for equality of outcome as our major priority.

When one deals with income maintenance, the primary focus of the
analysis is usually equality of outcome with attention paid to documenting
shifts in the distribution of income within that society. Specifically, we measure the shares of total income received by specific income groups (e.g., the
lowest fifth or the second-lowest fifth) and then plot them over time to
determine whether income inequality has increased or decreased (Plotnick
1987).

Major Income Maintenance Programs

Pre–Social Security Efforts

The picture dealing with the Victorian Poor Law painted earlier in this
chapter is harsh but accurate. In the early decades of the nineteenth century,
a major social agency—the New York Society for the Prevention of
Pauperism—listed the following as the leading causes of poverty:

- ignorance
- idleness

- intemperance
- imprudent and hasty marriages
- lotteries and pawnbrokers
- houses of ill fame
- too many charities

Agreeing with their colleagues and implementing Bentham's view of appropriate forms of relief (e.g., "less eligibility"), another major agency of the time—the New York Association for Improving the Conditions of the Poor—stated in its training manual for new workers:

> The evils of improvidence can never be diminished except by removing the cause, and this can only be done by elevating the moral character of the poor, and by teaching them to depend upon themselves. . . . The rule is *that the willingly dependent upon alms should not live so comfortably with them as the humblest independent laborer without them.* (Coll 1970:34; emphasis added)

Existing income maintenance programs were not only punitive during this period but were the purview of the private sector. There was very little government involvement at any level.

Furthermore, while there were cyclical periods of depression in the earlier days of this country's industrialization, jobs for the unskilled and the uneducated were more readily available. As Ozawa points out, "the economy which did not depend on high or advanced technology could produce endless jobs for the unskilled and the poor" (1982:7).

By the turn of the century, in a period that today we refer to as the Progressive Era, reformers such as Jane Addams, Lillian Wald, and Jacob Riis began to argue that the existing economic system did not operate as the theorists had hypothesized and that many people were unable to meet their needs. Still, these critics believed that capitalism was superior to any other form of political economy. Given this, they recognized the right and responsibility of the state "to interfere and to compulsorily modify and supplement its [i.e., market] operations" (Marshall 1972:31).

The reformers initiated a number of efforts that attempted to minimize these economic risks through collective measures in the public sector. Classical liberalism (competition, individualism, and laissez-faire) was rejected since "the realities of the economic market were making a nonsense of the normative theories of political economy" (Pinker 1973:75). And, finally, as Ozawa (1982) suggests, more and more we came to recognize that the welfare of each individual depends on the economic welfare of all and that we need to pool our resources if we are to deal with the risks we all may potentially experience.

In the area of income maintenance, two major programs dominated the first two decades of the twentieth century. (See Chapter 4 for a discussion of efforts in the area of housing.) In 1911, the first state worker's compensation (WC) law (or industrial accident insurance) was passed. Prior to the passage of this legislation, workers seeking compensation for work-related injuries (or their families seeking compensation for work-related deaths) were required to prove fault (usually negligence) on the part of employers in a court of law. In demonstrating fault, the injured worker had to prove that the accident was not caused by or related to (1) his or her own negligence, (2) the negligence of a fellow worker, or (3) the ordinary rights associated with employment. Given these legal barriers, few workers attempted to collect compensation, and of those who did attempt, few were successful. Worker's compensation laws removed these requirements and the concept of *fault* no longer was a consideration. Within Marshall's formulation, we had moved from the concept of rights associated with the first definition of citizenship (i.e., civil or legal) to the concept of rights associated with the third definition (i.e., social). By 1917, 40 states and territories had enacted similar legislation, and by 1929 only four states did not have worker's compensation programs. By 1988, 87% of labor force participants were covered.

During this period, a number of states began to provide means-tested, cash assistance to some categories of the poor—usually the old, the handicapped, and young children whose fathers had died. Perhaps the most common program found in the states was Mother's Aid, a program initially implemented in Missouri and Illinois in 1911. By 1935 all but two states had implemented this program. However, as Rothman points out, such support was not far removed from the earlier practices of the poor law:

> [W]idows did not receive their allowances as a matter of right the way a pensioner did. She had to apply, demonstrate her qualifications, her economic need and her moral worth and then trust to the decision of the welfare board. At their pleasure and by their reckoning she then obtained or did not obtain help. (Rothman 1978:78)

By 1935, 26 states had also passed old-age pension programs and 23 states had developed programs for the needy blind.

The Great Depression of the 1930s both changed and accelerated the nature and extent of public intervention, especially in terms of the federal government. In the early days of the New Deal, the Roosevelt administration emphasized economic recovery, i.e., intervention in the overall structure of the market system. Accepting the argument of the British economist Keynes, who rejected the idea of a self-regulating market and suggested that excessive savings and low levels of investment would decrease demand for goods and services, which in turn would increase unemployment, the government set out to prime a stagnant economy. The Keynesian solution was government spending—even if this were to result in deficit financing—and lower taxes on consumers to increase purchasing power (Keynes 1973).

Thus was born the myriad "alphabet programs": National Industrial Recovery Act (NIRA), Public Works Administration (PWA), National Recovery Administration (NRA), Civilian Conservation Corps (CCC), Federal Emergency Recovery Act (FERA), Works Progress Administration (WPA), and others too numerous to list.

One program, the Civil Works Administration (CWA) established in 1934, produced jobs for over four million persons in a matter of months. Although it was terminated in less than a year, it made a significant contribution: "Over 400,000 projects were started; 500,000 miles of road were built or repaired; 40,000 schools were built or improved; 500 new airports were established; parks, sewers, firebreaks, irrigation ditches, forestry trails and public buildings were started or improved" (Schottland 1963:33).

Social Security: A Shift in Federal Responsibilities

As the depression deepened, the federal government expanded its role beyond that of stimulating the economy and the employment market and for the first time in history began to deal more directly with the immediate economic needs of individuals and families. These efforts culminated in 1935 with the passage of the Social Security Act—an act that once and for all moved this society into the era of the modern welfare state. While initially the legislation was threatened on the issue of its constitutionality (i.e., is the federal government empowered to directly aid citizens or does this power reside in the individual states?) the Supreme Court eventually supported the administration, ruling in 1937 that it was constitutional for the federal government to go beyond its traditional role, and giving it legitimacy to act in the area of income maintenance.

To understand the magnitude of this action, we need only look at the data of Table 3.1. The Federal government expended almost $330 billion in 1985 compared to just over $2 billion in 1940. Furthermore, it is estimated that in 1986 this figure rose to $473 billion, or 11.3% of the country's gross national income. When state and local expenditures are added to these figures, over $770 billion or 18.4% of the GNP was expended on income maintenance programs (*Social Security Bulletin* 1989). Of the five federally administered or federally supported programs listed in Table 3.1, four came into being with the passage of the Social Security Act of 1935 (the exception being Workers Compensation, which preceded the act).

OASDI has always been the largest of the programs and since 1965 has represented over 50% of all federal income maintenance expenditures. Three of the other programs show a steady increase over the years, while the remaining program—unemployment insurance—fluctuates, as would be expected, with the cycles of the economy. For example, the largest UI expenditures ever were in 1982 (almost $21 billion), a year with a depressed

Table 3.1.   Public Income Maintenance Programs ($ Millions)

Year	Total	OASDI	UI ª	WC	PA ᵇ	SSI
1940	2,171	23	519	161	631	
1945	3,507	248	572	283	903	
1950	8,395	928	1,408	415	2,074	
1955	14,478	4,855	1,467	591	2,311	
1960	25,564	11,080	2,867	860	2,954	
1965	36,355	18,094	2,283	1,214	3,764	
1970	60,474	31,570	4,184	1,981	4,864	
1975	138,598	66,586	18,188	4,568	9,288	5,877
1980	227,977	120,272	18,756	9,632	12,144	7,857
1985	329,671	186,082	13,538	15,170	15,276	11,107
1988		214,486	12,159	15,979	16,964	14,533

ª UI was highest in 1982, $20,735,000.
ᵇ PA includes AFDC and GA; OAA, AB and APTD through 1973.
Source: Social Security Bulletin 52(9): 74 (September 1989).
 APTD: Aid to the Permanently & Totally Disabled
AFDC: Aid to Families with Dependent Children
 OAA: Old Age Assistance
  AB: Aid to the Blind
 G.A.:   General Assistance

economy and extremely high rates of unemployment (in an average week that year, over four million unemployed workers received benefits, compared to three million the previous year and two million in 1988). In the area of public assistance (PA), over $30 billion was spent in 1988 (including $17 billion for AFDC) and $14 billion for SSI, a program for poor elderly, blind, and disabled.

Social Security: The Social-Insurance Programs

As discussed in Chapter 1, the act included programs that were based on social-insurance concepts and programs that were based on social-assistance concepts in that they were extensions of the existing poor law. The social-insurance program of the 1935 act involved two complementary strategies and targeted two primary groups: (1) labor force participants, and (2) those unable to participate in the labor force. Both programs incorporated the ideas of (1) universal coverage, and (2) benefits as rights and non–means tested.

The first program, Unemployment Insurance, offered a combination of employee benefits designed to protect the worker against disability, illness, and temporary unemployment. The second program, Old Age Insurance (OAI), provided income support for those who were not connected to the work force because of retirement due to age. In time, the Social Security Act was amended to include additional groups not connected to the work force, e.g., widows raising dependent children (Survivors Insurance was added in 1939) and the disabled (Disability Insurance was added in 1956). Today, the social-insurance program is known as OASDI (the Old Age, Survivors, Disability Insurance Program). While Medicare (the medical insurance program for those eligible under the retirement and disability criteria) was passed in 1965 as the Title 18 amendment to the Social Security Act, technically it is not an income maintenance program in that funds are not transferred directly to the beneficiary.

The UI program is somewhat unique in that it is financed by employers through a special tax, which is collected by the Federal government (via the Unemployment Insurance Trust Fund), which then passes these funds on to the states to administer. While some of Roosevelt's advisors argued that this program should be the same as the other insurance programs (i.e., federal government administered) to ensure that all recipients would be treated the same way regardless of residence, in the face of some general resistance on the part of states to the growing role of the federal government, Roosevelt decided to include them more actively in the New Deal.

Unemployment benefits are provided as a right (there is no means test associated with either eligibility or amount of benefit) to workers who are unemployed through no fault of their own. Since the administration of the program has been given to the states, we do find some differences in both the amount and duration of benefits. In general terms, we find that each state has enacted a minimum and maximum amount tied to a worker's previous earnings (i.e., the higher the wage, the higher the benefit); that the norm is 50% of earnings up to that maximum; and that benefits are available for up to 52 weeks during periods of extended unemployment. Previously, the upper limit had been 26 weeks but lingering periods of high unemployment during the past ten years have resulted in the increase. In 1988, however, the average duration of benefits was 13.9 weeks, reflecting a period of high employment. Approximately 97% of labor force participants worked in covered jobs in that year.

The data in Table 3.2 demonstrate the fluctuations in the number of recipients over the past 50 years. Unlike the other income maintenance programs, which show a linear growth curve that is as much a function of population growth (with the exception of AFDC, which is more directly related to the economy), the increase or decrease in the number of UI recipients is directly related to economic cycles. The balance in the trust fund understandably grows and shrinks as the number of recipients increases and decreases. Since 1982–83, when the amount of funds in the trust fund had fallen to approximately $7 billion as a result of a poor economy, the average number of weekly recipients has remained under three million and the trust fund had grown to almost $32 billion by 1988.

Table 3.2.   Unemployment Insurance

Year	Average number of recipients weekly	Average weekly benefit ($)	Balance in trust fund at end of year ($ thousands)
1940	1,282,385	10.56	1,817,108
1950	1,606,164	20.78	6,972,295
1960	1,905,754	32.87	6,643,257
1970	1,804,631	50.34	11,895,901
1975	3,986,152	70.23	4,522,934
1980	3,350,326	98.92	11,446,283
1981	3,047,162	106.70	11,588,424
1982	4,060,730	119.37	7,482,261
1983	3,396,318	123.59	7,263,873
1984	2,476,340	123.28	11,556,897
1985	2,611,351	128.23	15,998,560
1986	2,649,989	135.72	19,932,395
1987	2,331,813	139.90	25,228,655
1988	2,056,481	144.53	31,885,200

Source: Social Security Bulletin 52(9): 109 (September 1989).

The counterpart of the UI program is OASDI. While the former attempted to buffer the risks associated with temporary unemployment for those able to work, this program was to do the same for those who were not able to work because of age or disability or whose livelihood was threatened because of the death of the insured worker, e.g., children. This program is funded through a special payroll tax paid by both employer and employee. Self-employed workers are also required to participate in the program. These funds are deposited in special trust funds (the OASI Trust Fund and the DI Trust Fund). The monies in these funds are administered by a board of trustees and can only be used to pay benefits and operating expenses of the program. Unlike a number of other income maintenance programs, OASDI is totally operated with funds collected through the special tax and deposited in the trust funds. There are no subsidies from the general revenues of government (see Table 3.3).

In determining the amount each employer and employee in a given year will pay, two factors are employed. The first is the tax rate and the second is the amount of total wages that will be taxed. Changes are made periodically to ensure the solvency of the fund.

While there is considerable debate about the health of the Social Security system (specifically OASDI), much of this is clouded with misinformation. Numerous polls show that many, if not most, young workers believe that there will not be sufficient funds for them when they retire (Harris and Associates 1981; Hart Research Associates, Inc. 1979).

Table 3.3.   Social Security Trust Fund ($ Millions)

Year	Receipts	Expenditures	Balance at end of year [a]
1940	592	28	1,745
1950	2,367	784	12,893
1960	20,629	11,072	20,829
1970	31,746	27,321	32,616
1975	58,757	56,676	39,948
1980	100,051	103,228	24,566
1985	179,881	169,210	33,877
1987	206,816	186,100	58,265
1988	235,720	197,201	96,964

[a] In 1982 the trust fund balance was at an all-time low of $12,535,000.
Source: *Social Security Bulletin* 52(9): 77 (September 1989).

In the first three decades of the Social Security program, most polls showed that most Americans thought highly of the program but had little understanding about it—including the insurance issue. By the mid 1970s, however, this began to shift markedly, and by 1978, over 60% had lost their confidence in the program (Sherman 1989).

In part this can be attributed to the belief that if OASDI is an "insurance" program, each contributor's payment should be set aside for his or her retirement, much like private annuity programs are operated. To put it another way, an insurance company is required to have sufficient funds on hand to pay off all of its contractual obligations either in the event that it goes out of business or if all of its policyholders decide at the same time to cash in their policies. OASDI is not an insurance program by this definition. It is, however, an insurance program in the sense that the program is designed (1) to continue indefinitely, (2) will accept new members, and (3) anticipates that revenues will be sufficient over a long-range period to meet expenditures, since (4) the program is compulsory (Schottland 1963). Rather than seeing the contribution as "paying" for the benefits, it is more accurate to think of these contributions as "qualifying" the individual for the benefits.

The data in Table 3.3 show that from the program's beginning and through 1975, annual receipts exceeded annual expenditures and that the trust fund's annual balance was continuously growing. By 1980, however, annual receipts had fallen below expenditures and the trust fund balances had decreased sharply.

This phenomenon can be attributed directly to the introduction in 1975 of the automatic cost of living adjustment (COLA), which is triggered to changes in the consumer price index (CPI). Given the high rates of inflation,

Congress passed a series of amendments in 1972 that not only introduced the automatic COLA, but in order to catch up with previous periods of high inflation, increased the benefits by 22% that year and 11% for the years 1973–74. While the policy change has had a positive impact on the quality of life of millions of people and has kept millions of recipients above the poverty line, it had the negative effect of almost wiping out the surplus funds in the trust fund.

Inflation, as measured by increases in the CPI, was relatively nonexistent for most of the years between 1940 and 1965 (see Table 3.4). With the exception of the postwar years 1945–50, the average annual rate of inflation was less than 1 percent. During the late 1960s inflation began to creep up, but it was only during the 1970s and early 1980s that the country experienced a major problem.

Two bipartisan committees were established in 1977 and 1983 to deal with this problem. Their attention turned to possible changes in the current financing mechanisms. One option, that of channeling general-revenue funds to "bail out" the OASDI trust funds, was rejected on the grounds that the strength of the program—the notion of "right to benefits"—would have been compromised. Second, the committee believed that to do so would open the door to making basic changes in the program, such as moving from universal coverage (an entitlement program) to selective provision (means testing). The committees reaffirmed the value of the institutional approach and rejected the residual approach. Instead, their focus was on strengthening the program within its fundamental philosophy.

The changes the two committees recommended for both the tax rate and the tax base are significant (see Table 3.5). From 1937 through 1972 (35 years) the taxable base (the amount of wages that were taxed) remained

Table 3.4.   Average Annual Increases in
             the CPI

Years	Increase (%)
1940–45	0.80
1945–50	1.22
1950–55	0.56
1955–60	0.48
1960–65	0.38
1965–70	1.46
1970–75	3.03
1975–80	5.76
1980–85	4.80
1985–88	2.02

Source: Social Security Bulletin 52(7): 31 (July
        1989).

Table 3.5. OASDI Tax Rates and Taxable Base [a]

Year	Tax rate [b] (%)	Taxable base ($)	Maximum annual tax ($ per employee)
1937–49	1.00	3,000	30
1950	1.50	3,000	45
1955	2.00	4,200	84
1960	3.00	4,800	144
1968	4.62	7,800	360
1970	4.80	7,800	374
1971	5.20	7,800	405
1972	5.20	9,000	468
1973	5.85	10,800	632
1974	5.85	13,200	772
1975	5.85	14,100	825
1976	5.85	15,300	895
1980	6.13	25,900	1,589
1981	6.65	29,700	1,975
1984	6.70	37,000	2,479
1985	7.05	39,600	2,792
1988	7.51	47,000	3,530
1989	7.51	48,000	3,605
1990	7.65	51,300	3,924

[a] The table has been divided into three parts. The first (1937–76) shows a pattern of steady but slow growth in both the tax rate and the taxable base. The second covers the early 1980s, when the 1977 amendments became operational. The third period reflects the dramatic corrections made in the system to deal with both short-range and long-range problems.
[b] Rate for both employer and employee. The tax rate for the self-employed was somewhere between the combined employer-employee rate.

under $10,000, and from 1972 through 1976 the tax base did increase but only marginally. Following the recommendations of the 1977 committee, the taxable base jumped to $25,900 in 1980 and just under $30,000 in 1981. Still, these were only stopgap measures attempting to deal with the current crisis. The balance in the trust fund, in spite of these measures, reached a historical low of $12.5 billion in 1982. The second set of more radical recommendations was implemented in 1984. Not only did the taxable base jump sharply, but for the first time in the history of the program, higher-income beneficiaries were required to pay taxes on up to 50% of the benefits.

To put this into perspective, if a worker began paying into the Social Security system in 1937 and worked for 13 years, and if his or her income was the maximum to be taxed, he or she would have contributed approximately $435 during that whole period. If that same worker continued to work for another 10 years, he or she would have contributed an additional $855, for a 23-year grand total of $1,290. A worker beginning in 1980, however, earning the maximum to be taxed would have contributed more than the older worker in that single year: $1,589.

By the end of 1988, over 38 million persons—72% of whom are over the age of 62—were receiving benefits under the largest of the income mainte-nance programs, OASDI. As Table 3.6 shows, while the ratio of retirees to those receiving benefits as disabled and survivors has fluctuated over the past 50 or so years, the retirement program has always accounted for at least two of every three recipients. The data in Table 3.6 also show that the number of recipients in the other two programs plateaued in the 1980s. It is remarkable that over 10% of all Americans are receiving benefits under this program. Of these, 54.3% are women, 37.3% are men, and 8.4% are chil-dren.

While average monthly benefits grew over the years, the growth following the introduction of the COLA trigger in 1974 was extraordinary (see Table 3.7). Average annual increases for the old-age program was 4% in the 1950s and 6% in the 1960s. Corresponding annual rates of increase for the sur-vivors program and for those covered under disability were comparable, ranging from 5 to 8%. Given the high inflation of the 1970s and the automat-ic increases in the benefit level, we experienced double-digit increases: an average annual increase of 19% in the retirement program, 20% in the survivors program, and 18% in the disability program. While the early 1980s continued to experience high inflation, the decade through 1988 showed moderate increases in the benefit levels (7, 7, and 5% respectively).

If we now combine the data in Tables 3.5–3.7, we see a pattern of moderate growth in the 1960s, with the increase in expenditures a function of an increase in both the number of recipients and the average monthly

Table 3.6.   OASDI Beneficiaries (Thousands)

Year	Retirees	Disabled	Survivors	Total
1940	148		74	222
1950	2,326		1,152	3,478
1960	10,599	687	3,558	14,844
1970	17,096	2,665	6,468	26,229
1975	20,364	4,352	7,368	32,084
1980	23,336	4,682	7,601	35,619
1985	25,991	3,907	7,160	37,508
1986	26,551	3,993	7,164	37,708
1987	26,995	4,045	7,150	38,190
1988	27,384	4,074	7,169	38,627

Source: Social Security Bulletin 52(9): 75 (September 1989).

Table 3.7. OASDI Average Monthly Benefit ($)

Category	1940	1950	1960	1970	1980	1988
Retiree						
Worker	22.60	53.86	74.04	118.10	341.41	536.74
Spouse	12.13	23.60	38.72	61.19	171.95	276.94
Child	9.70	17.05	28.75	44.85	140.49	227.73
Survivor						
Widow	10.28	36.54	57.68	101.71	308.12	489.56
Child	12.22	28.43	51.37	82.23	239.52	367.60
Disabled						
Worker	—	—	89.31	131.29	370.74	529.50
Spouse	—	—	34.41	42.55	110.48	138.44
Child	—	—	30.21	38.63	110.30	150.93

Source: Social Security Bulletin 52(9): 87 (September 1989).

benefit; sharp increases in expenditures in the 1970s were caused by increases in the amount of benefits provided and relatively slow growth in this decade. The so-called crisis in the OASDI program appears to be resolved and the program will continue to be solvent through the first 25 of the next century, or at least until the next period of sustained inflation. Moreover, while the Hart Research Associates, Inc. (1971) and Harris and Associates (1981) polls mentioned above showed a society pessimistic about the strengths and values of such a system, Yankelovich, Skelly and White (1985) found these trends being reversed: 90% of Americans supported the COLA; 67% agreed that social security taxes should be raised if needed; and by a two-to-one margin, military expenditures should be cut before Social Security expenditures.

Table 3.8. Average Annual Increase 1960–1988 (by Decade)

Decade	Category	Increase (%)
1960–70	Recipients	7
	Expenditures	13
	Monthly benefit	6
1970–80	Recipients	4
	Expenditures	28
	Monthly benefit	19
1980–88	Recipients	1
	Expenditures	9
	Monthly benefit	7

Social Security: The Social-Assistance Programs

The Roosevelt administration concluded that even with the passage of the two insurance programs that were the centerpiece of the Social Security Act (OASDI and UI), a significant number of Americans would not be covered for a quite a few years. Immediate steps had to be taken. For example, in 1933 approximately 15 million Americans were unemployed and 19 million (almost 16% of the population) were receiving some form of state-administered public assistance. The OASI and UI programs were not designed to help all of these people.

While the social-insurance program was seen as a long-range solution to a structural problem, the administration proposed a number of short-range income maintenance programs to complement the various employment-related strategies. Between the two efforts—(1) stimulating the employment sector, and (2) transferring income to those unable to work—the administration assumed that the immediate crisis would be met. Unlike the insurance programs, however, these efforts were thought of as temporary and as providing support to a smaller and smaller residual of the population.

The evolving Social Security legislation was thus expanded to include a special program for those who were clearly in need and unable to help themselves. Need was to be defined as poverty, and eligibility was to be determined through a means test. As so often happens, those responsible for "creating" the program looked for comparable examples. As mentioned earlier, over half of the states had already implemented public assistance programs for the elderly and the blind, and virtually all states had programs for children whose wage-earning parent had died. Furthermore, the federal government had already taken steps to support these states when they were in fiscal crisis by providing loans to the states. The Emergency Relief and Construction Act of 1932 provided $300 million for this purpose and the Federal Emergency Relief Act of 1933 made an additional $2.5 billion available. It was unnecessary to invent a new system—the infrastructure for the program was already in place.

The social-assistance programs targeted these three groups. Old Age Assistance (OAA) was designed to provide financial assistance to elderly persons who were poor; Aid to the Blind (AB) to those who were blind and poor; and Aid to Families with Dependent Children (AFDC) to children who lived in a family whose breadwinner had died. The important distinction between the insurance and the assistance programs is that the former is an entitlement program whose eligibility criterion is a demonstration of membership in a covered category (e.g., insurance coverage, age, level of disability); while the latter involves two sets of criteria for eligibility: membership in a category (e.g., age) plus documented poverty. These three programs were expanded in 1956 with the inclusion of the permanently and totally handicapped who were poor (this mirrored the expansion in the same year of the social-insurance program that provided coverage to handicapped and disabled workers).

These programs are referred to as "categorical programs" in the sense that they provide support only to those individuals who are poor and fall into one of the four designated categories: aged, blind, disabled, or dependent children. Unlike the social-insurance programs, they are:

- funded through general revenues and not a special tax;
- partially financed by the federal government and partially by state and local governments;
- administered by the states, who set eligibility criteria and benefit levels within a set of federal parameters; and
- means tested and not needs tested.

While the federal share tended to be more uniform in the earlier decades of the programs, in 1958 the sharing formula shifted in favor of those states with fewer resources, higher rates of poverty, and lower annual per capita income. While the formulas were and still are (in the case of AFDC) somewhat complicated, this share over time has averaged around 50% of total costs of the transfers (the federal share of some of the administrative costs has been higher).

In 1988, over 15 million individuals were receiving financial assistance under one of these programs. Approximately 10% were elderly, 20% disabled, 1% blind, and 70% dependent children and their parents. Over 7 million of the total 15 million recipients were children. These ratios have remained fairly constant over the past ten years (see Table 3.9).

From 1980 to 1988, the total increase of all recipients was 3%, the number of disabled persons increased by 31%, the number of blind by 6%, the number of dependent children and their parents by 1.4%. The number of elderly recipients, on the other hand, decreased by 20% during that same period.

Three of the programs were consolidated and federalized in 1974, leaving AFDC as the sole state-administered program. The "new" program—Supplemental Security Income (SSI, which combined OAA, APTD, and AB)— established a single set of eligibility criteria and standardized the amount of the benefits (Table 3.10).

To understand the significance of this shift in program financing (the new program was financed totally by the federal government from general revenues) and administration, we need only look at the level of benefits provided by the programs before the transfer. The figures in Table 3.10 represent average monthly benefits paid to individuals under each of the four programs.

Under the earlier federal-state program, we find that the amount of a

Table 3.9.   Social-Assistance Income Recipients
              (Thousands) [a]

Year	OAA	APTD	AB	AFDC	Total
1940	2,070	—	73	1,222	3,365
1945	2,056	—	71	945	3,072
1950	2,786	69	97	2,233	5,185
1955	2,538	241	104	2,192	5,075
1960	2,305	369	107	3,073	5,854
1965	2,087	557	85	4,396	7,125
1970	2,082	935	81	9,659	12,757
1973	1,935	1,168	80	10,949	14,131
1974 [b]	2,286	1,635	75	10,864	14,860
1975	2,307	1,933	74	11,346	15,660
1980	1,808	2,256	78	10,744	14,916
1981	1,678	2,262	79	11,079	15,098
1982	1,549	2,231	77	10,358	14,215
1983	1,515	2,307	79	10,761	14,662
1984	1,530	2,418	80	10,832	14,860
1985	1,504	2,551	82	10,855	14,992
1986	1,473	2,713	83	11,038	15,307
1987	1,455	2,846	83	10,814	15,198
1988	1,433	2,947	83	10,900	15,363
1989	1,427	3,005	83	(NA)	

[a] These statistics are for the end of December each year, with
   the exception of 1989, which is based on the latest available
   month (June).
[b] OAA, APTD and AB were federalized in 1974 under the term
   SSI.
Source: Social Security Bulletin 52(9): 92 (September 1989.).

recipient's benefit was related to the specific category he or she qualified for,
regardless of his or her resources. All recipients had to pass the same means
test, so we know that they were all equally poor. Historically, however,
recipients who were blind received the highest benefit, and for the past 25
years the disabled received the next highest level of benefits. Children received the lowest.

To put this into perspective, the benefit an elderly person received under
the OAA program represented about 75% of that received by a disabled
person under the APTD program, about 70% of that received by a blind
person under the AB program, and 150% of that received by a child under
the AFDC program. In part these differences were justified with the rationale
that each group had more or less financial need depending on its status, i.e.,
a blind poor person needed more because he or she was blind, a child
needed less because he or she was a child. In part, however, these differences can also be explained by the fact that when increases in benefits

Table 3.10.   Social-Assistance Programs—
Average Monthly Benefits ($)

Year	Aged	Disabled	Blind	AFDC
1940	20.25	—	25.35	9.85
1945	30.90	—	33.50	15.15
1950	43.05	44.10	46.00	20.85
1955	50.05	48.75	55.55	23.50
1960	58.90	56.15	67.45	28.35
1965	63.10	66.50	81.35	32.85
1970	77.65	97.65	104.35	49.65
1973	80.00	106.10	112.85	53.95

Source: *Social Security Bulletin, Statistical Supplement:*
56 (1974).

were made, some groups were more acceptable than others—or in the language of the Elizabethan Poor Law, some were "more worthy" than others.

The 1974 federalization of the social-assistance programs for the old, the disabled, and the blind also had a major impact on the economic well-being of many of the recipients in that a national standard of benefit was developed. The data in Table 3.11 show dramatically the range of benefits in each program in the year preceding this action. Under each program, the three states with the highest benefit levels are identified and then the three states with the lowest levels.

Although the average monthly benefit payment to an elderly recipient was $80 in 1973, benefits ranged from a high of $119 in Alaska to a low of $40 in New Hampshire. Similarly, benefits for the disabled ranged from $57 in Louisiana to $168 in Alaska; for the blind the range was a low of $66 in Mississippi to a high of $174 in Alaska; for a child the low was $14 in Mississippi, the high $86 in Hawaii. These differences were defended with the argument that benefits should reflect regional differences in the cost of living.

While the cost of living does differ by region (especially in Alaska and Hawaii), it is difficult to argue that the cost of living is 282% higher for someone living in Massachusetts compared to an elderly person living across the border in New Hampshire, or 200% higher for that same person compared to someone living in Texas or Mississippi. We find the same wide range in the other three categories. A disabled person in Massachusetts received over 250% more than a disabled person living in Louisiana, Indiana, or Mississippi; a blind resident in Massachusetts received a benefit over 200% higher than his or her counterpart living in Mississippi, New Hampshire, or New Mexico. And finally, a child receiving AFDC benefits in

Table 3.11.   Social-Assistance Monthly Benefits—Ranges in 1973

	OAA	APTD	AB	AFDC
High	AK ($119)	AK ($168)	AK ($174)	HA ($86)
	MA ($113)	MA ($159)	CA ($165)	MN ($83)
	HI ($112)	CA ($148)	MA ($155)	NY ($81)
Low	NH ($40)	LA ($57)	MS ($66)	MS ($14)
	MS ($54)	IN ($60)	NH ($74)	AL ($22)
	TX ($54)	MS ($65)	NM ($74)	LA ($25)

Source: Social Security Bulletin, Statistical Supplement: 56 (1974).

Minnesota received a grant 600% higher than a poor child in Mississippi, 377% higher than a child living in Alabama, and 332% higher than a child in Louisiana. These differences, in some instances staggering in their magnitude, cannot be explained totally as responses to differences in the cost of living. They were the direct result of allowing each state to determine the level of the benefit. Some states were more generous; others were more miserly. Some states were more progressive; others were still ruled by strongly held poor-law beliefs. This is clear when we examine southern states and analyze the differences of benefits within a state between the categories. Earlier we pointed out that nationally an elderly person's benefit under the OAA program was 150% higher than a child's benefit under the AFDC program. In Mississippi, the difference was 386%! To a large extent this can be explained on racial grounds. While AFDC recipients included both white and minority children, the popular belief (and myth) held that the majority of AFDC recipients were black.

The passage of the SSI program solved the problem for the elderly, the disabled and the blind. The problem remains, unfortunately, for dependent children (see Table 3.12). The same 1972 amendments that provided for automatic COLAs for OASDI recipients operate for SSI recipients. AFDC benefits, on the other hand, are not automatically increased to keep abreast of inflation. Increases have to be passed by legislatures in each state, and most do so only sporadically. For example, the average monthly AFDC benefit for a family of three in 1987 was $359 but the same states we analyzed in Table 3.11 still showed wide variations. The monthly average in Minnesota was $532 while the averages in Mississippi, Alabama, and Louisiana were $120, $118, and $190, respectively.

To understand these differences better, we need to introduce the criterion of "basic need standard." As discussed above, the 1935 legislation passed on to the states the authority to establish eligibility criteria and benefit levels. To carry this out, the states were required by the federal government to identify the amount of money families of various sizes would need to meet their basic needs. While the federal government required the states to determine these standards, they did not require the states to pay this amount.

Table 3.12. Aid to Families with Dependent Children

Year	Number of families (thousands)	Number of children (thousands)	Total expendend ($ millions)	Average monthly grant per family ($)
1936	147	361	49.7	28.15
1955	612	1,673	617.8	84.17
1960	787	2,314	1,000.8	105.75
1965	1,039	3,256	1,660.2	133.20
1970	2,208	6,214	4,853.0	183.13
1975	3,498	8,095	9,211.0	219.44
1980	3,712	7,419	12,475.2	280.03
1986	3,763	7,334	16,033.1	355.04

Source: Social Security Bulletin, Annual Statistical Report· Table 9.61 (1988).

Given this, only 20 states provided benefits that were 100% of the standard; 7 states between 75 and 99% of the standard; 14 states between 50 and 74% of the standard; and 9 states less than 49% of the standard. Keep in mind that these standards were established by each state and not by the federal government. Finally, in looking again at the same four states, in 1987 Minnesota's benefit was 100% of the need standard, Mississippi's was 33% and both Alabama's and Louisiana's were 31%.

While there are a number of important aspects of the AFDC program that have not been discussed, they will be introduced in the next section of the chapter.

A final income maintenance program under the heading of social assistance is the Food Stamp Program, established in 1964 by the Food Stamp Act. Persons whose income and assets fall below nationally derived standards may receive coupons redeemable for food at most retail food stores. The amount each individual or family receives is determined by household size and income. Over the past decade 21 million persons or approximately 10% of Americans have received food stamps. Sixty-seven percent of these recipients had incomes below the poverty line. Total costs of the program have risen from $32 million in 1965, to $4.8 billion in 1976, to $9.6 billion in 1980, and to $13 billion in 1986 (DiNitto and Dye 1987).

Income Maintenance Programs: A Critique

Earlier in this chapter, three major rationales used to justify income maintenance programs were identified. This last section of the chapter will assess the current system in terms of these rationales to determine the extent to which they have been successful.

1.   To Buffer the Risks Associated with Temporary or Permanent Unemployment.   Within this broad rationale we suggested that three somewhat differing purposes are proposed, each of which needs to be addressed in turn: (1) to replace wages, (2) to prevent poverty, (3) to meet basic needs. As we stated earlier, if the purpose of income maintenance programs is to replace wages, then the amount given to a recipient should vary according to his or her earnings history. If the programs are to prevent poverty, the amount of income to be transferred should be the difference between actual income and the agreed upon poverty level. Finally, if the programs are structured to provide a minimum subsistence level, the task is to document the amount required to meet basic needs. All of these would, moreover, have to have an anti-inflationary mechanism in place that would increase the amount of the transfer as the cost of living increased.

If we annualize the average monthly (or, in the case of UI, the weekly benefit), the average recipient in 1988 would have received the amounts shown in Table 3.13. Since the 1988 median family and per capita income were, respectively, $30,000 and $16,000, it is clear that none of these programs replaces income if income is defined as prevailing wages. One could, presumably, argue that a 90-year-old OASDI beneficiary who retired in 1965 might actually be receiving more than he or she earned and that the benefits, in fact, have replaced his or her wages. However, a realistic definition must take into account inflation. Instead, it is more reasonable to compare benefits to current workers.

A wage replacement program would also be more closely tied to individual earnings. In theory, a recipient's benefits under the OASDI and UI programs would vary according to previous wages. Higher earners, for example, pay more into the OASDI and receive higher benefits. However, there is a minimum and a maximum amount regardless of previous earnings.

Were the programs ever intended to replace wages? No, although many believe they were to do so. The architects of the 1935 Social Security Act, in looking to the insurance program implemented by Bismarck, incorporated most of the German system, including the philosophy that pensions should reflect income inequalities. This approach—the insurance approach—assumes that the more you have the more you should get, unlike the assistance approach, which assumes that the more you have, the less you should receive.

However, the original recommendations found in the Social Security Act also included provision for a voluntary government plan for old-age annuities to be sold competitively by the government (Derthick 1979). Apparently, the administration did *not* envision the new program to be a wage replacement program—otherwise there would have been no need for such an annuity program. Rather it was to protect the retiree by providing a floor or safety net. While there was early sentiment among some in Congress and

Table 3.13. Average Annual Benefit by Program (1988)

Program	Recipient	Benefit ($)
UI	Unemployed worker	7,515
OASDI	Individual retiree	6,441
	Retiree and spouse	9,764
	Survivor and one child	10,286
	Survivor and two children	13,344
	Disabled individual	6,354
	Disabled, spouse, and one child	9,826
AFDC	Parent and 2 children	4,308
SSI	All categories	3,336
	Elderly	2,388
	Blind	3,864
	Disabled	3,780
Median family income		30,000
Medan per capita income		16,000

Source: Social Security Bulletin 52(7): 76, 77, 86, 87, 93 (July 1989).

in the administration for a universal, flat-rate benefit, most believed that such an approach would be unacceptable to most people since it seemed to resemble the existing public assistance system—the dole. Political acceptability meant promoting the program as an insurance program. The trick was to make a program whose purpose was really to meet basic needs look like a wage replacement program.

During this period when the Social Security Act was being debated in this country, the British system was evolving. Beveridge, faced with the same issue (i.e., to what extent should benefits reflect prior earnings?) came down on the side of equal contributions and equal benefits for all. Moreover, he believed that the benefits should be fixed at the *subsistence* level or, in his words, a "national minimum" (Beveridge 1942:143).

While Beveridge argued that social insurance was a collectivist solution to the problem of meeting basic needs, he argued as strongly that to do more than meet those basic needs was to interfere with the natural workings of the market. To provide for total need would interfere with individual responsibility and would act as a disincentive to competition—the lifeblood of capitalism. Instead, he created a system that provided for the basic needs of everyone but allowed "individuals to create individual differences" through voluntary savings and retirement plans (Marshall 1965).

In answer to our original question then, it would be reasonable to conclude that the primary purpose of our income maintenance programs is not to replace earnings but to provide funds sufficient to meet basic needs. Although we do not have a flat-rate benefit like the British system, our system, even with its different benefit levels, is in reality similar in intent despite some rhetoric to the opposite.

To what extent does this system prevent poverty—the remaining stated purpose under this rationale? This is a more difficult question to answer in that many recipients also receive in-kind benefits that, if cashed out, might offer a more complete and realistic picture. These include food stamps, various housing subsidies, and medical care. For this analysis, we will focus only on the income maintenance programs.

The data in Table 3.14 provide a mixed response. The benefits an unemployed worker receives are above the poverty level if and only if the worker is single. It is important to note, however, that while the intent of the program is to protect the worker who finds himself or herself temporarily out of work, the average benefit has not kept up with inflation and, depending on the size of the worker's family, may provide an income that is below the poverty line. For example, the average benefit in 1988 was $144.53. This works out to $3.61 an hour or $7,500 a year.

The OASDI programs do offer benefits that, on the average, are above the poverty level. However, when we speak of average, we are not talking about a floor below which no one falls. Sixty-two percent of OASDI beneficiaries aged 65 or over receive one-half of their total income from Social Security, 24% rely on Social Security for at least 90% of their income, and 14% obtain all of their income from Social Security.

Moreover, if the COLA provision had not passed in 1974, many more would be living below poverty. This was dramatically pointed out by James Roosevelt, a Social Security commissioner. Commenting on the proposed COLA cut a few years ago, he stated:

Table 3.14. Benefit as Percent of Poverty Level, 1988 [a]

Program	Recipient	Percentage of poverty level
UI	Unemployed worker	126
OASDI	Individual retiree	108
	Retiree and spouse	122
	Survivor and one child	128
	Survivor and two children	133
	Disabled individual	106
	Disabled, spouse and one child	98
AFDC	Parent and two children	43
SSI	Elderly	56
	Blind	65
	Disabled	63

[a] The poverty level in 1988 was $5,980 for an individual, $8,020 for a two-person family, and $10,060 for a three-person family.
Source: Social Security Bulletin 52(7): 77 (July 1989).

The 1985 cola cut would have driven 500,000 elderly below the poverty line. Some will tell you that only 12.5% of the elderly are below the poverty line— they (most of the elderly) can afford it. But another 30% are just dollars and cents above the line and vulnerable. (Roosevelt 1988:6)

It is precisely because of the COLA amendments that the program on the whole is a relatively successful poverty prevention program. We use the word *relative* only because not all recipients will have benefits that bring them above the poverty level. As Roosevelt stated, 12.5% of the elderly are still poor. However, we need only go back to the early 1960s, when 50% of the elderly were poor (Orshansky 1966).

The social-assistance programs offer a different picture. No program— neither SSI nor AFDC—provides benefits above the poverty line. Many of the SSI recipients are also receiving OASDI benefits, and some of these may actually be raised above poverty. Still others, as discussed above, are eligible for a variety of in-kind programs, which if cashed out might put them above the poverty level.

We conclude, then, that the income maintenance programs:

- do not replace earnings;
- do provide for basic needs; and
- do prevent poverty for some beneficiaries and not others.

2. To Stabilize the Labor Force and Prevent the Possibility of Civil Unrest. In Chapter 1, we pointed out that during the depression the Roosevelt administration, confronted with the possibility of civil unrest, enacted a package of radical (radical in that they redefined the role and functions of the federal government) employment and income-related policies. This strategy, however, was not invented in the twentieth century. Throughout history, governments have used similar tactics to maintain social control. Perhaps the most famous example is the successful efforts of Bismarck in the 1880s. Briggs, in commenting on Bismarck's introduction of compulsory insurance against sickness, accidents, and old age, points out:

Many of Bismarck's critics accused him, not without justification, of seeking through his legislation [because of state contributions] to make German workers dependent on the state. . . . [T]he workers would put up with much because they had pensions to look forward to . . . to make German Social Democracy less attractive to workingmen. (1967:36)

Schottland reached this same conclusion:

Bismarck saw in social insurance an opportunity to halt the rising tide of socialism by yielding to the workers' demands for income protection and at the same time, to strengthen the central German government. (1963:15)

The issue of social control also needs to be examined more closely at the program level. While the UI program is a non–means-tested program and provides benefits as a matter of right, there are a number of social-control features incorporated in the program. The program offers benefits to workers who find themselves unemployed through "no fault of their own." In practice this means that workers (1) did not quit their job, (2) were not fired for cause, (3) had a recent history of attachment to the work force, and (4) and must be seeking work as evidenced by their registration for work at a state employment office. Each of these requirements bonded the worker to the workplace—and the bond was as strong as those forged by the eighteenth-century architects of the poor law in that it reinforced the work ethic with both a psychological and legal set of conditions.

The social-insurance benefits provided under OASDI also strengthened this bond in that benefits were only provided to individuals and families who had a previous attachment to the work force. Moreover, the level of the benefit was tied to previous earnings. This proved to be an incentive to the earner to work hard (assuming that hard work and productivity was related to higher wages).

Once assistance is given (i.e., the beneficiary is retired or is unable to work because of a disability), whether it is through the OASDI or SSI programs, the social-control element seems to become less important. As Handler points out, the "aged are becoming less associated with the labor market . . . thus the giving of aid to this group does not conflict with the moral issue of work" (1972:14). The primary social-control measure introduced under the Victorian Poor Law—the principle of less eligibility—was modified in this century so as to apply only to those who could reasonably be expected to work.

Handler has written extensively on this issue and the titles of his works are worth noting. In *The Coercive Social Worker* (1973) he suggests that social-service professionals, having disengaged from the War on Poverty, have returned to their "traditional mission of reforming the poor." In *Reforming the Poor* (1972) he carefully documents the numerous social-control measures built into the AFDC program from the earlier "man-in-the-house" rules and the "suitable house" requirements to the more recent "work tests."

Piven and Cloward, in their classic *Regulating the Poor,* offer data covering the period 1940–1970 to support their thesis:

> As for relief programs themselves, the historical pattern is clearly not one of progressive liberalization; it is rather a record of periodically expanding and contracting relief rolls as the system performs its two main functions: maintaining civil order and enforcing work. (1971:xv)

Joe and Rogers (1985) have offered a similar conclusion in their analysis of AFDC programs in the 1980s. Blending an analysis of legislation, secondary data, and interviews with a number of women in Georgia, they show the direct relationship between the AFDC program and employment in the secondary labor market.

Do our income maintenance programs perform a social-control function whose purpose is to stabilize the labor force and prevent the possibility of civil unrest? There is sufficient evidence on the whole (i.e., no one study is conclusive) to suggest they not only do, but that these functions are rational if economic goals are to be met.

3.   To Promote a More Egalitarian Society through the Redistribution of Wealth.   The third and final general purpose of income maintenance programs is that of moving our society toward a more egalitarian end state or, perhaps more accurately, to deal with some of the more glaring aspects of an unequal society. This argument becomes more tenuous than the above. While it is possible to analyze the extent to which we are or are not becoming more egalitarian, money income is only one aspect of wealth and income maintenance is only one form of money income. Still, public income maintenance programs accounted for 18.4% of the GNP in 1986 or over $700 billion. This is not an insignificant amount of money.

Kuznets (1953), in an earlier study of the distribution of money income in the United States, shows that in 1913, the top 1% of American families received 16% of pretax national income. By 1920 this had dropped to 14%, by 1939 to 13%, and by 1947 to 9%. This would suggest that some leveling had occurred.

However, if we look at the period 1947–84 and analyze the distribution of money income by quintiles, a less optimistic picture emerges (see Table 3.15). While a totally level society is an impossibility, a more equal society would be one in which each quintile would receive an amount close to 20%. However, over this 37-year period, families in the top fifth received approximately 42% of all money income, while families in the lowest quintile received about 5 percent.

Table 3.15.   Distribution of Money Income among Families, Percentage by Quintiles (1947–84)

Quintiles	Range (%)	Average (%)
First (lowest)	4.5– 5.5	5
Second	11.0–12.4	12
Third	17.0–17.9	17
Fourth	23.1–24.4	24
Fifth (highest)	40.4–43.0	42

Source: Adapted from R. Plotnick, Table 2, "Trends in Inequality of Distribution of Money Income among Families 1947–85" (1987).

We can conclude then that our income maintenance programs have not created a more equal society if income alone is the criterion. We are left with the question posed earlier in the chapter: Is Marshall's formulation of "equality of status" more realistic? Or perhaps is the position of Keynes, Galbraith, and Beveridge, more realistic that equality of opportunity in a capitalist society is an appropriate goal while the redistribution of income and wealth is inappropriate in that it will unduly interfere with the economic system? Or finally, are Titmuss, Tawney, and Crosland correct in suggesting that some combination of equality of opportunity and outcome will be required if our society is to remain a human society that fosters a sense of community and shared responsibility?

While this chapter has not addressed a number of issues germane to income maintenance, including the welfare reform measures of 1988, they will be dealt with later in many of the following chapters and then will be reexamined in the concluding section of the book, which will attempt to synthesize the various policy areas.

CHAPTER 4

HOUSING POLICY

While the federal government has had a long-standing commitment to meet the housing needs of this country, a commitment that began to take shape in the depression of the thirties, housing policy remains an extremely ambiguous term. As an area of national concern it

> encompasses government expenditures, loans and loan guarantees for investment in structures; zoning regulations and building and housing codes; legal provisions concerning property rights and tax treatment of residential property or of income from it. (Aaron 1972:4.)

Responsibility for the formulation and implementation of policy at the national level is presently parceled out among the Departments of Housing and Urban Development, Agriculture, Health and Human Services, Defense, and Treasury, the Veterans Administration, the Bureau of Indian Affairs, and finally, several congressional committees. This diffusion has produced a great deal of confusion and has resulted in the absence of a clearly stated position beyond the rhetoric of the general goal found in the Housing Act of 1949:

> The general welfare and security of the nation and the health and living standards of its people require housing production and related community development sufficient to remedy the serious housing shortage, the elimination of substandard and other inadequate housing through the clearance of blighted areas and the realization as soon as feasible of the goal of a decent home and a suitable living environment for every American family, thus contributing to the redevelopment of communities and to the advancement of the growth, wealth and security of the nation. (Section 2)

We include this chapter on housing policy because of these stated goals. By including the goals of a "suitable living environment" and "the redevelopment of communities," Congress has identified housing as a social policy. Furthermore, housing was defined as a basic societal good—one that was essential for the "general welfare and security of the nation and the health and living standards of its people."

Over 60 years ago, the Congress of the United States passed a series of bills that committed this country to a course of action to solve a massive housing problem. This commitment, which involved billions of dollars and which reaffirmed by Congress over the next four decades, was grounded in five basic principles:

- The goal of housing policy is home ownership.
- The federal government has a major responsibility for the nation's housing problem.
- Federal government manipulation of credit is the preferred solution.
- Public housing is for the purpose of clearing slums.
- Slum clearance (and therefore public housing) is a cooperative effort between federal and local governments.

As clear and simple as these principles may appear, housing policy has always been torn between the goals of an *adequate quantity* of housing and of *decent quality* of housing for all Americans. However, because of our tendency to equate these two goals and a reluctance to recognize the implications of our stated commitment to decent housing as expressed in the Housing Act of 1949 (and reaffirmed by the Housing Acts of 1954, 1959, 1961, 1965, 1968, and 1974), we have succeeded in achieving neither goal to the satisfaction of anyone.

For decades, policymakers have expressed a belief and reliance on market mechanisms as the most viable strategy to distribute housing resources. Because of this, they have approached both goals—the quantity and quality of housing—as an economic problem. The social dimensions of housing (housing as more than shelter) have been ignored or deemphasized.

The Current Situation: Deterioration on All Fronts

Fifty years later, as we enter the 1990s the housing problem is still with us—and, in the opinion of a growing number of analysts, it is a problem that is worsening. Schwartz and his colleagues recently identified and discussed a series of trends in the housing market that have developed over the last ten years. (Schwartz, Ferlauto, and Hoffman 1988). According to them:

I. We Are Experiencing a Decline in Home Ownership. Contrary to popular belief, home ownership became the norm only after World War II.

In fact, until that time the percentage of home owners had not reached 50 percent and had been declining over most of the first half of this century (see Table 4.1). During the latter half of the 1980s, the percentage of families owning their own homes began to decline. This decline, however, is not evenly distributed over the population but is more severe among young families, those headed by adults in the 25–34 age group. One reason for this decline is the skyrocketing costs of buying and maintaining a house:

- In 1975, the average family needed an income of $15,775 to buy an average new home; by 1985, that family needed an income of $37,657.
- However, while the median cost of housing has doubled during that period, median income has risen by less than 2%.

Another reason for this decline is the increase in interest rates since the early 1970s—rates that rose four to five times faster than real household income. As some economists point out,

- A 1% increase in conventional interest rates will keep at least 10% of potential buyers out of the housing market (an estimated 400,000 families in 1987).
- A 1% increase in VHA rates will keep over 1.5 million families out of the market.

A final reason is linked to lending institutions, which require larger down payments than previously: instead of 10%, they now require 20% or more. On a median-priced house in 1987, this would translate into a down payment of $20,000 to $25,000, plus closing costs. These problems have been greatly exacerbated by the current savings and loans scandals, which have forced many mortgage lenders to require higher and higher down payments.

Table 4.1.   Home Ownership Rates
1890–1987

Year	Percentage of all housing
1890	47.8
1900	46.1
1910	45.8
1920	45.6
1940	44.1
1980	65.0
1987	63.8

Sources: For 1890–1920, see E. Wood (1939: 37–38); for 1940–87, see Schwartz et al. (1988: 7).

2.   The Affordability and Availability of the Nation's Rental Housing has Decreased to the Point where 30 Million Tenants Live in Substandard Housing.   While there are no hard rules, common wisdom suggests that the average family should pay between 30 and 35% of income for housing. And yet:

- Over 6.5 million poor families pay more than half their income for rent.
- Families with incomes of less than $7,000 income pay more than 60%.
- More than one-third of single-parent families pay over 75% of their income.
- The number and percentage of female-headed families have increased from 3.5 million in 1950 (9% of the total families) to over 9 million in 1980 (15% of the total); and the number of single-parent households will grow by 50% again in the 1990s.

To compound these problems:

- Since the midseventies, the housing market has lost over one million low-income units *each year* due to abandonment, arson, demolition, condominium conversion, and gentrification.
- By 1996, over 900,000 federally assisted housing units will be lost to low-income families; by the year 2000, almost the entire stock of such housing (two million units) will revert to market rates. Under legislation, developers receiving low-cost loans and subsidies were required to accept low-income families for 20 years. This requirement is now expiring.

3.   We Are Experiencing a Decline in the Quality of Existing Housing.   Over time, the federal-private market partnership has achieved some successes in expanding housing opportunities and in improving housing conditions. For example,

- The proportion of family households living in physically inadequate (lacking complete plumbing facilities) or dilapidated housing units fell from 48.6% in 1940 to 7.4% in 1970.
- However, 24.2 million American families lived in inadequate or overcrowded houses in 1985 compared to 19.1 million in 1975. Furthermore, since 1975, conditions have deteriorated in seven of the nine modern indicators of housing maintenance and upkeep (National Association of HomeBuilders 1985).

4.   There has been a Dramatic Increase in the Number of Homeless Families.   In 1983, the first year that statistics were reported on a large-scale basis, various estimates of the homeless suggested that anywhere from

300,000 families (Department of Housing and Urban Development) to 3,000,000 families (Department of Health and Human Services) were homeless. Since then, it is clear that the numbers have grown, especially in the category of families with young children. At this time it is estimated that 30% of all homeless fall into this category, compared to 21% in 1985. A related phenomenon is the doubling up of families in the 1980s, i.e., a family unable to find/afford housing moves in with a family with housing. This is especially the case in single-parent, female-headed households. In 1987, there were ten million such families.

How did we get to this point and where do we seem to be going? We begin this search with a discussion of the major theories and assumptions underlying government intervention in this area and then explore how these theories have shaped our policy initiatives. Following this, individual housing policies are analyzed on two different but complementary levels.

First, each program is discussed from a historical perspective. This is important since all the basic issues in housing policy have been continuously fought over for at least 60 years. Policies that were proposed in the 1980s and those that will be proposed in the 1990s are not new ways of dealing with the "problem" and debates around these proposals are not concerned with "new" issues. The fundamental concern is and has been the appropriateness of increasing the supply of housing through the private market and the role of government in this process. The historical review attempts to analyze the extent to which this strategy has been successful.

Second, each major program is analyzed in terms of its own goals and objectives. How was the problem defined? What specific strategy was introduced? How successful was it?

Following this, housing policy as a whole is analyzed, i.e., we look across programs. To do this, we reintroduce the notion that housing policy is a social policy and, as such, requires a broader set of criteria to judge its effectiveness.

Theories of Housing Market Failure

In general, housing policy in the United States reflects the opposing views held by different groups of what the housing problem is and what public policy should be. Although different strategies emerge from these competing groups in terms of program strategies, all accept the fundamental premise that the private housing market, in theory, is the best allocator of housing resources.

Furthermore, while all accept that past and current housing markets have experienced some failures—that the private market is imperfect—they assume that marginal modifications to the market system will make the distribution of housing more efficient and equitable.

The major problem faced by the private market is its historic inability to provide decent quality low-cost housing due to certain inefficiencies and externalities that cause housing resources to be less than optimally distributed. These include: (1) externalities (2) lack of consumer knowledge, and (3) racial discrimination.

I.   There are few incentives for owners in deteriorating neighborhoods to improve their properties because it is likely to bring them little if any return on their investment. The upgraded property would continue to be surrounded by deterioration. In fact, the market often rewards those owners who do not invest in upgrading. An unrehabilitated building may increase in value at no cost to the owner simply because it is located next to a rehabilitated building. Although all owners would benefit if each upgraded their property, this collective good is not achieved because the private market, by definition, cannot dictate individual behavior.

2.   A second aspect of the market failure theory questions whether all households have equal capacity to obtain the housing and neighborhood they both want and can afford. A fundamental premise of free-market economic theory is that knowledgeable, rational consumers weigh their individual perceptions of the costs and benefits of various combinations of goods and services and then make a selection that maximizes their individual benefit. However, in a survey of rent-controlled apartments in New York City, Schussheim (1974) found that tenants in high-income units were more likely to be aware of their rights under the city's rent control ordinance. None of these high-income renters paid more than the legally permitted rent. In contrast, low-income Hispanic and black tenants in Harlem frequently paid rents substantially exceeding rent control limits.

3.   A third dimension of market failure is racial discrimination. From a purely economic point of view, discrimination is objectionable because it causes resources to be distributed inefficiently. In other words, some households presently living in substandard housing would be able to afford decent housing if the private market did not arbitrarily inhibit how they spend their resources. And yet, when entire classes of households are denied the right to choose where they want to live, their economic and social rights have been arbitrarily proscribed.

Title VIII of the Civil Rights Act of 1968 prohibits discrimination in the sale or rental of housing on the basis of religion, race, or ethnic origin. The data we have, however, shows that discrimination continues to limit the housing choices of minorities (Woods, 1979). The largest study of housing discrimination to date, the Housing Market Practices Survey conducted by HUD in 1975, found that blacks experienced discrimination in 27% of their attempts to locate rental housing and in 15% of their attempts to purchase housing (Schnare, 1977).

In summary, market failure theory attributes the causes of inadequate housing consumption to certain inefficiencies that cause housing resources to be less than optimally allocated. Given market failure, government intervention is justified to eliminate these inefficiencies. However, as discussed in Chapter 1, some forms of government intervention are preferred over others and, in general, the less intrusive, the more acceptable.

Two overall strategies have been, to greater or lesser degrees introduced by the government over the past six decades: (1) efforts to increase the quantity and quality of housing stock, and (2) efforts to increase the financial ability of some economically disadvantaged individuals and families who cannot afford adequate housing. The former is called a *supply-side* strategy; the latter a *demand-side* strategy. While both general strategies are theoretically acceptable, historically the emphasis has been on attempts to stimulate an increase on the production side.

Examples of supply-side interventions would include:

- tax incentives to developers;
- credit incentives to developers
- mortgage insurance to lenders
- public housing production.

Examples of demand-side interventions would include

- tax incentives to home owners
- subsidization of owners and renters.

While there may be disagreement among policymakers and analysts about which of the above is more effective and therefore more preferable, there is almost unanimous agreement that government production of housing (public housing) is the least desirable and the most intrusive.

As Friedman argued:

> [P]ublic housing . . . can be justified, if at all, only on grounds of paternalism; that the families being helped "need" housing more than they "need" other things but would themselves either not agree or would spend their available resources unwisely. (1962:178)

Those who argue a demand side strategy do not see the solution in the production of public housing units nor in the provision of incentives to builders, lenders, and developers. Rather, for them the solution lies with increasing the incomes of low-income households, who will improve their own housing condition. Proponents of the demand-side position argue that supply-side strategies substantially benefit the builders and the developers, while demand-side strategies primarily benefit the targeted population. Underlying this position is the notion of *elasticity*. This term, used by economists, is the percentage change in demand that would result from a change in price of one percentage point. In their study of the relationship between income and housing demand, de Leeuw and Ekanem (1970) concluded that the income elasticity of demand for rental property is approximately 1.0, i.e., for every given percentage point change in income, they predict an equal change in the quantity of housing units.

Those who argue for more nonintrusive, supply-side strategies point out that even developers and builders limit their effort to more costly (and there-fore more profitable) housing submarkets; they claim that all income classes will benefit through a process known as *filtering*. This argument is as fol-lows. As one family sells its house to purchase a more expensive one, the original house becomes available to a family with less income, and so on down the line, until a unit is eventually available to the poor. Aaron (1972) suggests that this notion of a filtering chain is a fundamental assumption underlying our housing policy, especially our housing related tax policies. As early as 1935, during the initial debates on whether the federal govern-ment should build public housing, the president of the National Association of Real Estate Boards argues:

> [H]ousing should remain a matter of private enterprise and private ownership. It is contrary to the genius of the American people and the ideals they have established that government become landlord to its citizens. . . . There is sound logic in the continuation of the practice under which those who have initiative and the will to save to acquire better living facilities and *yield their former quarters at modest rents to the group below*. (cited in Keith 1973:33; emphasis added)

While the idea of filtering is attractive, there is little evidence that the poor have benefited to the extent hypothesized. Stegman (1970) questions the effectiveness of the filtering strategy when he point out that for housing units to pass through the market, all units would have to sell for less than market value, i.e., individual owners would have to absorb losses.

Both supply-side and demand-side theorists agree that increasing housing consumption of low-income households has positive benefits for the poor as well as for society as a whole. However, the public policies derived from these theories tend to reflect a calculus weighted toward measuring only a few dimensions of housing deprivation. Until fairly recently, federal policy has followed the recommendations of those who argue supply-side strat-egies. Until the 1980s these have had some success in increasing the number of housing units produced each year. Combined with sporadic de-mand-side strategies, large numbers of low-income families, handicapped persons, and the elderly have been able to find adequate and reasonably priced housing. This progress, never sufficient, and now stalled, needs new stimuli.

To create an agenda for the future, we need to analyze these policies in some detail. The next section discusses, within a historical framework, major federal initiatives in the housing field. Moreover, it analyzes these programs against the backdrop of competing and often contradictory statements of purpose and strategy.

Triggers to Governmental Action

While initial governmental action in the housing market can be traced to the depression, with its high unemployment, escalating number of mortgage defaults, and general malaise in the world economy, an equally significant trigger was the growing awareness of documented scandals associated with urban tenement living.

Reformers such as Edith Wood observed in 1919:

> Roughly stated, one-third of the people of the United States are living under sub-normal housing conditions . . . and about a tenth are living under conditions which are an acute menace to health, morals, and family life; conditions which tend to produce degenerative changes in those subject to them. (1919:31–32)

Others, such as Veiller, not only agreed with Wood's findings but were quick to offer cause-effect conclusions—though at times it was unclear whether the cause of these "degenerative changes" was the housing conditions (i.e., the tenements) or the tenants.

> Democracy was not predicated upon a nation of tenement dwellers, nor can it survive as such. . . . This [lodger evils and overcrowding] prevails chiefly among the foreign elements of the population, more especially among the Italians and Poles, and in some cities, the Hungarians and other Slavic races. It also prevails among the Jews in the larger cities. It is fraught with great danger to the social fabric of the country. It means the breaking down of domestic standards. It frequently leads to the breaking up of homes and families, to the downfall and subsequent degraded career of young women, to grave immoralities—in a word to the profanation of the home. (Veiller 1910:37)

In 1910, three million people in New York City lived in tenement houses. Of these, one million had no bathing facilities in their homes: 250,000 used outside privies and one family in two shared bathrooms. In city after city, surveys conducted by social reformers highlighted immorality, crime, saloons, overcrowding, inadequate water supplies and waste disposal systems, dark rooms, filth, high rates of disease, and infant mortality. (Fish 1978).

At various times from 1890 to 1930, numerous coalitions fought for housing reform—reforms that attempted to draft and pass federal legislation bringing existing housing stock up to acceptable standards (the so-called *restrictive approach*) or legislation that would guarantee a certain percentage of new units be set aside at or below actual market value (the so-called *constructive approach*).

Initially, Veiller (1914) and other reformers refused to support the latter, arguing that people living in tenement houses would have to learn how to live in these new homes, which otherwise would quickly be destroyed by tenants who did not know any better. However, they were forced to abandon the restrictive approach when such legislation was thought to be ruled as probably unconstitutional.

The second (and later) trigger was the large and growing number of mortgage defaults experienced in the early years of the depression. By the end of 1932, the rate of foreclosures was approximately 26,000 per month, or an average of 1,000 per day (Fish 1978).

At that time, lending institutions were unwilling to offer long-term mortgages (the norm was three- to five-year loans) and were extremely conservative about the amount they would loan (a lender, on the average, risked about 40% of the value of a piece of real estate). Borrowers without sizable amounts of cash were forced to find second mortgages.

The home buyer usually paid the interest on the loan on an annual basis and the principal at the end of the loan period. Those who could not pay the principal would then refinance their loans. This system resulted in most borrowers refinancing their loans many times before retiring them. During the depression, many people lost their confidence in banks and began to withdraw their savings. The banks, in turn, having invested this money in home mortgages, found it necessary to call in their loans. When borrowers could not pay, the banks foreclosed and sold the property to recoup some of their money.

These distinct but equally pressing problems came to a head during the Roosevelt administration. As mentioned in Chapter 1, the historic role of the federal government was, by choice, minimal. Housing policy was virtually nonexistent, with the exception of three housing laws passed in 1918 to provide housing for laborers in war-related industries. These programs were short-lived and ceased after the armistice.

Two major strategies evolved during Roosevelt's first two terms—strategies that paralleled the two problems just discussed. The first involved a series of policies that attempted to strengthen the stability of lending institutions and thus prevent or slow down the number of foreclosures through various "insurance" programs. The second, and at that time more controversial, was the direct involvement of the federal government in battling the problems of slums and tenement housing through the production of public housing. These two approaches have been, and continue to be, major thrusts of housing policy. While a variety of programs has been evolving over the past years, they fall under one of the above two categories.

These two basic strategies can best be understood as strategies dealing with two distinct problems. The first (mortgage insurance and later the use of tax incentives) is concerned with the housing needs of "most" Americans— from the working class to the upper class; while the second (direct intervention in the market) is concerned with the poor and low-income families who cannot find adequate housing without substantial assistance. While the dichotomy cannot be equated exactly to the distinction made in Chapter 2 (i.e., institutional versus residual) there are enough similarities at least to suggest that the former are more institutional in approach and the latter more residual. When benefits and services are institutional they tend to be viewed by recipients as *rights*; they carry no stigma; and they are rarely questioned. When benefits or services are residual, however, they are not seen as rights; they are stigmatized; and expenditures are scrutinized continuously. Given this, housing policies will be discussed not in chronological order but as two distinct sets of policies: those that have been formulated for the problems of low-income and poor families and those for "the rest."

Housing Policies for Low-Income and Poor Families

Early Efforts: Public Housing

Public housing is considered today, by both conservatives and progressives, to have been a major social failure. The term *public housing* conjures up the depressed and deteriorated areas of the South Bronx in New York, Cabrini East in Chicago, and Pruitt-Igoe in St. Louis. This general perception of the failure of public housing is, however, one-sided and relatively new. Public housing had been strongly supported by most liberals from the early years of this century up through the 1950s and was proposed during the earlier period as a solution to the problems of the slums and tenement housing.

The public housing movement began in earnest in 1931, when social workers from the settlement houses, urban reformers, city and regional planners, and others established the National Public Housing Conference [later organizations influenced by this group included the National Association of Housing Officials (1933) and the Labor Housing Conference (1934)]. Moreover, they were able to forge a coalition between these groups and the trade unions, the National Urban League, the National PTA, and the NAACP—a coalition that eventually succeeded in pressuring Congress to pass the Housing Act of 1937 (P.L. 75-412).

The seeds of the 1937 act are found in the National Industrial Recovery Act of 1933, which authorized funds for the Public Works Administration for slum clearance and for building 21,769 rental housing units for low-income families in 37 cities (Meyerson and Banfield 1955). Almost immediately, like so much of the New Deal legislation, the program was attacked on constitutional grounds.

In 1935, a federal court first ruled [*U.S. v. Certain Lands in Louisville*, 9 F. Supp. 137 (1935)] that the federal government did *not* have the right to take property under the principle of eminent domain—the taking of property by a government from a citizen for a public use—and later ruled [*Township of Franklin v. Tugwell*, 66 D.C. App. 42, 85 F. (2nd) 208 (1936)] that the federal government was not empowered to purchase land and build housing. A final test case, carefully crafted by the federal government, was successful and later became the legal basis for the 1937 Housing Act. The court ruled [*New York Housing City Housing Authority v. Muller*, 279 N.T.S. 299 (1935)] that the Federal government could *finance the building* of housing and the states could use the power of eminent domain and could *own* housing.

Based on this finding, social reformers and housing advocates drafted legislation for large-scale public housing projects. The legislation, sponsored by Senator Wagner of New York, was defeated in 1935 and 1936 through the efforts of a coalition made up of the National Association of Real Estate Boards (NAREB), the United States Chamber of Commerce and the Mortgage Bankers Association, who argued it was an attack on the free-enterprise system; and the National Retail Lumber Dealers Association (NRLDA), who opposed the legislation because it excluded the use of wood in the newly built housing (Johnson 1952).

Wagner, aware of the pitfalls facing any bill proposing a national public housing program, went to great lengths to neutralize the opposition of the housing industry by assuring them that the program would only cover the poor—those who could not possibly be served by the private sector. He stated:

> The object of public housing, in a nutshell, is not to invade the field of home building for the middle class or the well to do which has been the only profitable area for private enterprise in the past. Nor is it even to exclude private enterprise from major participation in a low cost housing program. It is merely to supplement what private industry will do, by subsidies which will make up the difference between what the poor can afford to pay and what is necessary to assure decent living conditions. (cited in Keith 1973:32–33)

Roosevelt, ever the pragmatist, and concerned with another downswing in the economy, demanded solutions that dealt simultaneously with the housing problem and unemployment. At this time, one in three unemployed persons were in the building trades, and housing represented the largest part of this. While there were no data at that time, more recent analyses have confirmed Roosevelt's position: It is now estimated that each $1 billion of expenditures on multifamily construction will create over 25,000 jobs; for each $1 billion spent on single-family units, 22,000 jobs are created. More-over, the multiplier effect for each $1 billion will be responsible for an additional 276,000 jobs (Ball 1981).

Wagner, now with the active participation of the White House, re-introduced his legislation, which was signed into law on September 1, 1937. The stated purpose of the Housing Act of 1937, P.L. 75-412 was:

> to provide financial assistance to the States and political sub-divisions thereof for the elimination of unsafe and unsanitary housing conditions, for the devel-opment of clean, safe, and sanitary dwellings for families of low income, and for the reduction of unemployment and the stimulation of business activity. (Section 2)

Under the legislation, municipal governments established local housing authorities (LHAs), which in turn were responsible for obtaining a federal subsidy for the construction of housing units. These subsidies included up to 90% of development costs. The projects were developed, owned, and man-aged by these LHAs. Commissioners determined need, set rent scales, and established income limits and eligibility.

The federal government in turn marketed short-term notes to finance the construction of the units. Upon completion of this phase, it marketed the long-term bonds (up to 60 years) issued by the LHA. The federal government also entered into a contract with the LHA, agreeing to make yearly contribu-tions to pay off the debt service on these bonds. The 1937 act proposed an annual target of 135,000 units for a six-year period—a total of 810,000 units. Finally, the legislation required that for each new unit built, one slum dwelling had to be eliminated.

The Housing Act of 1937 is an important piece of social legislation for a number of reasons. First, it reinforced the emerging pattern of the new "federalism." As with the Social Security Act of 1935, responsibilities were to be shared among federal, state, and local units of government. Moreover, while the program was a national effort, critical powers were delegated to local government, e.g., coverage, eligibility, and standards. Second, the legislation reaffirmed the principle of federal intervention when an imperfect market exists (in this case the market had failed the poor and those with low income). Intervention was direct (unlike later housing policies) in that gov-ernment produced and managed the units. Third, housing was defined as a basic need—one for which society, through the public sector, has responsibility.

Such was the intent. What was accomplished given Wood's estimate of 11 million substandard housing units in the United States? From 1937 to 1942, 170,000 units of public housing in 260 communities were built. However, even this production figure, as small as it was, is misleading. Eighty-five percent of the units were built on slum sites that had been cleared for the new units, and only 18,000 units were built on vacant sites (Meyerson and Banfield 1955:19). Very little "new" housing was added to the nation's housing stock. From 1949 to 1966, over 400,000 houses occupied by low- and moderate-income families were torn down under the slum clearance component of the public housing program.

In the eight-year period from 1940 to 1948, 255,300 public housing units were built. This represented less than 0.5 percent of all housing units built during this period. The average annual production was a little over 28,000 units, but this figure is somewhat misleading in that in some years the production was very high and in others almost nonexistent.

Congress reaffirmed the 1937 National Housing Act in 1949 against considerable pressure from lobbying groups representing private housing interests. The act authorized $1.5 billion for slum clearance and urban renewal and authorized 810,000 additional units of public housing to be built by 1955. Six years later, only 263,800 units had been built—one-third of the targeted goal.

In 1954, the commitment to public housing was again reaffirmed and Congress authorized 140,000 new units to be built over the next four years: 179,000 were actually built. It is interesting that it was only during a Republican administration (Eisenhower) that public housing targets were actually achieved—albeit modest targets compared to previous administrations. By the end of the 1950s, public housing had ceased to be a desirable housing policy. Granted, later legislation did deal with public housing but not on the previous scale. The Housing Acts of 1961, 1965, 1968, and 1974 attempted to solve some of the existing problems, such as size, density, and location (e.g., through scattered housing strategies and eventual ownership) but with little success. This does not mean that the production of public housing stopped. It did, however, slow down. Whereas 716,300 units of public housing were built in the 20-year period 1940–1959 (still far short of the six-year target established in the 1937 legislation) the total stock had only grown to 1,200,000 in 1977 (an increase of 484,000 over a 17-year period) and to 1,300,000 in 1985. What had happened?

It was clearly not our success in dealing with the "tenement problem." As late as 1944, approximately two million people in New York City still lived in tenements condemned by the 1915 Tenement Housing Act (Strauss 1944).

It was also equally clear that it was not a lack of demand for such housing. In 1987, we had approximately 1.3 million public housing units and over 800,000 families on waiting lists (in some cities the wait was 15–20 years) for public housing.

It could hardly be argued that the federal government was unfairly intervening in the private market. Not only has the private market not been able to keep up with demand, the total federal involvement from 1940 to 1959 represented only 3.2% of all housing starts (see Table 4.2).

Table 4.2. Public Housing as a Percentage of All
Housing Starts 1940–59 (Thousands
of Units)

Year	Total	Number of public units	Percentage of all starts
1940	602.6	73.0	12.1
1941	706.1	86.6	12.3
1942	356.0	54.8	15.4
1943	191.0	7.3	3.8
1944	141.8	3.1	2.2
1945	326.0	1.0	0.3
1946	1,023.0	8.0	0.8
1947	1,268.0	3.4	0.2
1948	1,362.0	18.1	1.3
1949	1,466.0	36.3	2.4
1950	1,908.1	43.8	2.2
1951	1,419.8	71.2	4.8
1952	1,445.4	58.5	3.9
1953	1,402.1	35.5	2.5
1954	1,531.8	18.7	1.2
1955	1,626.6	19.4	1.2
1956	1,324.9	24.2	1.8
1957	1,174.8	49.1	4.0
1958	1,315.2	67.8	4.9
1959	1,494.6	36.7	2.4
Total	22,084.8	716.3	3.2

Sources: Adapted from tables cited in Fish (1978: 245, 300).
Original data source, U.S. Bureau of the Census
Reports.

The situation was, in all likelihood, in part associated with the characteristics of the tenants of public housing. Through the 1940s and into the
1950s,

> [t]hey were poor, but most of them were employed and accustomed to urban
> living. . . In those days Local Authorities carefully screened out, or imposed
> quotas on applicant families receiving relief, those who had unpleasant social
> histories or living habits, or those who were not normal. The ideal was to
> rehouse a cross-section of the low-income families of the community, in terms
> of income, of family-size and of source income. (Silverman 1971:6)

This had changed by the 1960s, in part (1) because of a conscious reversal of
discriminatory practices that had excluded many minorities from participating in the general economic growth that would allow them to be able to
purchase adequate housing on the market; (2) because of civil-rights ad-

vances that prohibited discriminatory housing practices (e.g., quotas for different subgroups to mirror the larger community), and (3) because of other programs that opened up the suburbs to young white families. Whatever the full list of reasons, Rainwater's description of the 33 11-story buildings Pruitt-Igoe project presents a quite different picture:

> [o]pen[ing] in 1954, [it] has 2,762 apartments of which only 2,000 are currently occupied, and has as tenants a very high proportion (over 50 percent) of female headed households of one kind or another on public assistance. Though originally integrated, the project is now all Negro. The project community is plagued by petty crimes, vandalism, much destruction of the physical plant, and a very bad reputation in both the Negro and white communities. (Subcommittee on Executive Reorganization 1966:2837)

This project, ultimately comprising 43 buildings, was dynamited in the early 1970s.

By emphasizing those in the greatest need, public housing has created ghettos of the poor; ghettos that other city residents do not wish to live near; and in which most of the poor would rather not live. Public housing has a threefold stigma: one has to be poor to be eligible (average family income is 28% of the average family income in the United States); 87% of public housing residents are either minority or elderly; and finally the physical environment carries a spatial stigma.

In addition, the policy as implemented, emphasized shelter and ignored the multiple dimensions of housing. This narrow definition has produced a continually troubled program. By providing only shelter, the community aspects were nonexistent. These failures, so painfully brought to the surface by Pruitt-Igoe, have been repeated again and again in large projects in metropolitan areas. Pruitt-Igoe, named for two World War II heroes, one black and one white, was designed by an internationally famous architect, and incorporated a large park with the latest playground equipment and extensive landscaping. As the original costs began to escalate, all of the elements, including the landscaping and playgrounds that are important for the creation of human environments and a sense of community, were dropped. Given these failures, numerous alternatives to public housing have been and continue to be proposed.

In 1984, for example, HUD under the rubric of "privatization" initiated the Public Housing Home Ownership Demonstration Program (with its legislative basis in the 1974 amendments to the 1937 Housing Act). Following the lead of British Prime Minister Margaret Thatcher, whose government sold 80,000 units of public housing, the administration began selling 1,600 units of public housing in 18 cities. At this time it is too early to predict the outcome of such a strategy, but some analysts suggest that the policy does have potential dangers. First, it will result in the removal from the supply of public housing the better units—further stigmatizing such tenancy. Second, the "owners" only have to hold the units for five years, which might result in initial sales and again fewer units in this market. Finally, what will happen when some owners default on their payments?

Low-Income Housing: Alternatives to Public Housing

By the 1960s, both Congress and the administration concluded that the 1949 housing goal of a "decent home and a suitable environment for every American family" had not been realized, especially for lower-income families. A series of major initiatives were introduced to deal with these shortages. While they differed in terms of specific programs, they all emphasized private-sector solutions. Some attempted to increase the financial position of those who were excluded from the private market (e.g., via rent supplements); others attempted to stimulate housing developers to produce new units (e.g., via interest subsidies and direct low-cost loans).

It is clear that these efforts reflected a belief

* that public housing was not the hoped-for solution to meet the housing needs of the nation;
* that public housing would continue to be a necessary but undesirable program—one for a small residual of the population; and
* that new strategies needed to rely on the private sector.

It also became clear that housing policy initiatives emerging in the 1960s and continuing through the 1970s and 1980s were not the result of systematic and comprehensive planning. Rather, these developments can be characterized as piecemeal engineering efforts, with the engineers working in isolation from each other. Some used a supply-side blueprint while others looked for a solution in demand-side strategies.

Interest Subsidies

By the mid 1960s this criticism of federal housing policy had grown to the point that members of both sides of Congress as well as advocacy groups were demanding more radical approaches to the housing problem. Most of the proponents for change proposed that the federal government play a much more limited role and that greater reliance be placed on the private sector. The solution, they argued, was not public housing with its resulting dependency, but private housing and self-help. The strategy of preference—the stimulation of new low-income housing production by offering developers interest subsidies, i.e., below-market interest loans.

The 1959 Housing Act (P.L. 86-372) had authorized a similar program on a small scale. Under Section 202, Congress authorized the making of such loans to nonprofit corporations to build housing for the elderly or handicapped. These loans were long term (often 50 years). The program was small—for its first ten years the average number of units built on an annual basis was less than 5,000.

The Kennedy administration modified the program in the Housing Act of 1961. The interest subsidy program was expanded to include low-income families and families displaced by urban renewal projects, but as with the Section 202 program, the appropriations were small. It took President Johnson and the Great Society to bring the interest subsidy program to center stage with the passage of the Housing Act of 1968 (P.L. 90-448), which pulled together all existing interest subsidy programs into two programs: Section 235 (assistance to low-income families to buy homes) and Section 236 (subsidies to developers to build rental units for low-income families).

In its discussion of the bill, Congress found

> that the goal of "a decent home and a suitable living environment for every American family" (as expressed in the Housing Act of 1949) . . . had not been fully realized for many of the Nation's lower income families; that this is a matter of grave national concern; that there exists in the public and private sectors of the economy the resources and capabilities necessary to the full realization of this goal. (Fish 1978:354)

Congress directed the president to set forth a

> plan for the elimination of all substandard housing and the realization of that goal" within ten years by constructing or rehabilitating 26 million housing units, 6 million of these for low and moderate income families. (Fish 1978:354)

The Section 235 program provided subsidies to low-income families to the point that they paid as little as 4% interest on their mortgages; were required to make very small down payments (3%); and would pay no more than 20% of their adjusted income for their mortgage payment. Families could then purchase new or rehabilitated units. Through 1977, almost 500,000 units were insured under this program, with a value of about $8.6 billion.

Under the Section 236 program, HUD provided the developer a subsidy that reduced his or her actual loan interest to 1%. The developer, in turn, agreed to accept eligible families (their income could not exceed 135% of the income ceiling for public housing residents) and charge them 20% of their income for rent. Unlike public housing, renters would not be forced to leave the unit if their income increased and exceeded this ceiling.

By using existing mechanisms of home financing and attracting more private capital, HUD believed that the supply of housing for low- and moderate-income families would be increased substantially. Moreover, the subsidies would make less demands on the federal budget; would minimize resentment on the part of the lower middle class by allowing them to benefit from the program; and would attract private developers into the low- and moderate-income housing market.

In absolute terms, the increase of available housing units was substantial. In the first nine years of the program, 939,000 units were produced, compared to the 1.2 million units produced in the first 40 years of the public housing program. This figure is, however, somewhat misleading. Various analysts suggested:

> [F]or every 100,000 units subsidized during the 1960's and early 1970's, perhaps as few as 14,000 represented net additions to the housing stock. The reason for this is that many builders dropped plans to construct nonsubsidized units when more profitable opportunities to build subsidized units became available. (Rice 1978:355–56)

The program, in hindsight, was a failure. Homes were poorly rehabilitated, FHA inspectors received kickbacks to look the other way, and inexperienced families were bilked into buying homes that would not last the life of the mortgage. While the cost was designed to be 20% of a family's income, the program did not include in that amount the cost of utilities, heating, and repair bills, which often ran as high as 55% of income for low-income families (Stegman 1970). When repair costs exceeded the ability of families to pay for them, many simply walked away from the units. Tens of thousands of units were abandoned nationwide, making the federal government the largest slum owner in history (Housing in the Seventies 1974).

The Section 236 program experienced a default rate in excess of 7%—much greater than any other housing program except the Section 235 program. Thousands of the Section 235 subsidies for ownership were defaulted. In Detroit alone, HUD foreclosed on 5,000 units. By 1974 HUD estimated that the defaults for both programs were costing the federal government $2 billion annually.

The scandal became so great that the interest subsidy programs were suspended and production strategies were shifted to rental subsidies in the 1974 housing bill.

Rent Supplements

The alternative to subsidizing the developers (a supply-side intervention) was to subsidize those seeking housing (a demand-side strategy). While the former assumed that developers would produce more and higher-quality units if they were provided incentives in the form of below-market interest rates, the latter held that if the economic power of poor and low-income families was increased, developers would respond by either building more or rehabilitating existing housing units.

While the major rental assistance initiative is found in the 1974 Housing Act (P.L. 93-383), its beginning, on a much smaller scale, goes back to the Johnson administration and the Housing Act of 1965. Under this program, eligible families would pay 25% of their income toward the fair market rent established by the Federal Housing Authority (FHA). The federal government would pay the difference.

The administration sought $110 million to subsidize 375,000 housing units over a four-year period (1966–69). The proposal met with tremendous opposition during the congressional hearings. Numerous members of Congress argued that the federal government was overstepping its bounds by attempting to force economic, ethnic, and racial integration. Lobbying groups such as the National Association of Homebuilders and Redevelopment Officials (NAHRO), the U.S. Chamber of Commerce and the National Lumber and Building Material Dealers Association argued that all federal efforts should subsidize production costs and not rent. Although the bill did pass, Congress approved only $36 million and of the targeted 375,000 units, only 4% or 16,567 units were subsidized under this program.

This rent supplement program, better known as the housing allowance program, differed from the earlier effort in that eligible families obtained certificates from LHAs and with these certificates, would find their own housing in the market. It was assumed that if owners received the fair market rent for their units (the family still paid only 25% of income, with the remainder covered by the program), they would have an incentive to upgrade the quality of the units and then maintain them if they were to remain competitive. This increase in demand would produce an increase in the supply of standard housing for low- and moderate-income families.

Eligible families (their income could not exceed 80% of the area's median income) were seen as having much more opportunity than in earlier housing programs in that they were free to choose the housing that in their opinion best met their needs or preferences: in economic terms they were able to maximize their choice of location and neighborhood. The only restrictions were that the housing authority had to certify that the housing met existing codes and standards and that the owner had to sign a contract obligating him or her to maintain the property and observe the legal rights of the tenant. By the end of 1977, three years after the program began, almost 1,000,000 units had been reserved under the Section 8 program and almost 300,000 were occupied—a significant improvement over the 16,567 units produced in the earlier rent subsidy program.

A more recent variation of this demand-side intervention emerged in 1983, when Congress authorized HUD to provide housing vouchers to a number of families on an experimental basis. As with Section 8 certificates, the vouchers subsidized tenants in units that met housing codes and standards. It differed from the Section 8 program in a number of ways. The administration admitted that this strategy would not stimulate the production of additional housing units; families were allowed to pay more than 25% of their income for more expensive units; the owner agreed to a five-year commitment rather than the earlier 15-year commitment.

The theoretical benefit of a housing allowance/rent subsidy program is that, in allowing a family to choose the housing that maximizes its choice, the spatial stigma found in the earlier public housing efforts and the first subsidy program could be avoided. Neighbors would not know that the family was receiving the supplement. This assumes, of course, that the issue of discrimination has and is being successfully dealt with—an issue that was first addressed by President Kennedy in his executive order, "Equal opportunity in Housing," which

> prevented discrimination in the sale, lease or occupancy of residential proper-
> ty owned or operated by the Federal Government (Subcommittee on Housing
> and Community Development 1975:314)

and which was not only reaffirmed but broadened in the Civil Rights Act of 1964.

The disadvantage of relying on the private market is that if the supply of housing is low, choice is restricted thought a voucher program. In 1986–87, for example, 62% of the families holding housing vouchers in New York City and Boston—low-vacancy areas—could not find housing. Furthermore, over 50% of all participating families were paying more than 30% of their income for rent (Schwartz et al. 1988).

Housing Policy for Middle- and Upper-Income Families

The picture that emerges when we trace through our efforts to improve housing conditions for poor and low-income families is one of ambivalence. Government has produced and managed housing units, it has also attempted to stimulate the production of housing in the private sector, and finally it has increased the buying power of low-income families. Under the first and third efforts, the targets of the policy were people who needed housing, while the second emphasized the developer. At times the policies seemed to be concerned with social objectives, at other times with economic needs including employment. Furthermore, at various periods the federal government used both supply-side and demand-side strategies simultaneously. These efforts have to be seen as a lack of consensus among policymakers as to the nature of the problem, its causes, and solutions. This ambivalence has been notably absent in policies targeting middle- and upper-income families. Since the 1930s housing policies have been quite consistent for these families. The following sections analyze these policies.

Mortgage Insurance Programs

Since the late 1920s, a major housing goal of the federal government, stated and restated on numerous occasions over the next 60 years, was home ownership. This promotion of home ownership was actively supported by different groups and for different reasons.

The early social reformers cited earlier in this chapter saw home ownership as the solution to most of the country's moral and social problems:

> [W]here a man has a home of his own, he has every incentive to be economical and thrifty, to take his part in the duties of citizenship, to be a real sharer in government. (Veiller 1910:6)
>
> [Home ownership] goes to the very roots of the well being of the family, and the family is the social unit of the nation. It is more than comfort that is involved. It has important aspects of health and morals and education and the provision of a fair chance for growing childhood. Nothing contributes more to happiness or sound social stability than the surroundings of their own homes. (Gries and Ford 1932:xv)

Other suggested that a major strategy to deal with the economic problems of the Depression—including the growing problem of unemployment—was the stimulation of increased home ownership. Still others argued that home ownership was American and more in ideological harmony with our beliefs about capitalism and free enterprise. It was a combination of these beliefs that led to a series of government efforts to support families who were or would become home owners.

As discussed in an earlier section, by 1933, homes were being foreclosed at a rate of over 1,000 per day. Congress in 1932, with the active support of President Hoover, passed P.L. 72-304 (the Federal Home Loan Bank Act), which established a new agency empowered to buy mortgages from lending institutions so that they in turn could make new loans. Eventually, a system of district home loan banks was organized and a nationwide mortgage pool established. This legislation also established the federal government's right to regulate the savings and loan associations. However, by 1933, with 49% of the $20 billion home mortgages in default, the program was in serious financial trouble (Fish 1978).

The Roosevelt administration took a number of new approaches to the same problem. The first was the Home Owner's Loan Corporation (HOLC), established in June of 1933 to help families who were in danger of losing their homes through mortgage foreclosures. Through a combination of bonds and other guarantees, loans of up to 80% of appraised value with a life of 15 years were offered at 5% interest. Applications were accepted up to June 1935, and the last loan was closed one year later. Over a relatively brief period 1.9 million applications were received; slightly over one million were approved and $3 billion loaned. Although there were some defaults, by 1951 when the program ended, the corporation was liquidated at a profit.

In 1934, Congress expanded its efforts. Insofar as the HOLC only assisted families who already owned their homes and were in default, legislation was needed to support those who wanted to buy their own homes. This legislation, the National Housing Act of 1934, had three main objectives: (1) to assist families to purchase homes, (2) to encourage investment in housing construction, and (3) to provide employment for the building trades. This act established the FHA, which was authorized

- to establish the Federal Deposit Insurance Corporation (FDIC) to insure banks;
- establish the Federal Savings and Loan Insurance Corporation (FSLIC) to insure other lending institutions; and
- to establish national mortgage associations to buy up mortgages.

In that they were insured, lenders were to offer mortgages on 80% of the appraised value; the interest would not exceed 5% and the loans would be for 20 years. Borrowers were charged a percentage of the monthly payment (usually ½ to 1% of the face value of the mortgage) as an insurance premium.

This legislation literally revolutionized the housing industry. It enabled more people to buy homes; it lessened the need for second mortgages; it brought stability to both borrowers and lenders; and it stimulated more investments in the housing market by diminishing the lenders' risk.

In 1944, Congress passed another mortgage insurance program—the Serviceman's Readjustment Act (more commonly known as the G.I. Bill of Rights)—which authorized the Veteran's Administration to guarantee loans for the purchase, building, or improving of private homes. About 40% of World War II veterans bought their homes under this program. This program, more than any other, was the major stimulus for moving this country from a nation of renters to one of home owners by 1950. The peak year of the Veteran Administration's program was 1959, when 393,000 of all new homes (24% of all new homes) were financed through this program.

Secondary Mortgage Market Activities

Concurrent with the insurance program, the federal government introduced another, somewhat more intrusive program—intrusive in the sense that while the insurance program supported the workings of the market, this approach actually shaped the market. Earlier, the Federal Home Loan Bank Board was given the authority not only to regulate the savings and loan industry, but also to set interest and deposit rates and even to make cash advances to a bank experiencing cash flow problems. These regulatory actives were considered to be needed because of the vulnerability of the industry to shifts in the money market and operated until the deregulation of the savings and loan associations by the Reagan administration in the early 1980s.

Faced with another economic downturn in 1937, Congress created the Federal National Mortgage Association (FNMA, known as Fannie Mae), which sought to encourage the flow of money from regions of the country where the demand for mortgage money was low to regions where it was greater. The FNMA purchased FHA mortgages from lenders and then sold them to interested investors. The agency, moreover, had the power actively to intervene in the market and affect monetary policy. It was able to increase the flow of money when credit was tight and offset restrictive monetary policies on the part of the Federal Reserve Bank. Within one year it had purchased 26,276 mortgages, worth $100 million.

As Aaron (1972) notes, the federal government's creation of a secondary mortgage market and its regulation of the savings and loan banks greatly benefited the housing market. By expanding the flow of credit, it stabilized a turbulent market, lowered interest rates, and attracted capital into a market experiencing problems in attracting investors. As with the mortgage insurance programs discussed in the previous section, these programs principally benefited single-family home owners who had middle and upper incomes. In 1968, Congress created the Government Mortgage Insurance Association (GNMA), which expanded opportunities for families with incomes below the median by allowing for the purchase of multifamily units.

Tax Policies

Of all policies affecting the housing market, tax policies have had the greatest impact. These policies offer the home owner the following benefits:

- interest deduction on home mortgages;
- property tax deductions; and
- capital tax deferment if the seller buys a more expensive home.

Furthermore, in order to attract more private investment into the rental housing market, the Tax Reform Act of 1969 allowed owners to depreciate their residential buildings at an accelerated rate. These massive tax shelters offered over the first years of the project stimulated many investors to enter the market. Furthermore, investors who substantially rehabilitated their properties were given even more tax benefits if they kept the property for more than ten years. The rationale for these tax benefits was that incentives were needed since the risk was high and investors were shying away from this market.

The Tax Reform Act of 1986, however, has made investments in rental units less attractive in that depreciation schedules have been lengthened and capital gains are taxed at higher rates. Some analysts predict that these changes will result in a 28 percent increase in rents over the next few years and a production decline of up to 300,000 units each year (Schwartz et al. 1988).

The total amount of tax revenue forgone is staggering. In 1987 (Harney 1989), for example, the federal government's loss of potential tax revenue included:

- $35 billion for mortgage interest;
- $12 billion for capital gains when home sellers bought more expensive homes;
- $4 billion for the $125,000, one-time exclusion for people over 55 years of age;
- $2 billion for interest on home equity loans;
- $1.5 billion for tax-exempt bonds for moderate-income home buyers and renters; and
- $700 million for low-income housing tax credits.

This came to slightly over $55 billion; three and one-half times HUD's entire budget for that year—$15.2 billion. Whereas HUD's programs benefit low-income and poor families, these tax policies provide benefits to those who are better off, e.g., 30% of all mortgage interest deductions goes to the population earning over $50,000 annually; only 8 percent goes to the tax payer earning under $20,000.

Housing Policy: A General Critique

Basic Assumptions

A number of assumptions clearly emerge from this analysis of past and present housing policies:

- Home ownership is a desirable national objective.

Throughout this century, the argument has been made that ownership develops a sense of pride and commitment on the part of the owner. Indeed, Congress in 1968 affirmed the belief that ownership would solve a number of social problems (a large number of cities were experiencing riots and other forms of racial disturbance) and would create "a new dignity, a new attitude toward their jobs and a sense of participation in their communities" (Housing Act of 1968, Section 2).

- Market mechanisms, for the most part, are adequate to determine the quantity and quality of the nation's housing stock.

The beliefs that a balance between the supply and demand for housing, and that profit and self-interest are legitimate values, are *the* fundamental driving forces in the housing market.

- While market mechanisms are adequate, the market is not perfect.

Occasionally there will be distortions in the supply-demand equilibrium. At times, the demand for housing will outstrip the available supply; at times, certain groups (e.g., low income, minorities) will experience barriers in their search for housing.

- Availability of adequate housing for all is a legitimate goal for the state.

Adequate has come to be defined as decent, safe, and sanitary. While the goal implies that housing is a right of citizenship, it seems to have been justified more from an externality rationale, i.e., poor housing and a poor physical environment is believed to be associated with disease and social pathology and thus detrimental to the stability of the community.

- Government can and should intervene in the housing market.

This intervention, however, should be as indirect as possible and specific strategies should not distort natural market mechanisms. Policies should favor fiscal and monetary strategies to counteract supply-demand fluctuations. The actual production of housing by government is the least favorable since it is the most intrusive form of intervention.

- Assistance to moderate- and low-income families should be indirect, thus minimizing the role of government.

This assistance should be limited to those bypassed by the private market and should require that families contribute a percentage of their income to the purchase or renting of the housing unit.

Housing: Economic or Social Policy?

Taken literally, the goal of a "decent home and suitable living environment for every American family" is clearly a social goal. In fact, it is a radical statement of societal responsibility. The irony of U.S. housing policy is that both the 1949 and 1968 Housing Acts

> contain a national commitment which not only could never be afforded, but are likely not supported by a sufficiently large constituency to be carried out even if more funds were to become available. . . . Yet . . . there seems to be little overt interest among low income housing advocates and our political

leaders in modifying the nation's goal of putting every ill-housed family into a new quality house in a good neighborhood in spite of the fact that fewer and fewer superior quality units can be built each year per million dollars of public assistance. (Stegman 1970:330–31)

To better understand the dissonance between rhetoric and actual practice, we need to ask, Who benefits from our housing policies? The answer: middle- and upper-income families. "Subsidized" housing programs attempt to direct some resources to poor Americans but in terms of level of benefits and numbers of units produced, they do not counterbalance the overall thrust of national policy. Indeed, this overall thrust is so strong that even "subsidized" housing programs reveal the pressure to aid middle-class families at the expense of lower-income and poor families.

Was our housing policy ever intended to produce enough units to meet the needs of the poor and the low income? To answer this question we need to reexamine the initial statement of housing goals:

the realization as soon as feasible of the goal of a decent home and suitable living environment for every American family, thus contributing to development of communities and the advancement of the growth, wealth and security of the nation.

Which of these goals are more important: the social goal of decent housing, the economic goal of growth and wealth, or the societal goal of security and stability? As Rein (1970) points out, multiple goals cannot be maximized at the same time, are often contradictory, and choices have to be made.

As we have argued, the housing problem has been defined as an economic problem and as such we have emphasized economic solutions. While there might be some sentiment that decent, safe, and sanitary housing is a basic need of all citizens and society; that government has an obligation to meet this need, especially for those who are unable to obtain housing in the market, government also sees that it has an obligation to the well-being of society as a whole. Thus decent housing is not defined as a right to which all members of society are entitled but a necessary component of general well-being and stability for a prosperous nation. Is this so different from Bismarck's development of a social-security system in the latter part of the nineteenth century—a system whose purpose was to maintain social order among the working classes who were threatening civil unrest?

From this perspective, housing assistance for the poor and lower-income families is justified as long as it does not threaten other more important social values: the social well-being of the nonpoor.

Housing policy was never meant to produce sufficient housing of acceptable standards for all people. It has been grounded in a filtering strategy with some intervention at certain points along the filtering chain. The interventions were to increase low- and moderate-income housing opportunities by closing obvious gaps in the filtering process. Although there may be some elements of conscience-soothing in a nation proud of its high standard of living, these elements have always been subordinate to the larger goal of increasing economic prosperity.

How else can we explain the decades of the 1980s? The Reagan administration, with its concern for reducing taxes and thus revenues, its concern for increasing military expenditures, and its stated promise to balance the budget, looked to other areas of the budget to locate possible cuts. Housing expenditures were slashed. The total budget authority of HUD was reduced from $35.7 billion in 1980 to $15.2 in 1987, from 7% of the federal budget to 1%.

Public housing construction and improvement, rental assistance for the elderly, handicapped, and low income were cut by 70% in the 1980s. Rent burdens (the percentage of income renters were to pay) were raised from 25 to 30% and new eligibility criteria resulted in only the poorest being eligible.

These program cuts (with the exception of the voucher programs) will virtually end all federal effort to assist low-income and poor families, the elderly, the handicapped, and Native Americans (Schwartz et al. 1988). These policies need to be questioned, given the evidence (1) that such a strategy (i.e., vouchers) will not significantly increase the quantity and quality of our deteriorating housing stock; (2) that a significant number of units that the elderly and handicapped have come to rely on will soon be "privatized" (i.e., converted to condominiums or rented at fair market value) thus creating more homeless; (3) that there will be more stress on families who will have to provide housing to their elderly parents; and (4) that a serious decline looms ahead in the quality of life of millions of people.

CHAPTER 5

THE PERSONAL SOCIAL SERVICES

In previous chapters we have discussed the ambiguities pervasive in so many areas of social policy. Some income maintenance policies, for example, are organized around the principle of wage replacement, while others provide for predetermined and standardized levels of subsistence. Some policies can be characterized as *demogrants* and viewed as entitlement, while others target individuals and families who meet a means test requirement. In the area of housing, we have seen the major beneficiaries shift back and forth from individuals and families needing shelter to those involved in the housing industry, i.e., developers, unions, bankers, and other lenders. This continuous shifting reflects our inability to meet multiple objectives simultaneously.

Social services create a different set of problems for analysis. First, and most telling, is the confusion surrounding the definition of social services. While much has been written in this area, less attention has been paid to setting some meaningful parameters around the concept. This chapter thus begins with a general discussion of social services. To address the definitional problem, we examine latent and overt purposes and propose a set of common denominators. Following this, issues of organization and financing are analyzed. Finally, the chapter concludes with a discussion of unresolved policy considerations.

Social Services: Definitions, Scope, and Parameters

While Gilbert and Specht (1981) have provided a valuable contribution to the literature on social services, the framework they use to discuss and analyze the subject matter contributes to the definitional problems inherent

105

in the social services. Their book is divided into two parts: (1) social service programs, and (2) methods of practice in the social services. They consider 18 areas of service, organized in four categories:

- services with a high degree of functional specificity (e.g., information and referral, day-care, homemaker/home health aides);
- services organized around population groups (e.g., families, elderly, children);
- services in non–social-welfare institutions (e.g., schools, prisons, housing, medical-care systems, industry); and
- income maintenance and the financing of social welfare.

We have listed the above *social services* simply to underscore the earlier mentioned definitional confusion. Are these 18 areas with their overlapping services (e.g., elderly people are major consumers of medical care and are also recipients of income maintenance) the sum total of social services, or should social services be defined as those 41 Title XX service categories or Kahn's list of 23 (Kahn 1967:185)? This issue is not one of semantics but has had and will continue to have serious consequences.

Current and future funding patterns are endangered when all-encompassing definitions are used. Gilbert and Specht (1981), for example, report that expenditures for public social services approached $24 billion in 1977, a 750% increase since 1965 and 250% increase since 1970. In 1970, social-"service" expenditures represented 0.8% of the GNP; by 1977 they represented 1.5%. And yet, $5.9 billion of this $24 billion went for food stamps. By 1987, expenditures had reached $29.7 billion (U.S. Bureau of the Census 1988). While we support the expenditure of public funds for such a basic commodity as food, we question whether this is a social service. What, if any, is the glue that holds together food stamps, child welfare, day-care, meals-on-wheels, and employment training programs? Is the package we label so large and are the products so varied that *social services* has become a meaningless concept?

Historical Formulations

The term *public social services* is found in British documents as early as the turn of the century. A royal commission established in 1905 spent five years reassessing the Victorian Poor Law. While the commissioners disagreed on a number of key issues, both the more conservative majority report and the now more famous minority report drafted by the Webbs recommended the development of a comprehensive social-service system (Report of the Royal Commission 1909). The majority report favored the expansion of social services through the voluntary sector (especially through the Charity Organization Societies). The Webbs disagreed and argued for a state-administered public system.

By the 1920s, however, the recommendations of the Webbs had been implemented and statutory (public) social services were not only well established but had been recognized as a separate category in that country's official budget as published in the Treasury's *Annual Return of Expenditures on Public Social Services.* As the decades passed, the annual report included more and more services for this category until all expenditures under the headings of public education, public health, old-age pensions, unemployment, health insurance, and poor relief were identified as social services.

Despite this long-standing commitment, Marsh points out that social services in Britain did not evolve from an agreed-upon set of consistent principles, nor from an agreed-upon definition of what social services covered. In an attempt to bring some clarity to the problem, he cites Clarke, who suggested that the "social services are the services which a community provide for its own members, and to which the members of a community are entitled, to a greater or less degree, by reason of belonging to that community" (1970:4).

The distinguishing characteristic of social service, then, was not the kind of services but the arrangements and form of their provision. This point, the responsibility of a community to care for its members, was amplified by Hall, who argued that the basis of the social services is "to be found in the obligation a person feels to help another in distress, which derives from recognition that they are, in some sense, members of one another" (1952:8).

Whereas the Treasury reports listed discrete services, Clarke and Hall emphasized the *purpose* of the service: the development and maintenance of human communities. Furthermore, both introduced the notion of redistribution either through taxes or private charity, while recognizing that the extent and direction of such redistribution has shifted over time.

A 1937 report by an independent research group, for example, defined social services as "a set of devices for providing people whose incomes are low or precarious, or both, with as many as possible of the essential facilities and resources which well-to-do families would naturally obtain in case of emergency" (PEP 1937:2).

Three important points are found in this definition. First, the redistribution is unidirectional—from the haves to the have-nots, from the nonpoor to the poor. Second, while the basis for redistribution may be one of a community caring for its own members, the level of social care is viewed as minimalist—the provision of essential services. Third, social services are to be provided on a temporary basis and are not to be viewed as part of each family's infrastructure.

With the implementation of the Beveridge Report 15 years later, the poor law was discarded and thinking about the social services shifted:

> [T]he state has gradually assumed responsibility for meeting the basic needs of *all of its citizens* . . . widening the scope of the social services to include *the whole community* without distinction of social or economic class. (Hall 1952:8). (emphasis added)

What we see then is a recognition that some mix of social services (not well defined) has been and continues to be recognized as important instruments of modern society; that the state has some degree of responsibility in assuring their availability; and that they involve some elements of redistribution.

The 1937 statement is an excellent example of what Wilensky and Lebeaux (1965) refer to as the "residual model" of social welfare. It expresses the belief that social services should come into play only when normal social institutions such as the family break down. Hall, on the other hand, describes a system that has been referred to by Wilensky and Lebeaux as the "institutional model" of social welfare. Social services are viewed as the normal, frontline functions of modern society, necessary to deal with the risks and contingencies all families are experiencing. These concepts will be dealt with in greater detail in a later section.

Recent Formulations

Titmuss, more than any other person, has influenced our conceptualization of the social services. Beginning with his seminal work on the emergence of the modern welfare state during World War II (*Problems of Social Policy,* 1950) and throughout his later works (*Essays on the Welfare State,* 1958; *Commitment to Welfare,* 1968; *The Gift Relationship,* 1971) he not only raised important questions but he also pushed for conceptual clarity. As important, he influenced the thinking of others by pointing them in fruitful directions.

Titmuss suggested that when we think about social policy

> we are [basically] concerned with the study of a range of social need and the functioning in conditions of scarcity, of human organizations, traditionally called social services or social welfare systems, to meet these needs. (1968:20)

For Titmuss, social services are societal responses to social need. This concept of social need is critical in that it argues that although economists emphasize demand as the most important stimulus for the planning and provision of services, this is an inadequate criterion. The economists assume that "real need" is only that which individuals translate into demand. Titmuss has been able to demonstrate that such a formulation fails to account for psychological and physical factors that impede such a translation.

Rein, in much of his work, explicitly affirms the influence Titmuss had in developing his approach to social policy and social services. In one of his earlier articles, he defines social services as

> collective interventions which are outside the market place to meet the needs of individuals as well as to serve the corporate interests of the wider community. The activities of physicians, teachers, social workers, as well as other helping professions are considered as social services. (Rein 1970:47)

Kahn, another leading theorist, agrees with Titmuss and Rein and offers the following definitions:

> Social Services may be interpreted in an institutional context as consisting of programs made available by other than market criteria to assure a basic level of health, education, welfare provision, to enhance communal living and individual functioning. (1969:179)

Titmuss, Rein, and Kahn emphasize that social services are not only a part of community life, they are requisites for community well-being in that they reaffirm the principle that each member of a community has responsibility for other members of that community.

Community can be analyzed on two levels: (1) the immediate, local, face-to-face community of family, friends and neighbors, and (2) the several layers of broader, more distant communities inhabited by people with whom we share a common heritage—that of citizenship—but who are strangers to us. While the former level is easily understood, the latter is not. Most people will agree that we have a responsibility toward family members, and perhaps even to friends and neighbors. But why to strangers? Quite simply, for both moral and physical reasons. By accepting the notion of a community of strangers, we place a value on cooperation, mutual aid, and collective responsibility. Titmuss (1970) places these issues in an appropriate framework by suggesting that we do not have to be as much concerned about those social transactions between people who know each other and feel a natural obligation for mutual sharing and support. He is more concerned with our accepting responsibility for those we do not know. In accepting this responsibility, we recognize common human needs and accept the reality that each of us has a moral obligation not only to our immediate community but also to the larger community. In intent, this is the rationale for the Social Security system, with its intergenerational and intragenerational exchanges. The notion of collective responsibility is especially clear in the retirement program. One generation is supported by another and, in turn, those who are giving trust that generations to come will support them. It is a program of mutual aid built on trust, and trust is the result of community.

Initially both Kahn and Rein offered a rather broad and comprehensive definition of social services. Kahn suggested that the "term social services involves a stubborn ambiguity . . . [but] the definition should at least be broad enough to encompass services such as education, medical care, cash transfers, housing and social work" (1969:179). Rein (1970), under the rubric of social services, mentions the activities of physicians, teachers, social workers, etc.

Both argued the need to distinguish social services from other social-welfare services. Rein (1970) described social services as those activities that assisted people to make use of these other services, and Kahn, with his colleague Kamerman, introduced as more meaningful the British distinction between education, income transfers, health, housing, employment, and the personal social services (Kamerman and Kahn, 1976). The term *social welfare* thus covers these six areas, with the personal social services operating to assure access to them. This distinction, we believe, begins to bring conceptual clarity to the analysis of social services.

Functions of Social Services

Social services can be viewed as those services that attempt to

facilitate or enhance daily living, to enable individuals, families and other groups to develop, to cope, to function, to contribute. . . . Still others offer substitute or safe or protected living arrangements. (Kamerman and Kahn 1976:4)

Within this definition, social services have two primary functions: social development/nurturance and social control. Garbarino (1987) expands on this distinction when he suggests that the social services are mechanisms that can

- improve the social skills of individuals;
- enlarge the resource base of each individual's social network;
- orient the individual and family to mainstream community values and institutions; and
- provide positive control when necessary.

Rather than discussing the specific purposes and functions of these services in the abstract, we will do so within the framework of the family, since that social unit is the place where most of these functions are carried out. As our society has moved from a traditional to an industrial and then into a postindustrial state, certain forces (e.g., modernization and urbanization) have produced periods of rapid social change. While all social institutions have been affected, the family has borne the brunt of the transition process—it has been expected to make the major adaptations (Vincent 1967).

The family is still the primary agent of socialization and mediation. As an institution, it maintains its members physically by providing food, clothing, and shelter and protects them from physical and social trauma and threat. The family is the usual context for reproduction, creating its and society's new members. Relative to society, the family socializes its children to assume expected, accepted, and useful social roles. In the process of socialization, the family helps develop children cognitively, affectively, and socially—the result being that children are equipped well or poorly to perform functions that attach to their social roles.

Socialization can be defined as the:

process by which persons acquire the knowledge, skills and dispositions that make them more or less capable members of this society . . . The function of socialization is to transform the human material of society into good working members; the content can be considered analytically to include an understanding of the society's status structure and the role descriptions and behavior associated with the different positions in this structure. (Brim 1968:361)

Lasch maintains:

As the chief agency of socialization, the family reproduces cultural patterns in the individual. It not only imparts ethical norms, providing the child with his first instruction in the prevailing social roles; it profoundly shapes his character in ways of which he is not even aware. The family instills modes of thought that become habitual . . . it colors all of the child's subsequent behavior. . . . If reproducing culture were simply a matter of formal instruction and discipline, it could be left to the schools. But it also requires that culture be imbedded in personality. Socialization makes the individual want to do what he has to do; and the family is the agency to which society entrusts this complex and delicate task. (1975:1)

Socialization begins in childhood and continues throughout adult life. It is concerned with knowledge, ability, motivation, and the transmission of norms and values across generations.

Social control is another family function. Acting as an agent of society, the family is expected both to transmit values and attendant behaviors that equip its members to be well behaved and productive members of society and literally to police its own members, keeping them in line on a daily basis. In the process of performing these functions, family identity is developed. Paradoxically, the family is also expected to produce independent members with their own personal identities.

The family also provides social and psychological support (Berger and Kellner 1970; Carroll 1973; Parsons and Bales 1955). While it may have lost some of its functions in the modern era, in theory the family has emerged as an institution specializing in emotional support for its members. It provides adults with an escape from the pressures of a competitive marketplace, while at the same time it helps equip the young with the necessary resources to deal with these pressures in the future. It is primarily within the family that intimate and meaningful relationships are possible and that alienation is mitigated.

Further, the family provides a stabilizing social environment, one that benefits individuals as well as society as a whole (Hauser 1976; Mercer 1967; Segre 1975, Sorokin 1941; Vincent 1967). Hauser, building on Parson's notion of social systems, suggests:

> the more rapid the role of [social] change, the greater becomes the probability that sections of the social order will be characterized by anachronistic relationships and dissonance which may be represented in the attitude, value and behavior of the individual. (1976:80)

In his discussion of industrialization and its impact on the social order, Goode argues that this "revolution has and will continue to bring pain, bitterness and frustration" (1975:84) to many until the transition is completed. These social and behavioral scientists suggest that this period of transition, characterized by rapid social change, is felt first by the family. In this context, Vincent (1967) argues that society needs a family system that is highly adaptive to the demands of other social institutions as well as to the needs of its own members. The family facilitates social change by adapting its structure and functions to these external changes:

> A major reason is that the family's strategic socialization function, that of preparing its members for adult roles in the larger society, is inseparable from its mediation function, whereby the changing requirements (demands, goals) of that society and its other social institutions are translated and incorporated into the ongoing socialization of all members of the family, both children and adults. (1967:37)

This notion of the mediation or executive function is also discussed by Berger and Neuhaus (1977). Parents are, in effect, the executives of the family firm.

Although some tasks have changed, several have remained fairly constant. Parents have needed and continue to need time, energy, resources, and knowledge in order to fulfill their parenting roles; and usually, their successful performance as parents has also involved satisfaction derived from the continuing and healthy development of their children. In earlier times, this satisfaction was often derived from the knowledge that healthy and well-raised children would provide security in one's old age; today, it often involves the enjoyment of children and an awareness of one's own personal development and social contribution.

Stress tends to have a deleterious effect on parents because it detracts and drains from the time, energy, resources, and knowledge that they are able to bring to child rearing. Many parents have developed means of coping with stress, largely through the development and use of support systems.

First, social services, within this framework (i.e., strengthening families), should help families master developmental tasks. Families can be viewed as moving through developmental phases from childless married couples, through several phases defined by the presence of children of varying ages, and finally to aging families. Each phase requires family tasks to be mastered, such as physical maintenance, protection, socialization, and the development of independent behavior.

Second, social services should support families by minimizing potentially harmful stresses, thereby improving the quality of intrafamily systems and family relations with external systems. Families can be viewed as small systems operating in relationships to other societal institutions such as the extended family, the neighborhood, schools and other service bureaucracies, the community, the world of work, and the marketplace.

Third, social services can be instrumental in improving the operation of liaison or linkage functions related to social resources and supports needed by the family. Research has underscored the importance of linkages between families in need of help. Supporting families therefore requires the development of liaison functions to identify and mobilize these resources.

Kammerman and Kahn's (1976) later formulation of the personal social-service tasks is quite helpful. They identify eight possible purposes. Social services

1.   Contribute to socialization and development. Under this we would include services such as day-care.

2.   Disseminate information about and facilitate access to other social-welfare services. Information and referral services would be included under this task.

3.   Assure the frail elderly, the handicapped, and the incapacitated a basic level of social care. Homemaker and home help services are examples of this task.

4.   Arrange substitute homes or residential care when necessary. Foster care would be included in this category.

5.   Reestablish functional capacity through counselling services.

6.   Develop self-help and mutual-aid activities, e.g., community centers.

7.   Assure coordination of programs or services. Case management is an example of this task.

8.   Control or supervise deviant individuals, e.g., protected residential arrangements for adolescents.

Rein (1970), in turn, identifies five functions:

1.   Preparation: the use of counselling, guidance, and information to enable individuals to make use of other available institutions.

2.   Procurement: the process of referring individuals to other community resources.

3.   Provision: the giving of concrete services that facilitate the use of other programs and extend well-being.

4.   Participation: the planned involvement of consumer groups in defining need, instituting institutional change, encouraging conformity, and developing support for social services.

5.   Protection: assuring that the rights of individuals and families are protected.

Both frameworks offer a clear statement that distinguishes the social services from other social-welfare or human services, e.g., health, education, income maintenance, housing, and employment. Furthermore, both Kahn and Rein emphasize the *facilitating* function of the social services, through either (1) the provision of concrete services (e.g., day-care, information, and referral) that assist the family or individual to use social-welfare resources, (2) *self-actualizing* services (e.g., counselling, parent education) that support individuals and families in carrying out their normal functions, or (3) *therapeutic* services that attempt to reverse existing pathology.

Finally, both social-development and social-control functions are included in their definitions. We have made the argument that while social services can either support or substitute for families, while they can be placed on a prevention-treatment continuum, while they might emphasize both enhancement and restoration; we are not suggesting that our current social-service system in practice balances these differing purposes. In fact, we argue that our system emphasizes a residual, reactive, treatment function. This will be dealt with in a later section.

Government Policies

The Evolution of the Social Services

During the depression, the then existing patchwork of state, county, and local public and private social-service agencies was overwhelmed by the economic disaster engulfing the country. A major response to this, as discussed in Chapter 1, was the passage of the Social Security Act in 1935. The drafters of this legislation expected that, as economic conditions improved, employment increased, and the employment-related social insurance programs expanded their coverage, the need for the public assistance program would lessen. However, it became evident after World War II that this "temporary" public assistance program, rather than diminishing, had grown.

While the stated intent of the program was to provide money and not services, social casework quickly became a part of the program. Social workers, among them Jane Hoey, who was the first chief of the Bureau of Public Assistance, were convinced that social casework should be part of the eligibility determination process if individuals and families were to become financially self-sufficient. Arthur Altmeyer, the director of the Social Security Administration from 1935 to 1953 supported this concept. The Social Security amendments of 1956 sanctioned this practice by extending federal financial participation to the provision of social services.

As the public assistance caseloads continued to grow, federal officials and social workers became even more convinced that social services were necessary to rehabilitate existing recipients and to prevent others from needing financial assistance. Their efforts were successful and by 1962 they had convinced Congress that professionally trained social workers could reduce welfare costs by helping families to become self-sufficient.

The Social Security Act was once again amended, this time it

- increased the federal match for social services from 50 to 75%;
- left federal expenditures open-ended (i.e., the federal government would not place a cap or ceiling on social service dollars);
- significantly expanded the eligible population; and
- authorized state welfare departments to purchase services from other state agencies.

While the broad goals of these amendments—to strengthen and maintain family life, and to reduce and prevent dependency—were specified in the legislation, the states were given considerable flexibility in defining the specific social services to be provided.

By 1967 it was clear that the proponents of the service strategy had greatly oversold the potential of social services to reduce welfare dependency. AFDC participation had increased at an unprecedented rate, from 3.5 million persons in 1962 to 5 million in 1967. Not only had the numbers increased dramatically, but the nature of the AFDC caseload was changing as well. Recipients were increasingly and visibly concentrated in the metropolitan areas and were likely to be families where the father had deserted the family, unlike the earlier caseloads where families became dependent because of the death of the father.

Congressional criticism of the failure of the 1962 amendments with their social service strategy was intense. In shaping the 1967 amendments, Congress was determined to stress employment as the goal for those on welfare. While the resulting legislation did shift the emphasis to workfare, professional social workers and federal officials were able to retain the service strategy and the service provisions were again expanded. A major programmatic initiative created was the Work Incentive Program (WIN), which sought to place recipients, including mothers, in training programs and eventually jobs. States were required to provide child care for the younger children of WIN enrollees. The incentive to the states was the federal government's willingness to pay 90% of total costs. The amendments also expanded the states' capability to provide day-care and child development services to non-WIN AFDC recipients under the existing 75–25% federal-state match. However, while the service strategy survived, we saw a shift from casework services to more "concrete" services, e.g., job training, homemaker services, and day-care.

While congressional intent may have been conservative, i.e., to put welfare mothers to work through training, placement, and day-care, other features of the 1967 amendments had the effect of expanding the states' claims for federal reimbursement for a broad range of social services. Moreover, the provisions of the 1967 amendments included

- an expansion of purchase of service contracts with private agencies;
- continuation of the open-ended appropriations; and
- a broader definition of the goals to be achieved: "services to a family, or a member thereof, for the purpose of preserving, rehabilitating or strengthening the family to attain or retain maximum self-support and personal independence."

During this period, the Department of Health, Education and Welfare (HEW) experienced a major reorganization. In part this reorganization reflected the new emphasis on the work-related, rehabilitative purpose of the social services. The casework oriented Bureau of Social Services was abolished and responsibility for social services was placed in the Vocational Rehabilitation Administration (VRA) of the newly established Social and Rehabilitation Service (SRS). Mary Switzer, who had considerable success with employment and training programs as the head of VRA, became SRS director. SRS was less interested in oversight than the Bureau of Public Assistance, preferring instead to allow the states more latitude in developing their service strategy. Thus began the explosion in the purchase of service contracting.

The states responded by enlarging their planning and budgeting offices and consolidating the social-service agencies into larger departments. The governor's office in a growing number of states, disenchanted with the federal government's overly active involvement at the implementation level, saw this as a means to gain greater control over the federal grant programs. Derthick (1975) discusses in great detail the aggressive and successful efforts of a number of large states (specifically, California and Illinois) to exploit these more liberal administrative controls.

The years following the 1967 amendments were a period of explosive growth in federal spending for social services. For example, between 1969 and 1972, federal expenditures increased from $390 million to $1.7 billion, or 435%. While some of this increase resulted in expanding the amount of social services, a considerable portion of the increases went to financing existing social services because of the better federal match.

Faced with this funding explosion, the Nixon administration proposed a number of initiatives to rationalize the social-service system and to hold the states more accountable. By the early 1970s, it had become clear at the federal level that some type of more limited financial involvement would be necessary (Mott, 1976). Congress rejected an administration proposal in 1971 to limit appropriations to 110% of the previous year's level and a total ceiling of $2.5 billion in 1972. In 1972, however, Congress did adopt a statutory limitation of $2.5 billion as a rider to the General Revenue Sharing Act. Furthermore, 90% had to be spent on present welfare recipients. Finally, the conference report accompanying the act directed the secretary of HEW to issue regulations that would force the states to become more accountable to the federal government.

Initially, there was little reaction to the legislation—in part due to the fact that at that time only six states were spending at their allocation limits. However, on February 16, 1973, HEW issued proposed regulations so restrictive that all states would be negatively affected. The goal of social services was narrowed so that the 1967 goals of prevention, strengthening family life, restoration, and maintenance were revised to cover only the rehabilitation of welfare clients. The regulations offered an extremely restrictive definition of acceptable services and states would no longer have the flexibility they had under the 1967 act. Finally, if enacted, total federal spending would have been reduced to $1.7 billion.

HEW received 200,000 adverse comments on the regulations and Congress was inundated with letters of protest. The proposed regulations also precipitated the formation of a unique coalition of interest groups that eventually resulted in the passage of Title XX. The principal forces in the coalition were the National Governor's Association and the Social Services Coalition convened by the National Association of Social Workers (NASW) and composed of 20 or so diverse groups representing labor unions, associations of state and local government, and professional and advocacy groups in the social-service field.

The coalition was successful in postponing the implementation of the proposed regulations twice. By 1974, the coalition and HEW were pressed by Congress to develop legislation that both could support. The following is a list of the major compromises:

1.   HEW changed its position that favored tight federal control and now favored placing responsibility with the states. While the coalition supported this position, some social-service organizations feared that state control

could diminish the level of services. The issue was resolved in favor of HEW, with the compromise that accountability would be lodged in citizen review of state plans.

2.   HEW gave up its position that limited services to current public assistance recipients and agreed that each state must use one-half its service allocation for recipients of AFDC, SSI, or Medicaid and the other half could be used for those with family income up to 115% of the state's median income. Persons with less than 80% of the state's median income would be eligible for free services; fees could be charged for those families between 80 and 115% of the median.

3.   HEW agreed not to list permissible services. The compromise agreed to was HEW's identifying five broad goals toward which all services must be directed: (1) achieving economic and social self-support; (2) achieving self-sufficiency; (3) preventing abuse and neglect of children and adults; (4) reducing inappropriate institutionalization; (5) securing institutionalization when necessary.

After two years of intense negotiations, in December 1975 Congress passed P.L. 93-647—Title XX. Whatever its limitations, this legislation was a landmark event in the social services. The willingness of Congress to spend $2.5 billion annually, together with a broad definition of goals and potentially eligible target populations, demonstrated the considerable progress made since the early days of the Social Security Act when social services could be financed only as part of the costs necessary for the administration of the public assistance program.

Social Services: Critical Issues

In Chapter 2 we introduced the concepts of institutional and residual approaches. While the former begins with the premise that most, if not all, families are at risk, the latter assumes that only a small proportion of the population experiences difficulties. Policies and programs that evolve from the institutional approach emphasize strategies to minimize these general risks (preventative); while those that accept the residual approach emphasize programs that rehabilitate those who actually experience problems (curative). Kamerman and Kahn (1976) address these emphases when they distinguish between public social utilities (those social services that are meant to serve average people facing ordinary circumstances) and case services (those that involve people with maladjustments, problems, illnesses, and other difficulties).

We further argued in Chapter 2 that services should be available to all (the concept of universal) as a right of citizenship and not be earmarked for a residual of the population if we were to build a sense of community. The latter emphasizes common need; the former tends to be divisive in that it labels people capable or incapable, normal or deviant, "we" or "they."

In arguing the case for universal services Titmuss states:

> One of the principles of the National Blood Transfusion Service and the National Health Service is to provide services on the basis of common human needs; there must be no allocation of resources which could create a sense of separateness between people. It is the explicit or implicit institutionalization of separateness whether categorized in terms of income, class, race, colour or religion rather than the recognition of the similarities between people and their needs which causes much of the world's suffering. (1970:238)

It is his belief that exceptionalistic services (the residual approach) tend to generate stigmatization, to be divisive, and to create barriers to community and mutual aid. While universal services offer no guarantee that these values will be achieved, they do establish an environment in which families and individuals can be integrated into a network of supportive social relationships.

Proponents argue that universality of benefits and services is essentially egalitarian; that it stresses social unity rather than divergence; that the universal approach offers a guarantee that potential recipients will avail themselves of the benefits and services since they are offered equally and without discrimination. Furthermore, the universalist argues that the redistribution so achieved (in that the high taxpayer contributes more and realizes less in relative terms) is more equitable than an exceptionalist system, which may merely shuffle resources among the poor.

A universal approach has the advantage of maintaining a high level of quality of services since the middle class are recipients and, as taxpayers, they are likely to be more influential than the poor in their demands. The exceptionalist approach is based on the notion of two classes of citizens, often resulting in two separate service delivery systems.

Still, to offer equal services or benefits to people in unequal situations is not to offer equality. It merely underwrites their existing inequalities. To counter this, additional services are often necessary, e.g., the poor need more than the nonpoor; the handicapped more than the nonhandicapped; the developmentally disabled more than the "normal" student. A universalist system, then, does not exclude the possibility of positive discrimination to rectify territorial and group injustices or the special needs of individuals and families. Titmuss argues:

> The challenge that faces us is not the choice between universal and exceptionalist social services. The real challenge resides in the question: what particular infrastructure of universalist service is needed in order to provide a framework of values and opportunity bases within and around which can be developed socially acceptable selective services aiming to discriminate

positively, with the minimum risk of stigma, in favor of those whose needs are greater. (1968:135)

Social Services: A Critique

It is clear that although earlier public social services emphasized treatment and rehabilitation of a small number of individuals and families; the language of the Title XX legislation covered both the social-development and social-control functions—strengthening families through prevention and early intervention as well as rehabilitating families once they experienced breakdown.

Time has shown, however, that this potential centerpiece for a national social-services policy has failed to materialize. Although 38 distinct services were being provided by the states, Morris (1978) found that 60% of total expenditures were being spent on only six of these services. Day-care, a potential source of support for large numbers of families, was being provided in all 50 states but almost all recipients (98.9%) were either recipients of income maintenance programs or were income eligible. Chore services were restricted to extremely low income families (99.1%) and were provided by only 35 states. Table 5.1 lists five additional services that could be critical in developing a supportive environment for families and yet they account for less than 10% of the total Title XX expenditures, coverage was limited, and utilization tended to be restricted to the poor.

Table 5.1.   Title XX Services

Category	Number of states providing services	Total expenditure (%)	Recipients without regard to income (%)
Day-care, children	50	22.0	1.1
Foster care, children	41	9.0	7.0
Protective services, children	48	8.0	59.6
Education/training	44	7.0	1.8
Counselling services	43	7.0	8.3
Chore services	35	7.0	0.9
Homemaker services	49	5.0	1.8
Transportation	45	2.0	1.2
Day-care, adults	36	2.0	1.1
Home/congregate meals	32	0.4	0.8
Recreation services	21	<0.1	0.7

Source: Adapted from Morris et al. (1977: 6, 8).

This has led Morris to conclude:

> Poverty can be seen as the primary criterion for receiving most federally funded social services. Even those programs which define their eligible populations in terms of handicapping conditions (e.g., Vocational Rehabilitation Services and Developmental Disabilities) or demographic vulnerability (e.g., Administration on Aging), in practice tend to attach such criteria to a consideration of income status. (1977:16)

Although the federal regulations require that only 50% of federal funds must be spent for services to AFDC, SSI, or Medicaid recipients, the bulk of the funds go to welfare recipients (63%) and those who while not recipients are income eligible (27%). While the strictly nonpoor do receive some services, they tend to be limited to information and referral and protective services.

Title XX was replaced in 1981 with the Social Services Block Grant. This reorganization of the social services was yet another attempt to curtail costs By 1981, Title XX expenditures had risen to $2.86 billion within an allowed ceiling of $2.9 billion. The Omnibus Budget Reconciliation Act of 1981 (P.L. 97-35) reduced federal involvement significantly. First, the legislation reduced the cap to $2.4 billion; and second, it gave states complete discretion in deciding upon those services it wanted to offer. No specific services were mandatory.

Most states experienced an immediate 20% reduction of federal funding and more importantly, the mix of social services changed markedly. If we compare Tables 5.1. and 5.2, we see a sharp decrease in all services be-

Table 5.2. Percentage of Political Units Offering Selected Services

Category	1982	1983	1984
Day-care, children	54	50	50
Foster care, children	36	34	34
Protective services, children	52	52	47
Protective services, adults	48	44	45
Counselling services	48	30	28
Transportation	36	25	25
Day-care, adults	41	37	29
Home/congregate meals	28	23	24
Education/training	40	28	31

Source: Adapted from Office of Policy and Legislation, *Summary of Information. Social Services Block Grant Preexpenditure Reports. Fiscal Year 1984*, Washington, D.C.: Department of Health and Human Services (1984).

tween 1977 and 1984 with the exception of day-care services for children. The promised infrastructure was crumbling.

Title XX, then, despite its promise and possibilities, has become a residual program and is an exceptionalist response to social need. It is means tested and, at least in terms of day-care, has produced a dual system, i.e., all children in a specific program tend to be from poor families.

Earlier in this chapter we pointed out that social services can, by definition, perform two important functions: social development and social control. The former tends to emphasize the "normal" while the latter the "deviant" individual or family. As discussed above, social services are targeted to meet the needs of a residual proportion of the population, i.e., the poor, the near poor, and those incapable of functioning at a level defined as acceptable by society. This leads us to the conclusion that our social services are primarily concerned with the social-control function. For example, Head Start attempts to overcome the negative influences poor parents and/or environments might have on children's development. It is a deficit model. Day-care provided for children of AFDC mothers is also a social-control measure, in that it is a means of stimulating the mother to seek employment—to change her behavior.

One aspect of this social-control function is particularly disturbing to a number of critics—the issue of dependency. As discussed in Chapter 2, neoconservatives argue that social services create and foster dependency in recipients. This position has been supported by a number of theorists such as Lasch and Donzelot. Donzelot (1979), in a book aptly title *The Policing of Families,* extends the thesis formulated earlier by Lasch (1978) that social services tend to weaken families. For both, the crime of intervention is not that professionals do not help families, but that their involvement produces negative outcomes.

This concern is not one that can be put aside lightly. Parsons (1951), discussing the appropriate role of the physician, notes that the patient was expected to become dependent on the professional since only the professionally trained person knew enough to diagnose and cure. The "good patient" accepted this status differential and followed orders. Goffman (1961) expanded on this notion by observing that patients were required to place absolute trust in the knowledge and technique of the professional since only the professional could translate symptoms into diagnoses. Patients may ask for specific services, but only the professional can develop an appropriate treatment plan. Given their lack of training, patients see services in terms of presenting symptoms (it is interesting that often we find the phrase "presenting complaint" used), while professionals are equipped to go beyond symptoms and identify the underlying cause of the problem. The professional, of course, is trained to be sensitive to the patient's "diagnosis," recognizing that if this is ignored, the "real" treatment plan could be jeopardized.

If one examines the professional literature of the major human service providers (medicine, psychiatry, psychology, nursing, and social work) it is clear that professionals view family members as less than capable caregivers when one of their members has a physical or mental handicap (Moroney 1980, 1986). Even those who accepted family members as part of the "helping team" saw them only as extensions of the professionals, providing care under professional supervision. This would suggest that while social services are theoretically of value for both social-development and social-control functions, the emphasis is on the latter.

Given these developments, the neoconservatives would argue that many of the personal social services should be dismantled. Many support the other social services, i.e., income maintenance (e.g., a negative income tax program), employment (e.g., subsidies to employers, training programs, unemployment insurance), education (though they would prefer a more competitive system through the use of vouchers), and medical care (e.g., national health insurance). Many would even support some of the personal social services, e.g., day-care, but through indirect measures such as tax credits. They do so on the rationale that indirect measures are supportive to families in that they provide them with the means to enter the market to purchase those services they believe to be important rather than having someone else determining what they need. In theory, the more the family is allowed to make these decisions, the more the family will develop its capacities. The ability to choose is thus seen as the key to building independence.

Proponents of the personal social services cannot ignore this argument. Although there is a significant body of evidence that markets do not respond the way the theorists argue they will (see the chapter on housing), there is some basis to the argument that the personal social services do, in practice, foster dependency. We have argued that the residual approach, which assumes a deficit model, dominates our system. Even those services that could by definition be developmentally oriented are often delivered to achieve a social-control function (e.g., Head Start). Finally, the majority of people view the public social services as services for other people and not for themselves, since only "incompetent" people need them.

If this is to change, we will need to see a greater commitment to those personal social services that are developmentally oriented: those that emphasize self-actualization, access, advocacy, self-help, and mutual aid. This, by itself however, would be inadequate if effort were not also made to reorient the attitudes of the professionals involved in the provision of the social services.

Current and Future Trends

The evolution of the personal social services in this country has been shaped by two deep-seated beliefs: first that services provided by the private sector are superior to those provided by public agencies, and second that public provision is acceptable only as a residual effort. The traditional distinction (beginning with the Elizabethan Poor Law) between the "working" and the "nonworking" consumer forms the base for the development of our two-tier system. Public social services were established to serve the residual client, those unacceptable to or ineligible for private services. (Note the similarity of this belief to the majority report on the Victorian Poor Law cited at the beginning of this chapter.)

Disillusionment with the performance of public social services, accompanied by the stigma of the public sector's association with an unpopular clientele, has accentuated the belief that the private sector is the better service delivery system. It is probable, however, that this preference rests more on beliefs and anecdotal information than on the proven superiority of the private service delivery system. It is also likely that this belief is based on a somewhat incomplete understanding of past and current governmental involvement in a wide range of public social services.

Private-sector expenditures, relative to public-sector expenditures are small and continue to shrink. For example, in 1965, for every dollar spent by the private sector, the public sector spent $2. Twelve years later, this ratio exploded to $12 of public expenditures for each dollar of private expenditures (Gilbert and Specht 1981:3). What has occurred is not so much cutbacks in the private sector but that private expenditures have remained static while public expenditures have increased dramatically. This phenomenon, however, is best understood in the context of public-private relationships.

Prior to the enactment of Title XX, about 25% of the private not-for-profit social-service agencies' budgets came from public expenditures. Since that time this has grown to a little more than 50% and in some states has reached 80% (Barber, Slavin, and Barnett 1983). Despite this blurring between the public and private social-service sector, private agencies are still perceived as independent and autonomous by their consumers and employees.

Currently, there is a movement to reduce these notions of separate systems. Drucker (1968) proposed over 20 years ago that we would be able to abolish the dual system and gain support for social services if we would "reprivatize" social services. This new system would be characterized by clearly differentiating the planning, financing, and monitoring functions (in his view these functions are more appropriate for the public sector) from the design and delivery functions, which would be the responsibility of the private sector.

The private sector itself can be divided into the not-for-profit sector (often referred to as the voluntary) and the for-profit sector. Until recently, most discussions of a public-private partnership in the social service area have been concerned with the government's relationship with the former, and reprivatization has meant purchase of service contracting. Now, public-private partnership also includes the for-profit sector. One of the more extensive surveys, for example, indicates the existence of 8,000 industry-based social-service programs. While many of these began as Employee Assistance Programs (EAPs) and were primarily concerned with substance abuse, more and more are evolving into comprehensive social-service agencies (Rowan, Randleman, and Smith 1982).

This new partnership—a blending of economic and social well-being—is predicated on the assumption that employment and labor market policies are one of the cornerstones for social welfare. (See Chapter 2 for a more complete discussion of this point.) Work is a fundamental value in American culture and is therefore of central importance in the lives of all Americans. Consequently, if the opportunity to work is absent, or if the work environment is unsatisfactory, severe repercussions are likely to be experienced by the individual, his or her family, and ultimately by society. While such systematic efforts have not yet been fully developed, industry-based social services are meeting important social needs. However, the private sector cannot, nor should it be expected to, replace public social services.

Summary

This chapter has attempted to bring some conceptual clarity to our understanding of social services—to address what Rein calls the "psychedelic mosaic where boundaries are vague, overlapping and uncertain, reality and myth emerge, and a participant's mood in observing development shifts from euphoria to depression" (1970:4).

We have taken the leads offered by Titmuss, Kahn, and Rein and suggested that social services are best understood as those services concerned with social development and social control. Our position is that both functions are important to an industrial society, important for the well-being of the individual, the family, and the community.

To achieve this integration of the individual and community, we argued that services should be available to all as a right of citizenship and not earmarked for a residual of the population. The former emphasizes common need; the latter is divisive in that it labels people as capable or incapable, normal or deviant, "we" and "they."

Finally, recent developments, including the reprivatization of the social services and the growth of industry-based social services might, we believe, strengthen the notion of a dual system. At the turn of this century, the British debated this issue in their *Report of the Royal Commission on the Poor Laws and Relief of Distress* (1909). As discussed earlier, the grounds for the debate were (1) a dual system or a single system, and (2) a reactive or proactive system. These issues are still very much with us.

CHAPTER 6

FAMILIES AND THE CARE OF THE DEPENDENT

In the best tradition of the modern welfare state, this country has repeatedly expressed its commitment to meeting the basic needs of its families. Yet this same tradition has produced a series of policies, programs, and services that are often contradictory and counterproductive when assessed as a whole. This does not mean that specific policies, taken individually, have not been of value; rather it means that intervention has often created new problems in other areas or operated at cross purposes to other policies. More often than not, the secondary effects were never intended nor anticipated.

For example AFDC is a program intended to provide financial support to needy families, but as designed and modified, it actually penalized two-parent families and encouraged fathers to desert (Stack and Semel 1974). Housing policies of the 1930s were successful in providing improved shelter to tens of thousands of families who were living in tenements and slums, but often also had negative effects on neighborhoods and informal support networks (Subcommittee on Executive Reorganization 1966). Finally, recent efforts to deinstitutionalize the mentally ill and the mentally retarded, defensible on both therapeutic and economic grounds, have created increased pressure on families in that the discharges have not been accompanied by a comparable expansion of community-based resources (Moroney 1986).

The secondary effects of these and other social policies have, in turn, generated continuous and often bitter debates. The debates can be reduced to a number of fundamental questions:

- Should services be provided as a right or made available only when individuals and families demonstrate their inability, usually financial, to meet their basic needs?

127

- Should benefits be provided to the total population or restricted to specific target groups, usually defined as "at risk"?
- Should government develop mechanisms to improve and promote the quality of life, or should it restrict its activities to guarantee some agreed-upon minimum level of welfare—a floor below which no one should be allowed to fall?
- Should government seek to prevent or minimize stressful situations, both environmental and personal, or should it merely react to problems as they arise?

These questions, of course, are raised and discussed in general terms in Chapter 2 and in one form or another have recurred in later chapters. Despite this ambivalence and disagreement, however, there seems to be a general consensus that when policies are proposed, the family should be considered in all deliberations. Whether for political or moral reasons, legislators argue that the family should be protected and strengthened as a basic social institution. Even a cursory review of the past 50 years shows that social legislation has been promoted on the premise that it would benefit the family and thereby benefit the country. Opponents of such action counter with the argument that the same legislation would weaken the family.

This latter position has gained considerable currency over the past 15 years. Sir Keith Joseph, a leading theorist for the Conservative party under Prime Minister Margaret Thatcher and a former secretary of the Department of Health and Social Services, has argued:

They [the family and civilized values] are the foundation on which the nation is built; they are being undermined. If we cannot restore them to health, our nation can be utterly ruined, whatever economic policies we might try to follow. . . . The socialist method would try to take away from the family and its members the responsibilities which give it cohesion. Parents are being divested of their duty to provide for their family economically, of their responsibility for education, health, upbringing, morality, advice and guidance, of saving for old age, for housing. When you take responsibility away from people, you make them irresponsible. (1974:5)

In this country, similar charges, in strikingly similar language, have been leveled at the social policies formulated in the New Deal of the 1930s and expanded in the Great Society of the 1960s. We are told, in an echo of Joseph's position, that families should not be relieved of traditional caring tasks because when this happens, families begin to feel that they are neither able to nor expected to continue their traditional responsibilities. For example, under the banner of "profamily" the New Right has argued:

[F]amilies are strong when they have a function to perform, and when government takes over the functions of a family, then as sure as the night follows the day, families are going to disintegrate and fall apart because they have no reason to exist . . . today we have well intentioned causes saying that we'll provide your food and we'll take care of your health, and we'll provide you with everything you really need, and then you can be a strong family. It doesn't work that way. Families are strong when they have a job to do. (Marshner 1981:63)

For over four decades the federal government has assumed a proactive stance in minimizing risk and enhancing social functioning, as exemplified by the Social Security Act (e.g., retirement benefits, benefits for the handicapped, unemployment insurance), various housing programs (e.g., public housing and numerous forms of subsidized housing), and education programs (e.g., the G.I. Bill of Rights and mainstreaming the handicapped student). Today this role and function are being redefined and the federal government is in a more reactive stance, intervening only when it is absolutely necessary. Many of the New Deal and Great Society programs have been cut back, dismantled, or turned back to the states through the block grants strategy discussed in Chapter 5.

Proponents of both positions argue that their formulation of the welfare state provides the most effective set of guidelines for strengthening the family. How is it that one group can argue that proactive social welfare measures are the solution while another can argue that the real solution is the dismantlement of those very measures?

Characteristics of the American Family

How do we deal with these anomalies? What "families" do we have in mind when we formulate policies? If policies are always proposed with "the family" in mind, and if they are supposed to "strengthen" families, how realistic is our view or understanding of the American family? How capable is the family in terms of our expectations to care for its own?

It is impossible to offer many generalizations or universal statements that some authority will not challenge. While one expert argues that the family as a social institution is not only dissolving but has actually become an anachronism (Zimmerman 1974), another applauds its state of health (Levy 1966), and a third maintains that though there have been some changes in family structure, the family is evolving toward a more viable form (Folsom 1943). Each position is accompanied with an impressive array of data. Each conclusion is credible if the reader is willing to accept each authority's implicit definition of what a family is and what it should be.

The single proposition that might be allowed to stand unscathed is that all societies have been characterized by some form of family structure and this unit usually carried out certain key functions. While the form of the structure, the specific ways by which the family fulfilled these functions, and the extent to which they were shared with other institutions has changed over time, there has always been, in recorded history, some basic social unit that could be called a family.

Whether family life was natural or was created in the sense of a social contract is largely a matter of speculation. Regardless of how it came into being, as an institution it was more capable of achieving the survival needs of its individual members, than they were on their own. These basic needs included both physical and social, and specific family functions are usually described as procreation, protection, social control, socialization, nurturance, and physical and emotional care. (See Chapter 5 for a more detailed discussion of family functions.) While major historical social scientists such as Durkheim, Weber, Tonnies, Simel, and Parsons have debated whether families have retained or transferred these functions to other institutions, whether the nuclear or extended family is the dominant form of family structure, whether one form is superior, in theory, to the other given the demands of modern society, the more important issue is to arrive at a realistic and reasonable picture of the family and its ability to support (whatever that support is) individual members.

From whatever perspective we approach the situation of the modern family, the community and with it the traditional family are perceived to have gradually deteriorated. But is this the case? Are we, in fact, being nostalgic about the "world we have lost" (Laslett 1965), rather than being objective?

Families today do differ significantly from those of the nineteenth century, and a number of those differences potentially affect a family's capability and willingness to provide social care for its dependent members. Families have become smaller. They have more members who are older and dependent as the age composition of the population has shifted upwards. Women have entered the work force in significant numbers and their earnings account for an important part of the average family's total income. The number of single-parent families has increased sharply. It is clear that the family is undergoing profound and rapid change.

Perhaps the most notable of these changes is the size of the family (see Table 6.1). Almost 60 years ago, one in three families had five or more persons, compared to one in seven in 1988. We also see a significant shift in the percentage of two-person families, 40% in 1988 compared to 26% in 1930. Finally, the size of the average family size has dropped by 20%, or by almost one person.

Even though women were marrying earlier in each successive generation since the turn of the century and theoretically were more likely to have more children, the birthrate has actually dropped (see Table 6.2). Although the rate did swing upward between 1950 and 1960, it began to drop again in the 1970s.

Table 6.1. Family Size 1930–1988

Number of persons	1930	1940	1950	1975	1982	1988
2	26.1	29.3	32.8	37.4	39.9	40.8
3	22.5	24.2	25.2	21.8	23.0	23.9
4	18.8	19.3	19.8	19.7	20.6	21.1
5	12.8	11.7	11.1	11.3	9.7	9.1
6	8.1	6.8	5.6	5.4	3.9	3.2
7	11.7	8.7	5.5	4.4	2.5	1.8
Mean	4.04	3.76	3.54	3.42	3.25	3.17

Sources: U.S. Bureau of the Census, "Household and Family Characteristics," *Current Population Reports,* Series P-20, No. 291, p. 3 (1976); *Census of Population, 1980,* pp. 22–23 (1984); *Statistical Abstracts of the United States, 1989,* pp. 50–51, Washington, D.C.: U.S. Government Printing Office.

The average number of children 75 years ago was 2.9 per family; today it is 2.2. These trends have had a significant impact on family structure and family life. For example, in the middle of the last century, the average mother was still bearing children well into her forties; by 1900, she had completed her child-bearing functions at 33; and by 1980 this age had dropped to 29. Unlike her predecessor, the present-day mother is likely to have completed her child-rearing functions in her forties (although it should be noted that a small but significant number of mothers are postponing childbearing until their thirties and raising their children in their forties).

One argument for these changes is that as a society becomes more industrialized, it develops some form of social-security or social-insurance system. Before this, many parents, however erroneously, viewed their children as their old-age insurance: the greater the number of children, the greater the insurance (Schottland 1963). With collective social-insurance mechanisms available, the need for large families diminished. Related to this was the dramatic reduction in infant mortality rates. When the rates were extraordinarily high, the norm was to have a large number of pregnancies, on the assumption that only a few children would survive. For example, it has been estimated that 100 years ago one child in five died before reaching the age of one, and one in three died before reaching their fifth year. Another reason was the nonavailability and/or nonreliability of fertility control measures.

A final factor is related to changing expectations and roles of women over the past 50 years. In the past, women had fewer opportunities for careers outside the home. Furthermore, prior to World War II, mothers were under heavy societal pressure not to work. Since then, not only has this sanction disappeared, but women have been encouraged for economic reasons to

Table 6.2. Birth-, Infant Mortality, and
Maternal Mortality Rates [a]

Year	Birthrates	Infant mortality rates	Maternal mortality rates
1840	51.8		
1880	39.8		
1900	32.3		
1920	27.7	85.8	79.9
1940	19.4	47.0	37.6
1960	23.7	26.0	3.7
1970	18.4	26.0	2.1
1975	14.7	16.1	1.3
1980	16.0	12.6	0.1
1985	15.8	10.6	<0.1
1987	15.7	10.0	<0.1

[a] Birthrates are per thousand population; infant mortality rates are per thousand live births; maternal mortality rates are per 10 thousand live births.

Sources: 1840–1940, adapted from U.S. Bureau of the Census, *Historical Statistics of the United States, Colonial Times to 1957,* pp., 23, 25 (1960); 1960–1976, *Statistical Abstracts of the United States,* pp. 55, 70 (1977); 1980, adapted from *Statistical Abstracts of the United States,* pp. 34, 35 (1984); 1985 and 1988, *Statistical Abstracts of the United States, 1989,* pp. 61–62. Washington, D.C.: U.S. Government Printing Office.

limit the size of their families. Large families are now viewed as a barrier to social mobility and to a higher standard of living. Mothers, having completed their childbearing function by 30, thus had the time and opportunity to begin or resume other careers, many with paid employment (see Table 6.3).

In 1900, 20% of women between the ages of 16 and 64 were employed. Over the next 40 years, this figure gradually rose to 26%. The figures for married women rose from slightly under 5 to 15% during this same period. Older women (45–64) were less likely to be in the labor force: 14% in 1900 and 20% in 1940.

These trends accelerated over the next 50 years, until 50% of all women are now employed. Even now, married women living with their husbands make up 57% of the labor force. While the number of women in the labor force increased by 28% between 1960 and 1980, it has increased by 68%

Table 6.3. Female Labor Force Participation Rates

Age	1950	1960	1970	1980	1990
16–19	41.0	39.4	44.0	51.8	55.2
20–24	46.1	46.2	57.8	68.4	75.2
25–34	34.0	36.0	45.0	57.4	63.5
35–44	39.1	43.5	51.1	58.3	63.0
45–54	38.0	49.8	54.4	57.1	60.3
55–64	27.0	37.2	43.0	41.9	42.3
Total	33.9	37.8	43.4	48.4	51.4

Sources: Bureau of the Census, *Current Population Reports: A Statistical Portrait of Women in the United States,* Special Studies Series P-23, no. 58, Table 7-2, p. 28 (April 1976); Bureau of Labor Statistics, *U.S. Working Women: A Databook.* U.S. Department of Labor, Table 61, p. 65 (1977).

for married women and by 162% for mothers of children under the age of 6 (almost one-half of them are working outside their homes).

The reasons for these shifts are multiple and have been reported on extensively (Kanter 1978; Ridley 1968). While the specific reasons may differ by social class, they can be grouped under three major headings: (1) the need for income, either to supplement a husband's earnings or, in the case of families where the woman is the main provider, to survive, (2) increased opportunities, and (3) the need for self-fulfillment. Not only have the stigma previously attached to working mothers and exclusionary labor practices diminished, but women are not tied down by large families and extended periods of child-rearing.

These changes have, however, created new and unanticipated pressures on today's families. Although child-rearing years have been reduced, families are faced with the growing demand from the other end of the dependency continuum—the elderly. Whereas in earlier decades of this century children were likely to be our largest group of dependents (e.g., in 1910 there were 12 children for every elderly person), today children are sharing demands on the family with their grandparents (e.g., in 1990 there were only three children for every elderly person).

These shifts in the dependency ratio are creating new pressures for families, especially mothers, since it is not simply a matter of transferring the care from children to elderly parents. For most families there is a significant hiatus in years. As discussed earlier, mothers were able to complete their child-bearing years in their twenties and were in their early thirties when the children went to school. Fifteen to twenty years later, the new dependent group—their aged parents—needed care. Furthermore, the type of care required was not the same as required by their children.

Previously this had created fewer problems. There were fewer aged and when a family did have an aged member, some family members were available to provide care. Few mothers worked and, more important, many families had unmarried daughters or other relatives living with them. Theoretically this group, especially those between the ages of 45 and 54, were the care givers, as they were the generation immediately following the elderly group. This does not mean that only women were the care givers in this age group.

This pool of potential care givers has shrunk throughout this century (see Table 6.4). Over half the women in this age group are in the labor force. Moreover, 86% of married women between the ages of 45 and 64 are working. These women, once a major source of care giving, are either unavailable or working and caring. (To be clear on this point, we are not concluding with regret that this pattern of informal care is no longer available. Our point is more one of historical description. These women were able to provide substantial amounts of care because they were not working.)

Another characteristic of the modern family with implications for its capacity to provide care is the growing divorce rate. There is no question that divorce is becoming a common occurrence. In fact, it has been projected that between 40 and 50% of all marriages of women born between 1940 and 1944 will end in divorce. However, this trend needs to be tempered with the likelihood that 80% of divorced persons will remarry (Norton and Glick 1976).

Table 6.4. Caretaker and Dependency Ratios

Year	Women 45–54 per thousand elderly	Single women 45–54 per thousand elderly
1900	966	76
1910	974	83
1920	983	94
1930	937	84
1940	837	72
1950	708	55
1960	625	44
1970	600	29
1980	456	22
1990	543	

Source: 1900–1950, U.S. Bureau of the Census, *Historical Statistics of the United States: Colonial Times to 1957,* Series A51–85, p. 10 (1960); 1960–1980, adapted from U.S. Bureau of the Census Decennial Reports.

This increase in the divorce rate can be attributed to changing attitudes and the liberalization of the divorce laws (Goode 1975). Whereas most Americans feel that divorce is preferable to an unhappy marriage and that divorce no longer carries the stigma it did in the past (Yankelovich, Skelly and White 1977), divorce still brings stress to those involved and impairs the family's ability to provide care (Hetherington, Cox, and Cox 1977; Schorr and Moen, 1977).

Eighty-five percent of all divorced women (including those with children under the age of six) are employed. Furthermore, even those who remarry will spend a considerable amount of time as the head of a single-parent family. Moreover, one in two children born in the 1970s will see their parents divorce or have one of their parents die. However, few children are in single-parent families for their entire childhood, the average period being about five or six years (Bane 1978).

While most children do live in a home with a mother and a father, the last decade has seen a substantial increase in the number of children living in single-parent families, most of which are headed by women. The trend toward a still-increasing number of single-parent families is likely to continue throughout the remainder of this century. The proportion of children under six living with both parents declined from 87.5% in 1960 to 71.0% in 1990. During this period, the number of children who lived only with their mothers increased from 5 million to just under 15 million (see Table 6.5).

Not all children, however, have the same likelihood of growing up in a single-parent, female-headed family. For example, in 1990 the percentage

Table 6.5. Living Arrangements of Children under 18

	1960	*1970*	*1990*
Total families (thousands)	45,111	51,586	69,947
Total children (thousands)	64,310	69,523	64,776
Living with two parents (%)	87.5	83.1	71.0
Living with two natural parents (%)	73.3	68.7	56.0
Living in reconstituted family (%)	8.6	9.4	11.0
Living with one parent (%)	9.1	13.4	25.0
Living with one parent, mother (%)	7.9	11.5	23.0
Living with neither parent (%)	3.4	3.5	5.0
with relative (%)	2.4	2.3	4.0
with foster parents (%)	0.8	0.8	1.0
in institutions (%)	0.2	0.4	0.1

Source: Glick (1979).

of children living in a single-parent female-headed family differed significantly by race and ethnicity. Twelve percent of all white children; 19% of all
Hispanic children, and 42% of black children were living in single-parent
female-headed households. Still, in absolute numbers, and contrary to popular belief, 72% of all children living in families headed by women are
white.

Furthermore, 16% of all children live in single-parent female-headed families in which the mother was never married; of these, half were born to
young women who became mothers in their teens, two-thirds of whom did
not finish high school. Moreover, although the average for single moth-
erhood is one child, slightly more than 40% have had two or more children
(Grabill 1976).

Although most women who are single parents work, one in three children
living in a single-parent female-headed family lives in poverty; a ratio that
rises to 6 in 10 for all black children living in single-parent families. Although incomes in general have increased over the years, the income of a
female-headed single-income family continues to be just over half the income produced by male-headed single-income families. (This issue is examined in greater detail in Chapter 8.)

The final trend affecting the family's capacity to provide social care is the
change in the expectations that people have toward family life and marriage.
These changes have produced significant tensions, especially in terms of
role expectations and sex-differentiated tasks. Bott (1955) describes these
tensions in terms of joint and segregated conjugal role relationships. In the
former, tasks are shared; in the latter they are differentiated along sex lines.
More and more, both men and women are stating a preference for the joint
conjugal role. A 1976 poll, for example, found that while 90% of women
preferred marriage *with* children, over half wanted both children *and* employment outside the home, a percentage that was even higher among
women under 30 (61%) and women who were college graduates (65%).
Approximately one-half of the men responded that they would support their
wives if they wanted to work (Roper and Associates 1976). A number of polls
indicate that mothers and fathers, whatever their stated preference for a
shared marriage, still have fairly traditional responsibilities toward child care
and maintenance of the home. Yankelovich, Skelly and White (1979) reported that 78% of the respondents disagreed with the assertion that "it is
the wife's responsibility to insure that the house is clean if she holds a job
outside the house." And yet Yankelovich, Skelly and White also found that
women continued to have primary responsibilities in the areas of meal
preparation (77%) and house cleaning (65%). When asked, How much time
does your husband spend in various household activities? How much time
do you think he should? we find that behind the rhetoric of shared marriages, lies the reality of sex-differentiated roles (see Table 6.6).

Table 6.6. Time Husbands Spend in Household Activities

	Does little or none (%)	Should do more (%)
Housecleaning	61	30
Shopping	53	26
Dishes	80	19

Source: Yankelovich, Skelly, and White (1977).

Young and Wilmott (1973) support these findings and speak of the "three-job family"—a phenomenon also discussed by Poloma:

> [T]he assumption of a professional role by the wife does not mean a drastic change in family roles. . . . The wife was responsible for the traditional (homemaking) tasks. (1970:87)

Gordon also commented:

> [T]heir domestic responsibilities are not lightened to any degree . . . and thus are doubly burdened. They work full time and take care of their homes as well (1973:93)

Carisse (1972) discusses the ambiguity and expectations many women (her sample was limited to college graduates holding professional jobs) were experiencing in four major areas: (1) the family as an institution, (2) marriage as an institution; (3) parent-child relationships, and (4) man-woman relationships. These women did not fall neatly fall into one clear cultural-historical category (i.e., traditional, Industrial, or postindustrial) but were more likely to have beliefs that fell into more than one, depending on the area. The "modern, liberated" woman finds that while she may be employed, she is still expected to carry major responsibilities in the domestic life of the family.

Summary

The trends described here are familiar facts of modern life. They are but a few of a large number of social and demographic realities reported regularly by the media. The tendency has been to treat these trends as individual statistical phenomena with little attention to their broader or combined implications. In examining these trends it is important to avoid the romantic view that families were once better off than they are today. It is not appropriate now—if indeed it ever was—to look back nostalgically and devise policies whose primary purpose is to re-create things as we imagine, usually erroneously, they once were. Families are not worse off than they were in the past. They have undergone changes, to be sure, and these changes have taxed the coping capabilities of many families. But families have always been under pressures of one sort or another.

Despite the increasingly complex demands placed on parents, and the continuing pattern of stress and limited family support, parents are expected to carry out their tasks as if they were automatically capable and autonomous. There is mounting evidence, however, that this expectation is unrealistic. As a result, families need resources and supports to permit adequate family functioning in general, not just low-income families.

Families are smaller than they were. When coupled with changing fertility patterns and significant increases in the numbers of working women (especially mothers), it would seem that families would be deterred from carrying out caring functions for their dependent members, that families are neither in a position to be care givers nor should they be expected to be.

In fact, on a number of levels, families are neither in a position to be care givers nor are they expected to be. Still, the trends discussed above cannot be equated with problems. A dual-career family, a single-parent family, and a childless family cannot be defined as problem families. Some might be at risk in that they experience stress other family types do not. A working mother heading a family may have problems in interacting with external social-service agencies and the educational system because their hours of operation conflict with her work schedule, but is she the "cause" of the problem? Similarly, families providing care to handicapped members may have problems, but more often than not, it is because the social-welfare system does not support them.

Finally, the issue of defining the family or families for social-policy purposes needs to be addressed. What is clear is that there is no one dominant type. There are nuclear isolated families—units with no or few contacts with other family units; extended families—units that are residentially near other kin; and modified extended families—although the families are spatially dispersed, they are characterized by considerable interaction and exchange. There are families in which both spouses work; families in which only the husband works and the mother stays home to care for the children; single-parent families where the head works and others where he or she stays home; families with and without children. As valid as these family types are in a descriptive sense, it is simplistic and somewhat counterproductive for policy purposes to divide America's 70 million families into these categories. To do so assumes that families are static, since most data are a cross-sectional snapshot of families. A more realistic approach is to recognize and analyze the fluidity, change, and transitions as individuals live in a variety of family types over time. There are periods in the life cycle when an individual family may be one in which the father works and the mother stays home with the children. This stage is relatively short-lived when the total family life course is analyzed. There are also periods when women (and men) find themselves raising children without a spouse present, but again, for many this is a transitional period. None of these types or stages, however, should be viewed as the dominant or "ideal" family type: no one family type is superior to another. Effective policies and services should be sensitive to the needs and stresses of certain types of families and recognize that some families are at greater risk (in the statistical sense) than others and therefore need greater amounts of supportive services. However, to conclude that because a group of families has a greater need for services that type is "deviant" or "inferior" is spurious. The evidence instead suggests that all families are experiencing stress and would benefit if supportive services were made available. The evidence is equally clear that some families are experiencing greater levels of stress and need additional services. Given this, what has been our response?

The Ideology of Our Welfare State

Our approach to families since the depression can best be understood as falling under two contrasting paradigms. The first might be labeled the "old" paradigm, the one that emerged during the 1930s and held center stage until the 1970s. Briefly stated, it encompasses four major principles:

1.   We believed that a number of group-identified needs warranted public action. This is a variation of the public-goods argument and the public-interest rationale and would include programs ranging from public education to social insurance to national health insurance.

2.   We believed that family life is enhanced if family caregivers are provided some relief from onerous care-giving tasks. Examples of these policies would include homemaker/home care services for the frail elderly and respite care for parents with mentally retarded children.

3.   We believed that social-welfare organizations, both public as well as private, are efficient and responsive in meeting human needs. Aspects of this principle include notions of imperfect market mechanisms, economies of scale, and a combination of centralized and decentralized service delivery systems.

4.   We believed that professionals are central to the provision of effective services. Examples of these policies are regulations that deal with staffing requirements in day-care, nursing home care, and child welfare.

Under the old paradigm then, we believed that families recognized their natural obligation to care for one another. We believed, however, that families were at risk and under stress due to the rapid changes in the twentieth century. Continuing shifts in our economic system created risks and produced consequences that negatively affected the quality of family life. This, in turn, required society, through the state, to create a safety net.

Under the "new" paradigm that emerged in the 1970s:

1.   We now believe that government efforts to improve the quality of life of individuals and families are not only undesirable but are likely to be harmful. This is a variation of the argument that governmental intervention invariably weakens families by creating dependency.

2.   We believe that families should not be relieved of traditional caring tasks as they were under the old paradigm. This is another variation of the dependency argument. Intervention becomes interference and will be interpreted by families as a lack of trust in their care-giving capability.

3.   We believe that decision-making and organizational responses should be decentralized. This assumes that the further away decision-making is from those in need, the less sensitive and responsible the effort.

4.   We believe that professionals are self-serving and intentionally create dependency.

Under the new paradigm, we now believe that too much has already been done, that families are spoiled, and that they need to reassume more of their traditional care-giving tasks—even if they do not want to do so.

Under the old paradigm, government assumed a proactive stance, which tended to generate policies that were universal in coverage. Under the new paradigm (actually this paradigm has its roots in nineteenth-century poor-law tradition and utilitarianism) government assumes a reactive stance, i.e., it only intervenes when there is clearly defined pathology.

This approach, the new paradigm, is consistent with the *residual approach* to social welfare—a concept that has been discussed in a number of chapters in this book. Fundamental to this approach is the belief that most people, most of the time, will be able to take care of their own needs. Given this, the front line of our social-welfare system should be existing informal support networks, i.e., the family, the neighborhood, the churches, etc. Only a small number will need help from the more formal and impersonal institutions beyond this immediate system. We also believe that, to some degree, when people seek help they do so because of personal or family deficits.

These perspectives are tied to deeply held notions about the family and community. The "traditional" family was seen as the basic unit of community life. As Demos suggests:

> Families were the building blocks from which all larger units of social organizations could be fashioned. A family was itself a little society. . . . The family performed a multitude of functions, both for the individual and for the aggregate to which it belonged. Thus, most of what children received by way of formal education was centered around the home hearth; likewise their training

in particular vocations, in religious worship, and in what we would call good citizenship. Illness was also a matter of home care. (1983:164)

Communities then were settings in which families interacted with other families for mutual support. All of us can relate to the classic example of barn raising—where the total community came together to build a home or barn for a new family or for an established family after theirs had burned down. Families willingly gave of their time and resources to help others with the understanding that if they ever needed help, other families would help them.

This idea of the family, real or not, is the type of family much of our policy is built around. Given this, we assume that state intervention should be considered carefully before actions are taken. Consistent with our belief that government intervention in the economy should be minimal and should be undertaken only after there are clear imperfections in specific markets, so also we believe that the state should not interfere with family life. Intervention should be limited to those instances where family functioning has been clearly impaired.

There is a widely held belief that family life is and should be a private matter. The family, moreover, is viewed as a sanctuary from the harsh economic world and therefore the state should not interfere. Furthermore, the family is perceived as a fragile institution, one that is "besieged" and that must be protected (Lasch 1978).

This approach supports the notion of intervention in family life only when necessary. It is not that we are not interested in all families (at least so goes the argument); nor does it mean that we do not recognize that all families could use supportive services. The concern is a fundamental one: that intervention might result in families giving up their responsibilities—responsibilities they would prefer to keep. Instead of helping families remain strong care-giving units, the "support" might result in weakening the family. Intervention becomes interference. Therefore, it is argued, the more appropriate role for the state is to become involved only when there is clear evidence of family breakdown. By waiting until the family declares that it can no longer care for a handicapped member, for example, the state is assured that its involvement is necessary. There is, in conclusion, such a fine line between intervention and interference that caution is the preferred course.

This line of argument is usually supported with the assertion that families have deteriorated—an assertion based on any number of social indicators, e.g., rates of out-of-wedlock pregnancy, divorce, family violence, delinquency, adolescent pregnancies, and chronic economic dependency. The resultant list of weak family types then includes single-parent and "broken" families, families in which parents abuse each other or their children, families whose adolescents behave in sexually or violently disruptive ways, and families on public welfare. The argument inevitably leads to proposals to rehabilitate these families by making them more like strong families—families that care for their own members with little outside help.

Given this emphasis, policies affecting families and children tend to be restricted to a smaller subset of families and children. These are the families that have demonstrated their inability to function, and since there is sufficient evidence that pathology already exists, there is little danger that the intervention will cause harm, create dependency, or weaken the family unit. The harm has already been done; the family members have lost their ability to be independent; there is little strength to be found in the family.

The major program targeting the family (in terms of expenditures) is AFDC. The stated purpose of the program is to maintain children in their own home by providing income when the wage earner dies, is incapacitated, or is absent from the home. (AFDC is discussed in greater detail in Chapters 3 and 8.) This program has, since the 1970s, provided income support to between three and four million families—between seven and eight million children.

Title XX (see Chapter 5 for a more detailed discussion) is another major "family" program. In some respects, Title XX evolved from the 1967 amendments to the Social Security Act, which attempted to expand social services to families at risk of becoming income dependent (AFDC)—a preventive function. As discussed earlier, Title XX mandated that at least 50% of social-service expenditures go to AFDC and SSI recipients or those who were income eligible for these programs. This gave some discretion to the states to provide services to nonpoor families (those whose income was 115% of the median family income). The reality, however, was that with the exception of child and adult protection services, over 90% went to income recipients or income eligibles—the poor and very poor.

Day-care for children was the largest program funded under Title XX (22% of all expenditures) and about 800,000 children received this service. Head Start is another source of funding for day-care. This program, within the Office of Human Development, provides comprehensive health, educational, social, and nutritional services to approximately 350,000 children from low-income families.

Child welfare, another major source of support for families, has two major goals: (1) to strengthen the family through the provision of preventive services (e.g., counseling, parent training, chore services); (2) to develop appropriate alternatives when necessary (e.g., foster care, adoption). However, the primary effort as measured in funds and services goes into achieving the second objective.

The above approach is supported by the efforts of most policy analysts, who typically limit their concerns to specific and exceptional classes of families, e.g., poor families, minority group families, single-parent families,

families with handicapped children, or otherwise "unlucky" families. Data are marshalled to show that these families experience special stresses, are uniquely at risk, and have special needs. It is then argued, and often vigorously advocated, that such families be given special consideration in allocating scarce resources. This exceptionalist approach is not without value and, in fact, has a number of advantages. First, by focusing on discrete special groups, analysis can be narrowed and concrete recommendations made. Second, inequities can be pinpointed, including gaps and shortages in needed resources and services. And, finally, how can one argue against this approach in light of the following statistics:

- In 1990, more than 12 million children lived in families with incomes below the poverty level.
- In 1990, over 8 million children lived in families supported by AFDC.
- In 1990, 650,000 children lived in foster homes.
- In 1990, 65,000 children lived in institutions.
- Between 1.5 and 2 million children are abused each year.
- Between 60,000 and 100,000 are sexually abused.
- Between 10 and 20% of all families experience some form of spousal abuse.
- More than one in ten teenagers become pregnant each year; over 500,000 babies are born each year to teens; 96% keep their babies.

Ambivalence in Practice

While the above argument appears to be logical, rational, and even compelling—an argument that dominates the current debate—many of our policies are not as logical or rational. A few examples will make this clear.

Policy position 1A: Children Should be Raised by Their Mothers and Not by Strangers. The family (so it is believed) throughout history has always been the major force that has provided societal stability and continuity between the past and the present by carrying out its responsibility to transmit acceptable values to its children. It is now being argued that the family has defaulted in this responsibility over the past 20 to 30 years. For the well-being of this and future generations, the family needs to reassume its responsibilities. However, families cannot achieve this if they continue to place their children in day-care programs. The rationale: existing research clearly demonstrates that day-care is harmful to the growth and development of children. *Therefore, mothers should stay home and raise their children.*

Policy Position 1B: A Variation of the Above. AFDC mothers should not be allowed to stay home, even if they have very young children, but should be required to work. Not only is this in the public interest (it would slow down the rising cost of welfare) but it is also in the mother's best interest in that she will learn to become independent. Furthermore, research strongly supports the conclusion that children benefit when placed in day-care. *Therefore, AFDC mothers should leave the home and enter the labor force even if they have very young children.*

Policy Position 2A: Families Should Not be Paid to Carry Out Natural Care-giving Functions. The very idea that society should provide financial support to families caring for handicapped members (beyond tax credits, deductions, or exemptions) is abhorrent. It is inconceivable, if not un-natural, it is argued, to pay families to provide such care. They are expected to do so. Families should want to care, whether from a sense of duty or love. The basis for this position emerges from a historical belief in what constitutes acceptable moral practices. *The payment of money to carry out "natural' family functions is viewed as unacceptable in that the moral reasons for caring—duty, love, responsibility to care for one's own—are replaced by nonaltruistic motives and the total fabric of society is threatened.*

Policy Position 2B: A Variation of the Above. Money can be given, however, to people who are willing to "serve as families." Foster parents can be paid to care for children without natural parents or whose parents are incapable of providing a caring environment. Others are paid to care for handicapped persons and the elderly residing in institutions. These people, in effect, are paid to function as substitute families—for providing for the physical and, in some instances, the social needs of the residents. Recently policies have been initiated to provide financial incentives to prospective adopting parents especially when the children are hard to place, e.g., older children, handicapped children, and minority children. Another example was the effort of the Department of Health and Human Services (DHHS) in the midseventies both to prevent institutionalization of physically and mentally handicapped adults and to ensure a reasonable quality of life while they lived in the community. The department, in its efforts to enable SSI recipients to "live within a family setting," increased their monthly grants by an average of 43% if they lived in a foster-care-type home and not by themselves. However, the same legislation reduced the monthly grant by one-third "if the individual is living with their family." On the one hand, the policy paid more money to stimulate the development of surrogate families on the assumption that families provide better environments than institutions. On the other hand, this same policy would reduce the benefit when the recipient lived with and received care from a relative. *Natural families are penalized when they care because they are "family" while unrelated persons are paid to function as families.*

We are forced to return to our earlier question, but this time we expand it to include the notion of bilateral exchange: What is the most desirable, effective, and feasible division of responsibility between the family and extrafamilial institutions in meeting the needs of individuals, and in what ways can these institutions relate to each other so as to maximize benefits to families?

Earlier, we pointed out that our policies toward families are shaped by our implicit belief in a residual approach to social policy: wait until the problem occurs before doing anything. However, it was also argued that many blame the family for many of the social and economic problems facing society today and that families had to reassume their responsibilities. To support this position of weakness and deterioration, a number of family indicators were listed. But most children do not spend their whole childhood in single-parent families. Most parents do not abuse their children; nor do most spouses abuse each other. In fact, on the whole, one might argue that most families, despite the stress in their lives, are coping. The concern, however, for family well-being remains and needs to be addressed. Nor can we expect that families will return to traditional ways from earlier times. To maintain a reactive approach may be less costly in the short run, but it is likely to be more costly over the long run:

- over 61 million children live in families with at least one natural parent;
- over 46 million children live in two-parent families;
- over 36 million children live with their two natural parents; and
- 5.2 million children under 13 are in families where both parents are employed full time.

An Alternative Formulation

We need to reexamine some of these basic assumptions if we are to move ahead in the public debate about policies affecting families. Is it useful to continue assuming that it is the family's responsibility first, and only when it cannot or will not provide the needed care, that the state should become involved? While we understand that the above has ideological value, is the introduction of a dichotomy (either the family *or* the *state*) of any practical value other than keeping expenditures down for the time begin? Assuming that it is not, what competing principles or assumptions might we build our social policies on? (Baldwin 1985).

In searching for this reformulation, two major questions emerge:

1. Is social welfare (we use the term broadly to include health and social services as well as financial support) a matter of charity, of generosity, of humanity?

If the answer is yes, then the family would have no legal or moral right to what it receives. By definition, one individual cannot have a right to another's charity—it is a gift freely given. Furthermore, the type and amount of service given will vary depending on the benevolence of the giver and need not reflect the type and amount of service needed by the object of the charity. If the answer is no:

>   2.   Is social welfare then a matter of strict obligation on those who have resources?

If the answer is yes, then the recipient has a moral claim on those who are better off in society, a claim that includes rights and entitlements and will involve, in most instances, redistribution—the "taking" from those who have and the "giving" to those who do not.

How do we, society, choose or decide between these two points of view? Are there rationales to help us in choosing between them? The next section introduces and discusses four major rationales that are currently used to justify intervention: (1) economic rationality, (2) compassion, (3) need, and (4) entitlement.

1.   Economic Rationality

Much of this country's social policy, including policies affecting families, is justified under this rationale. We begin with the assumption that there are not enough resources, including money, to meet all the legitimate demands on those resources. Given this, we are faced with making choices among competing demands, all of which we would probably like to fund. To complicate the situation, we are also faced with "opportunity costs," a term that simply means that if we allocate our resources to one program, we are not able to fund another program now, nor perhaps in the near future. This type of thinking forces us not only to choose the objectives of one program, but also to do so with a full understanding of the objectives we will not be able to achieve.

With this as a foundation, we argue that it is important that the decision to fund a particular program be the result of analysis that identifies the funding as a "wise investment"—an investment that will provide us with an acceptable monetary return. How then do we conclude that an investment is wise and that the return is acceptable? How do we conclude, furthermore, that the investment in program A is wiser than one in program B?

This argument assumes, moreover, that investments are rational *only* when there is a return and that the most rational choice involves finding that investment with the greatest return. In theory, not only does this position sound reasonable, but the flip side of the coin—that to invest in a program with a lesser return is irrational—is equally compelling.

This approach, sometimes referred to as the "human capital rationale," is often used as an argument to support families. We should allocate resources to children *because* they are our economic resources of the future. Our programs for the handicapped, another example, are justified on the grounds that rehabilitated persons will become independent and contribute to the general well-being of the economy by working and paying taxes instead of being dependent on welfare.

In practice, however, this approach has serious implications. First, analyses such as these require that a common denominator be used if proposed results (or benefits) from different programs are to be compared. The primary common denominator used is money (all benefits or objectives need to have a dollar value assigned) and, even then, in a special way (earnings over a lifetime maintained or improved because of the program).

Furthermore, if we assume that resources are scarce and inadequate, we often find agencies and advocacy groups competing against each other—attempting to convince policymakers that one disability is a better investment than another (e.g., the blind over the severely retarded); that some age groups are better investments than others (e.g., adult workers over retired persons); that some families are more worthy of investing in than others. Although each group is sincere and "rational" in what it does, the enemy becomes other groups and survival is achieved only at the expense of others: in the planning literature this is referred to as a win-lose or "zero sum game" scenario.

Given this somewhat narrow definition of benefits, some groups in our society are a priori better investments than others. In a sexist society, for example, where a woman's salary represents only 70% of a comparable male salary, our investment policies will always favor men over women. In a racist society where certain groups are relegated to the secondary labor market, it would be "irrational" to favor blacks, Native Americans, or Hispanics over whites. On a different level, it would also lead us to favor programs for people who are physically handicapped over those for the chronically mentally ill, and programs for people who are mildly mentally retarded over those for the severely mentally retarded. While the surface argument is reasonable—we are not choosing between and among people, we only want to get the biggest economic return for our investment—the more subtle analysis that requires weighing the economic value of groups is disturbing, especially in a society with many inequalities.

2. Compassion

This rationale offers a different perspective. Unlike the above rationale, which supports investments only if they return more than they cost—i.e., if they make economic sense—this rationale suggests that we provide services if and when the situation "touches" us.

The basis for this response, one that is ingrained in most of us, is found in Judeo-Christian teachings and, at least in part, explains our generosity to many fund-raising efforts in the voluntary sector. For example, telethons raise millions of dollars annually for children who are victims of muscular dystrophy, cancer, and other conditions. Recent efforts have raised funds for farmers in this country who were losing their homes and livelihood, and food and medical supplies for victims of famine in third-world countries.

If we were to use this rationale to justify supporting families who care for handicapped children, for example, we would, in essence, be arguing that (1) all children are vulnerable but these children are even more vulnerable; (2) while parenting in general is important, it is more difficult to raise a handicapped child; (3) disability is an unexpected crisis. The same line of argument might be made in those instances where adults are experiencing family stress because they are providing care for a frail elderly parent.

Compassion is also grounded, however, in other dynamics, three of which are pervasive in our culture. The first is simple: I feel good when I help someone else, a modern-day version of the "salvation through good works" argument. The second, and not necessarily exclusive of the first, is a variation of John Rawl's "veil of ignorance" thesis. (Rawls 1971). He suggests that lacking full knowledge of future conditions (e.g., whether my future unborn child will be handicapped or not) the rational person will analyze alternative possibilities in terms of how he or she will be negatively affected and then choose the alternative that will harm him or her the least. The rational person will support the "best of the worst scenarios." While the overall strategy is clearly defensive, it is rational—though in a different way from the previous use of the concept (i.e., economic rationality). A common every-day version of this position is the "there but for the grace of God go I" reaction, with its accompanying sense of relief (Moroney 1986b).

A third, and growing, dynamic is the apparent transformation of what was initially compassion into frustration—frustration that the problem or condition is still with us after we have given support. A vivid example of this is the Hands Across America event held in the summer of 1987. With much publicity, and with the promise that the problem of poverty would be solved, millions of people formed a human chain across America to raise money. National and local media offered human interest stories, most of which showed people who were happy, who were excited, who seemed to care. They were doing something to solve a problem. A year later, when the problem of poverty was not only with us but growing, when there was evidence that more people than ever were homeless, many participants were at first confused, then frustrated, and finally angry. This anger unfortunately was not focused on the causes of poverty insofar as that might raise questions about many basic beliefs related to our economic system; not on the organizers, who represented many of our community leaders and entertainers; but on the poor. Participants seemed to be saying, in so many words, "What right do they have still to be poor? I stood in the hot sun for a whole day for them. How ungrateful!"

This rationale, then, not only can appeal to the more generous nature of people, but has the potential for eventually turning us against the recipient. Compassion implies that the recipient has no rights or claims for support. Rather, the recipient depends on the generosity and charity of the giver—a giver who may require or even demand the recipient to act or behave in a certain way. This issue of reciprocity becomes critical (Pinker 1973; Moroney 1986a).

3. Need

This rationale shifts our thinking from the idea that the provision of services to people is because we "feel" for them to one that suggests that persons with needs should be supported simply because they have needs. This position begins with the argument that industrialization and modernization have brought with them a number of risks and consequences that potentially affect all people and not just a small percentage of the population. As a result of significant social changes, families are experiencing considerable stress.

It is further argued that the free-market system has not been able to achieve a just allocation of goods and services, resulting in significant hardships for a number of people. Social policies become essential then, if we are to correct social inequalities and provide a buffer to these societal stressors.

Titmuss is the best known and one of the earliest proponents of this position. As discussed in Chapter 2, within this framework, which demonstrates strong linkages between common stressors, common risks, and common needs, he argues the necessity of recognizing collective responsibility on the basis of moral claims and the ethics of mutual aid and cooperation (Titmuss 1968, 1971). Social policy, he suggests, is concerned with different types of moral transactions embodying notions of exchange or reciprocal obligations necessary to bring about and maintain community relations. Others, such as Boulding (1967), Macbeath (1957), and Tawney (1964), support this position.

To speak of moral claims and the ethics of mutual aid and cooperation is to speak of community. Boulding, in fact, argues that the major purpose of social policy is to build the identity of persons around some community because we need to be concerned with questions of identity and alienation. While integrated people believe in common risk and common need, the alienated attempt to destroy any sense of shared responsibility.

The glue of this moral sense of community is the notion of trust: I will give to others who have a need because I believe that, if and when I have a need, someone will give to me. Not only this, but I have responsibilities to people I do not even know (the "community of strangers") and they have responsibilities toward me. This is, of course, the rationale behind our intergenerational Social Security system. We are paying into the system to support currently retired persons, trusting that a generation to come will contribute when we are retired.

4. Rights or Entitlements

While for thousands of years many authors have offered insights into the issue of rights, I will briefly comment on the formulations of only two: John Rawls and Alastair MacIntyre. MacIntyre (1981) suggests that when we address the question of rights, we are confronted with the issue of claims that need to be validated. Those that can be validated, we accept as rights; those that cannot be validated, we reject. This validation process, in turn, almost always makes some reference to law, custom, or logic. Under the first category, the process usually involves an interpretation of existing law (including the Constitution) to cover additional categories. Within this framework, for example, we might argue that P.L. 94-142, Education for the Handicapped, was an *extension* of existing civil-rights legislation, which in turn was validated by the Constitution. The second, custom, involves another type of argument—one that eventually rests on the prevailing sense of what a moral community is or should be. Within this framework, we might argue that P.L. 94-142 was a *good* policy. Finally, an appeal to logic would involve not only the argument that such a policy was good, but would require our demonstrating how this is logically consistent with a whole value system (Dokecki et al. 1986). MacIntyre goes on to say that once a right is validated, we assign it a moral status. Finally, he concludes that the entitlement that evolves from the right will have contractual dimensions and often will result in some compensation.

Rawls (1971) offers a different perspective—justice as fairness—though he does conclude with a formulation of rights based on contract theory. Today, many professionals in the human services are familiar with his principles:

> Each person is to have an equal right to the most extensive total system of equal basic liberties compatible with a similar system of liberty for all.
>
> Social and economic inequalities are to be arranged so that they are both

> a) to the greatest benefit to the least advantaged
> b) attached to offices and positions open to all under conditions of fair equality of opportunity
>
> All social primary goods—liberty and opportunity, income and wealth, and the bases of self respect—are to be distributed equally unless an unequal distribution of any or all of these goods is to the advantage of the least favored. (1971:302–3)

This formulation is appealing for the issue of family care in that a case can be made that handicapped persons are at a disadvantage compared to non-handicapped persons; parents of retarded children compared to parents of nonhandicapped children; adults caring for frail elderly parents compared to adults whose aged parents are able to care for themselves. We might even be able to extend the argument to single-parent families: Children growing up in single-parent families are at greater risk than children growing up in two-parent families (i.e., two parents in theory constitute twice the resources as one) and therefore should receive more if both families are to be treated fairly.

The use of the argument as a single rationale has some serious limitations in that it is grounded in contract theory. Contract theory is appealing to most people, of course, since it is a long-standing part of our history. Beginning with the American Revolution, we have emphasized the *contractual rights* of people. This position was articulated initially in the constitution, and notably in the Bill of Rights, and has become the major emphasis in our legal approaches to social policy, which include:

- the landmark 1954 Supreme Court decision (*Brown v. Board of Education, Topeka*) guaranteeing blacks and minorities educational rights
- civil-rights legislation beginning in the 1960s guaranteeing voting rights, nondiscriminatory hiring practices, fair housing, etc.
- P.L. 94-142, which guarantees mentally retarded and other handicapped persons access to the public school system.

Given our history, such an emphasis is understandable. The revolution was sparked, in part, because of oppressive measures introduced by the British government—measures that infringed on the rights of citizens. Rothman (1979) points out that most of the "rights" expressed in the Bill of Rights are written as negative statements, ("Congress shall make no law. . . ," "No person . . . shall be compelled . . .") and suggests that this preoccupation with rights grew out of a profound mistrust of government.

Such an approach assumes an adversarial society, one in which people relate to others as competitors. Lowi (1969) describes this as "interest group liberalism." Furthermore, in emphasizing rights, we begin any problem-solving process with the position that some groups are being treated unfairly or unequally by others, whether these others are institutions such as government or educational systems or individuals such as employers or landlords. Moreover, our policy instruments (i.e., laws, regulations, and sanctions), which are intended to coerce compliance, often end up being divisive and weaken feelings of community.

Rothman continues that the expansion of rights only responds to a part of the problem in that it does not address the equally important issue of needs:

> imbalances in economic and social power, in inherited physical constitutions, that demand redress. . . . To this end advocates of the liberty [rights] model are far more comfortable with an adversarial approach, an open admission of conflict of interest, than with equality with its presumption of harmony of interest. (1979:92)

Can we as a society continue to recognize and respect rights and ignore needs? Of what value is it to grant people rights to inadequate or nonexistent resources—a problem that is endemic when we analyze the needs of the chronically mentally ill in this country? A second troublesome point is the possibility that if used alone, this rationale could, like the economic rationality argument discussed above, lead to competition between groups claiming they more nearly comply with Rawl's principles compared to other claimants for the same scarce resources.

Toward a Reformulation: A Synthesis of Justice and Need

In developing any rationale for intervening in the lives of families caring for dependent members and meeting the social, physical, and emotional needs of all their members, we will, of necessity, begin with the notion of community and the idea that we have responsibility for each other's well-being.

If we were to apply this rationale, the argument would probably be as follows: First, a relatively small number of families are raising a majority of the children in our society. (In this country as in Western Europe, approximately one-third of the families are currently raising 70% of the children.) Since children cause financial burdens on the families who raise them (it was Gunnar Myrdal, the Swedish economist, who first pointed out that "children were the major cause of poverty") and since children are our resources for the future (the idea of intergenerational responsibility), all of us have some responsibility to support those parents who are actively raising children. If we in this country continue to maintain that children are the sole responsibility of the parents who brought them into the world and that the rest of us have no responsibility in easing the financial burden children cause, we should not be surprised when these same children, as they become adults, refuse to support us (through the Social Security system), who will then be retired and dependent on that system for our basic medical and financial support. They are *our* responsibility, whether they are being raised by two-parent families, single-parent families, or adolescent mothers who never marry; whether they are white, black, Hispanic, Native American, or Asian; whether they are handicapped or not.

Next, we need to reexamine the concept of justice. Rawls's concern for justice does allow for treating people unequally, only if the beneficiary of such treatment is the least advantaged. This principle becomes clear when we apply it to the human services. To offer equal services to people in unequal situations is *not* to offer equality. Such an approach merely underwrites the existing inequalities between and among people. In Chapter 2, we introduced Titmuss's argument for "positive discrimination," a concept compatible with Rawls's position, with one exception. Titmuss believed that such positive discrimination needed to be built on a universal infrastructure and not a separate system.

Principles drawn from comparative justice are helpful in that this view holds that like cases be treated alike and different cases be treated differently (Watson 1980). Certain differences—those based on the notion that special needs, justified as societally important (MacIntyre's formulation of validation discussed earlier), call for special help—may result in policy-produced advantages that are warranted. In this case, however, *all* members of a justifiable special-need group are entitled to this advantage. Income tax credits for child care may be an example of unwarranted advantages: persons who do not earn enough to pay taxes, but who have need equal to or greater than those with higher incomes, are denied the benefit. An example of a warranted advantages would be the children's allowances granted by most Western countries to families with children. All families, regardless of income, are beneficiaries. (This strategy is discussed in Chapter 3.)

If we were to move in this direction, we would begin to balance our preoccupation with rights with an equally important concern for need in the tradition of Tawney (1964), who argued for justice; of Marshall (1965), who suggested that citizenship be the basis for social policy; and Titmuss (1970), who argued for and demonstrated the societal value of altruism with its foundation in beliefs of shared common need and responsibility for others.

Summary

By underestimating the stresses and risks encountered by all families in American society, the policies and programs that derive from the residual approach encourage the stigmatization of families designated as needing special consideration. Since self-sufficiency and independence are power-fully sanctioned social values, the stigmatization related to being placed in a dependent position by these policies and programs is often accompanied by a substantial loss of perceived status and self-esteem. In addition, families ignored for special attention are not likely to seek external resources and support, even when they experience the inevitable difficulties of American life. Reluctance to seek help is particularly strong among parents (regarding their child-rearing responsibilities), who often view it as an admission of weakness or pathology.

Kahn and Kammerman also argue against the residual approach and for universalistic provision of services for all families. They point out that rich and relatively fortunate people also receive "benefits and services assigned for important public reasons, in the public interest, and not achieved through market place transactions" (1975:ix). These social-welfare benefits include agricultural subsidies, and tax deductions for interest on real estate loans and business expenses. In arguing for the concept of "public social utilities" Kahn and Kammerman state:

> Society masks realities by distinguishing among what it calls public welfare and social services for the poor and troubled, and education and public health protection for everyone, and benefits for the affluent. It fails to recognize that, in a more basic sense, there are really two categories, not three: social services and benefits connected to problems and breakdowns (and these are not limited to the poor), and *social services and benefits needed by average people under ordinary circumstances.* (1975:x; emphasis in original)

This in no way argues against or diminishes the need to meet the needs of those families who are poor. The framework offered toward the end of the chapter, in fact, strongly supports the development of priorities based on need. It does, however, argue against the continuing strategy of establishing separate systems for the poor and the nonpoor. In separating we stigmatize no less than *Plessy v. Ferguson* did 100 years ago. By offering separate services we continue to divide an already fragmented society.

CHAPTER 7

POLICIES FOR THE ELDERLY

In the last public speech of his life in 1977, Hubert Humphrey challenged us with the following:

> The moral test of a society is how it treats those in the dawn of life—its children; those in the twilight of life—the elderly; and those in the shadow of life—the sick, the needy and the handicapped. (*Washington Post,* May 13, 1977:8)

While the evidence would suggest that our commitment to children and the poor has been mixed at best and negligent at worst, there is little question that the group of people referred to as the aged, the elderly, senior citizens, or retirees have not been neglected, nor have they been slighted. In the previous chapters we have seen that those "in the dawn of life" and those "in the shadow of life" have not been treated well, especially if they are doubly at risk, if they are in both groups.

Not only has there been a commitment, but this commitment has not been made to any other population group within our society. We need only look to the Older Americans Act passed in 1965 for such an expression of this formal commitment. Title 1 of the act lists ten objectives the Congress has established:

1. An adequate income in retirement in accordance with the American standard of living.
2. The best possible physical and mental health which science can make available without regard to economic status.
3. Suitable housing, independently selected, designed and located with reference to special needs and available at costs which older persons can afford.

4.   Full restorative services for those who require institutional care.
5.   Opportunity for employment with no discriminatory personnel practices because of age.
6.   Retirement in health, honor, dignity, after years of contributions to the
economy.
7.   Pursuit of meaningful activity within the widest range of civic, cultural
and recreational activities.
8.   Efficient community services including access to low cost transportation, which provide social assistance in a coordinated manner and which are
readily available when needed.
9.   Immediate benefit from proven research knowledge which can sustain
and improve health and happiness.
10.   Freedom, independence and free exercise of individual initiative in
planning and managing their own lives.
(U.S. Department of Health, Education and Welfare 1974:2–3)

Congress not only established a set of principles or a philosophical position
for this group; it has made a concrete commitment to achieving those objectives by consistently approving policies and programs and by appropriating
the funds necessary for their implementation. Today, this population group,
which accounts for 12% of the population, consumes 29% of all federal
expenditures and 48% of all domestic spending (Lewin and Sullivan
1989a,b). Such, however, has not always been the case.

Pre-Twentieth-Century Attitudes and Practices

Morris (1986) has provided us with a fascinating historical analysis of the
process and dynamics of care giving. With a broad brush, he covers almost
three thousand years of societal responses toward the vulnerable, i.e., the
elderly, widows and their children, and the handicapped. It is fascinating in
that he combines the more recognizable approaches of policy analysis with
methods drawn from the tradition of hermeneutics and exegesis. Based on
his analysis of texts such as the Hebrew Testament; writers such as Homer,
Plato, Aristotle, Demosthenes, Seneca, Cicero, and Marcus Aurelius of the
early Greek and Roman worlds; the Christian Testament and writings of the
Fathers of the church; Morris concludes:

> Throughout this history it is possible to trace a continuing tension between the
> unfairness, the brutality and the injustices encountered in the real world on the
> one hand and the attempts to introduce and to impose more civilizing, hu-
> mane ideals upon peoples and leaders struggling in an imperfect world. A
> moral code evolved about behaviors in relation to real life conditions.
> (1986:68)

What emerges, in Morris's analysis, is not a linear progression of the
practices and dynamics of care giving to the vulnerable, nor a common

rationale. Whereas the Jewish tradition emphasized justice as the guiding principle, the early Greeks stressed reciprocity; the Romans, citizenship; and the early Christians operated within a sense of moral and spiritual obligation. What is common to all is the apparent belief that dependency and therefore caring for dependent persons is not a negative phenomenon. Vulnerability was an all too common occurrence, and therefore the vulnerable needed protection and support. All of these societies seemed concerned with the issue of community and the importance of building and strengthening social cohesion.

This sense of responsibility took a sharp turn in the fourteenth century when deep cracks began to appear in the feudal system. For over 700 years, the needs of most Europeans were met by the church and the manor. Serfs were required to give complete obedience to their masters, personal freedoms were nonexistent, mobility was unthinkable; but all physical (and spiritual) needs were met. The coming of the Black Death in 1348, however, forever changed this system. Between 1348 and 1471, the Bubonic plague decimated the population of most European countries, creating a number of crises. The first, and probably the most important, was the erosion of authority. Authority figures, whether they were secular or religious, literally abandoned the estates and the villages when the plague came. The hold that these leaders had over the serfs was broken. Second, with so many deaths, the serfs found that they were able to sell their labor services to the highest bidder. No longer were they tied to a particular place but were free to move about, and as importantly, they found themselves in a position to demand wages for their work and not depend on the good graces of the manor lord. Thus began a 200-year period of social instability. While men, women, and children were free to move about and work for whom they wished; these same people found that no one had responsibility to care for them when there was no work. When these "hordes of vagrants" moved from place to place, they created an atmosphere of fear—fear of violence and fear of civil unrest:

> Poverty was a potential danger to the state, and was therefore, a peril to the King. At a time when no monarch was so firmly seated on the throne that he, or she, did not fear rebellion; persons went up and down the country side, starving and discontented, and linking up the country with a web of dissatisfaction . . . [They] were regarded as a menace. . . . In short, the poor must be relieved, if not on religious grounds, then for the sake of ensuring political stability. (Marshall 1969:17)

During this period, numerous laws were passed that attempted to control wages and limit mobility (the Statute of Laborers enacted in 1349 was the first of a series of laws passed over the next hundred years). People were required to obtain "letters of authorization" if they were going to travel from one village to another and those found without such letters were severely punished. The "able-bodied" were required to work, charity was banned, and begging became a crime.

If the period up to the fourteenth century is characterized as an era when vulnerable individuals and families were cared for because they were members of a community and as such had legitimate claims for support, the period following the plague can be characterized as the beginning of an era when rationales such as community and social cohesion lost their significance, to be replaced with punitive legislation that coerced families to care for their vulnerable under threat of harsh civil penalties.

Over the next four centuries various amendments were made to the poor laws (the most noteworthy being the Elizabethan Poor Laws enacted in 1601) that attempted to resolve the problem of care for the vulnerable, apparently with little success:

> It appears from the whole Evidence that the clause of the 43rd Eliz., which directs the parents and children of the impotent to be assessed for their support, is very seldom enforced. In any ordinary state of society, we much doubt the wisdom of such an enactment. The duty of supporting parents and children in old age or infirmity is so strongly enforced by our natural feelings, that it is well performed, even among savages, and almost always in a nation deserving the name of civilized. (Report of the Poor Law Commission of 1832, 1905:43)

The nineteenth-century family, particularly three-generational families, had only the institution of the poor law—primarily the workhouse—to look to for assistance, and for a number of families, this was either not acceptable or they could not meet the strict eligibility criteria. Dependents were kept in the home, but often at a high cost in both material and psychological well-being. Care was provided to the old and the handicapped: But what kind of care? Was it offered freely and with affection or was it perceived as something that had to be done, something to which there were no alternatives?

Testimony presented to the Royal Commission on the Poor Laws offers a rather bleak picture of the status of the elderly in that century:

> The large majority of those who endure biting poverty without seeking relief from Guardians are women. Men do not so frequently attain old age under disadvantageous circumstances as women do. Old men go more readily into the workhouse than old women. Women struggle longer and with greater determination with the difficulties of poverty and the incapacities of old age. Families in poor circumstances find it less possible to provide food and shelter for an old man who is a relative than for an old woman. He is more in the way, he expects not only a larger portion of the food, but to share in the better portions. He does not fit into the household of a working family as an old woman does and is not as useful in domestic matters. His welcome is cold-

er . . . a decent old woman will cling to a home where she may be regarded as a drudge . . . and she will exist on the plainer portions of the meals and will wedge in both day and night without encroaching much on the means of the family. (Report of the Royal Commission, 1909:259)

Stephen Marcus (1979), in a fascinating essay, skillfully blends an analysis of historical documents and literature to describe movingly the impact of the Victorian Poor Law in the lives of the average nineteenth-century family. His retelling of Wordsworth's story of the "Old Cumberland Beggar's" desire to stay out of the work house and of Betty Higden's (a character from Dickens' *Our Mutual Friend*) extraordinary efforts to die "free" are moving. One of Higden's final speeches is particularly insightful as to how the elderly felt about the poor law:

"Dislike the mention [of the poorhouse]?" answered the old woman. "Kill me sooner than take me there. Throw this pretty child under carthorse's feet and a loaded wagon sooner than take him there. Come and find us all a-dying, and set a light to us all where we lie, and let us blaze away with the house into a heap of cinders, sooner than move a corpse of us there. . . . "Your old granny is nigher fourscore year than three score and ten. She never begged nor had a penny of the Union money in her life. She paid scot and she paid lot when she had the money to pay; she worked when she could, and she starved when she must. You pray that your granny may have strength enough left her at last . . . to get up from her bed and run and hide herself, and sworn to death in a hole, sooner than fall into the hands of those Cruel Jacks we read of, that dodge and drive, and worry, and weary, and scorn and shame the decent poor." (Marcus 1979:58–59).

During this transition from an agricultural to an industrial society there were bound to be casualties. The traditional extended family may have become nonfunctional, but the isolated nuclear family—although suited to the needs of the economic system—was probably as ineffective in meeting the new pressures. Anderson seems to support this notion of a period of uncertainty for families and suggests that families only became viable care-givers in the twentieth century:

It was probably only after the introduction of the old age pension had transferred much of the economic burden of old age from kin . . . that a really strong, effective and non-calculative commitment to the kinship net could develop and "traditional" community solidarity become possible. (1971:178)

He, like others, concluded that early developments of the welfare state in this century had a positive effect on the quality of life of the elderly. By removing the economic strain and establishing an income maintenance floor, families were finally capable of providing other forms of support.

Characteristics of the Elderly

Life expectancy at the beginning of the nineteenth century is estimated to have been approximately 35 years. At the beginning of this century, it had been raised to 47 years and currently it has reached 70 years. Life expectancy, especially for females, has climbed remarkably. Of the Americans who reached age 65 during 1982, males could expect on average to live until age 77 and females until age 84 (Novak 1989).

At the turn of the century, the elderly numbered slightly more than three million people, about 4 percent of the total population. One in four of the elderly were over 75 years of age (779,000) and less than 4 of every 100 (or 120,000) were over 85 years of age. Over the next 40 years, the elderly population increased by 75% but the distribution remained the same. Seven of every ten were in the age group 65–74. Since 1960, there have been significant shifts in these ratios. By 1980, 37% were over 75 and by the turn of the next century, this age group will represent 44% of the elderly (see Table 7.1).

While the total population will have increased by 270% during this century, the elderly population will have increased by 820%, the population over 74 by 1,529% and the population over 84 by a staggering 2,690% (see Table 7.2). In real terms, this means that by the year 2000 there will be 14 million people over 74 (an absolute increase of 2.4 million) and 2.6 million people over 84 years of age (an absolute increase of 600,000).

Another facet of these demographic shifts worth noting is the sex composition of the elderly population (Table 7.3). From 1910 until 1930, 50% of the aged were female. Even among the elderly over 74, there were approximately 92 males for each 100 females. By 1960, the ratio of males to

Table 7.1. Age Distribution of the Elderly Population

Year	Total Population 000's	Percent of total population over 65 (%)	Percentage of elderly (over 65) Over 75 (%)	Over 85 (%)
1900	76,094	4.1	25.1	3.9
1920	106,466	4.6	29.4	4.3
1940	132,594	6.8	29.5	4.1
1960	180,671	9.2	33.6	5.6
1980	222,943	11.0	37.3	8.4
1990	246,106	11.8	39.9	8.6
2000	264,866	11.9	44.0	10.6
2010	281,288	11.9	42.0	11.6

Source: Adapted from U.S. Bureau of the Census, *Demographic Aspects of Aging and the Older Populations in the United States: Current population reports,* Special Studies Series P-23, no. 59, Tables 2-1 and 2-4 (May 1976).

Table 7.2. Increase of the Elderly Population (%)

	1900–1950	1950–2000	1900–2000
Total population	100	85	270
Over 65	247	165	820
Over 75	334	275	1529
Over 85	385	473	2690

females had dropped to 83 (75 for those over 74), and by the turn of the century the ratio will have decreased to 65 and 52, respectively. Not only will there be more elderly women, but they are also likely to be older than elderly men. The more significant differences are found in the over-84 age group. By the year 2000, not only will there be over three million people this old, but over two million or seven of every ten will be female.

Over the past few decades there has been a consistent shift in the marital status of the elderly. The proportion of elderly men who are married has increased significantly. Even within the 1960–1980 period, the elderly, both male and female, were more likely to be married than they were previously. However, marital status differs sharply between the sexes even when controlling for age (see Table 7.4). Almost twice as many men as women in the age group 65–74 were married, and three times as many in the older group

Table 7.3. Age and Sex Distribution of the Elderly Population (%)

	1910	1975	1985	1995
Total elderly population				
Males	50.3	41.0	40.1	39.6
Females	49.7	59.0	59.9	60.4
Males				
65–74	71.8	65.9	66.0	64.1
75–84	—	27.6	27.8	29.2
Over 84	28.2	6.5	6.2	6.7
Females				
65–74	69.7	59.6	58.4	55.6
75–84	—	31.1	31.6	33.1
Over 84	30.3	9.3	10.0	11.3

Sources: Adapted from U.S. Department of Commerce, *Social Indicator,* p. 22 (December 1977); and Bureau of the Census, *Current Population Reports,* P-25, no. 60, "Projections of the Population of the United States: 1975–2050," Table 8, pp. 67, 77, 87 (October 1975).

Table 7.4. Marital Status of the Elderly Population (%) ᵃ

	1960		1980		2000	
	65–74	Over 74	65–74	Over 74	65–74	Over 74
Females						
Married	46	22	49	23	4,748	2,075
Single	8	9	6	6	562	514
Widowed/divorced	46	70	45	72	4,380	6,279
Males						
Married	79	59	84	70	6,199	3,256
Single	7	8	4	5	318	256
Widowed/divorced	14	33	12	24	872	1,140

ᵃ The figures for the year 2000 are estimated numbers (thousands) for each category and are based on 1980 patterns. While these estimates are tenuous, they are included to show what the situation might be at that time.

Source: Adapted from U.S. Bureau of the Census, Current Population Reports, P-23, no. 59, p. 46; and U.S. Department of Commerce, Social Indicators, p. 22 (December 1977).

were married. In 1980, 7 of every 10 men over 74 were married (an increase of 18% since 1960 compared to only 1 in 4 women of the same age). If these ratios remain constant, by the year 2000 there will be almost seven million women over the age of 74 without a spouse (single, widowed, and divorced). When the unmarried men are added, the total number exceeds eight million people.

This brief analysis has highlighted a number of changes that have taken place over the past decade, trends that are likely to continue for the foreseeable future. In 1900, those over 64 years of age represented about 4% of the total population. By 1990, the elderly constituted 12%, an increase in absolute numbers of 26 million. This shift has been accompanied, moreover, by a significant growth of the very old, those 85 years of age and older.

Approximately six of every ten elderly persons are women. Women not only make up more of the elderly population but they are likely to be older then elderly males. While more of the elderly are married than previously, 3 of every 4 women over 74 years of age were single, widowed, or divorced. Finally, it is generally agreed that the elderly are more likely to be disabled and have higher rates of handicapping conditions than the general population.

Functional Status of the Elderly

While the elderly are more likely to be disabled and have higher rates of handicapping conditions than the general population, it is difficult to locate comparable time series data to measure historical patterns. In 1990, a total of almost 1.9 million elderly were appreciably handicapped, 1 million severely handicapped, and 542,000 very severely handicapped. Two of every three impaired elderly were female and over half were 75 years of age or older. By the year 2000, the severely and very severely handicapped elderly will have increased by 65% or an additional 700,000 persons, of whom 550,000 will be women. These are people who, by definition, will be either bedridden or confined to a chair (see Table 7.5).

Living Status of the Elderly

Over the past 30 years, between 5 and 6% of the elderly population have been residents in institutions at the time of the decennial census. Most of these people are in nursing homes, homes for the aged, and mental hospitals. Institutionalization is clearly related to age. Since 1950, the rates for the younger elderly have actually decreased, while the major increases have been in the older groups, especially among those over 84 years of age (see Table 7.6). In 1980, about half were over 80 years of age and one in four over 84. Less than 2% of the population between 65 and 74 were institutionalized, compared to 18% of those 85 and older. Furthermore, 71% of the elderly in nursing homes and 60% of the elderly in mental hospitals are women.

These numbers and rates must, however, be put in perspective. All too often policy analysts emphasize the negative aspects of conditions, providing a somewhat distorted picture of reality. This approach assumes that since the acceptable paradigm of social welfare in this country is residual, and since most people, including elected officials, support the belief that government should not become involved in the lives of individuals and families until there is evidence of pathology, policy analysis and policy proposals should be limited by these parameters. A major proponent of this view is Steiner, who discusses this emphasis in his studies of public welfare (1971), child welfare (1976), and family policy (1981). Given this view, many analysts and advocates, wittingly or unwittingly, argue as convincingly as they can that the problems and needs of the target population are overpowering and that action to ameliorate the situation should be taken. The distortion arises when these same analysts and advocates deemphasize the positive aspects. To some degree such has been the case with regard to the elderly.

And yet, the quality of life for most elderly has improved considerably, not only since the poor law began to be dismantled with the passage of the Social Security Act of 1935, but even more so over the past 30 years. During this period, most of the elderly, between 94 and 95%, lived in noninstitutional settings. Almost all elderly persons lived in households, the majority

Table 7.5. Impairment and Handicap by Age (Rates per 1,000)

	Impaired	Very severely handicapped	Severely handicapped	Appreciably handicapped	Projected by year 2000 (thousands) [a]
All ages	67.99	3.47	7.68	13.37	
65–74	220.25	8.28	23.99	50.67	553
Over 74	372.60	33.91	52.92	74.90	1,204

[a] Numbers projected for the year 2000 are for the elderly who are in the very severely and severely handicapped categories.
Source: Age- and sex-specific rates are based on Harris (1971); also reported in Moroney (1986).

Table 7.6. Institutional Population by Age (%)

Age	1950	1960	1980	Change 1950–1980
65–69	1.78	1.77	1.67	−6
70–74	2.55	2.64	2.68	+5
75–84	4.73	6.89	7.96	+49
Over 84	9.41	12.63	18.0	+191

Source: Adapted from U.S. Bureau of the Census, *Census of Populations,* 1953, 1963, 1984.

in primary households. In 1980, 27% lived alone, with women two and one-half times more likely to live alone than men. Of the more than 6.5 million elderly living alone in 1980, 80% were women. Those living alone were also more likely to be older—almost one in two were over 74 years of age (see Table 7.7).

A large number of the elderly are living as dependents with their children or other relatives—approximately 17% in 1980, or four million persons. Of this group, 62% were over 75, and 80% were women. Most of these persons are severely handicapped and incapable of living independently.

While most of the elderly live alone or with their spouses, most do so by choice. Their preference has been and continues to be to live near their families but not with them. The elderly do want contact with their children and other relatives and there is ample evidence to document the persistence of interaction between the generations.

By and large, the increase in the percentage of the elderly living alone can be interpreted as a positive trend. Unlike the picture of the nineteenth century offered earlier in the chapter, 75% of the elderly today are not impaired and 90% are not handicapped. In 1960, 80% of Americans 65 and over, and 58% of those over 75, maintained independent living. By 1984

Table 7.7. Living Status of the Elderly (%)

	1950	1960	1980
In households	94	95	94
In primary families	76	73	67
Head or wife of	69	56	54
With relative	7	17	13
Living alone	18	22	27
In institutions	6	5	6

Sources: Adapted from U.S. Bureau of the Census, *Census of Populations,* 1953, 1963, 1984.

these rates were 91 and 86% respectively. In 1985, 75% of the elderly lived in their own homes, and of these, 84% owned their homes outright (Novak 1989). Furthermore, Harris found in his 1971 survey that most of the elderly surveyed were positive about the quality of their lives. A 1982 Gallop poll found that 71% of those 65 and older reported that they were highly satisfied with their standard of living (Preston 1984). Older persons today are more independent than in the past, possibly because of better health status, more adequate housing, higher incomes, and expanding community support services.

Economic Status of the Elderly

The percentage of elderly living below the poverty line has decreased significantly since 1960. Furthermore, if you include the market value of noncash goods and services (in 1982 this amounted to $98 billion, much of in medical payments) the percentage drops from 12% to 4% (Preston 1984).

From 1960 to 1985, real income increased by 69% for those elderly not living with relatives and 59% for those who were living with family. For the general population, corresponding increases were 41 and 25%, respectively.

While income has increased, we have also experienced a sharp reduction in the percentage of elderly who are employed. Before the passage of the Social Security Act in 1935, over half of the men over the age of 64 were working—they had no choice but to work. In 1935, approximately 1% of all retired persons had pensions and only 15% of current workers were employed in jobs offering pensions (see Table 7.8).

The passage of the Social Security Act both made it possible for many of the elderly to retire at the age of 65 and made it less attractive to continue working for those who wanted to. In Chapter 3 we discussed the importance of the 1974 amendments to the Social Security Act when Congress made benefits inflation proof by providing automatic increased in benefits when the Consumer Price Index rose by a certain percentage. This allowed more people to stay retired once they began receiving benefits. There was an equally important, and still somewhat controversial, component of the act: The "work test" or the "retirement test" was implemented to ensure that beneficiaries were actually eligible, i.e., that they were really retired.

In the early 1960s, for example, retirees under the age of 72 would receive the full benefits they were entitled to if their earnings were less that $1,200 a year. If earnings were more than this amount, the benefit would be reduced by $1 for each $2 earned up to $1,700. For all earnings above $1,700, $1 of benefits would be withheld for each $1 earned (Schottland 1963).

Table 7.8. Labor Force Participation
Rates (%) of the Elderly,
65 and Over

Year	Males	Females
1890	73.9	8.3
1900	68.3	9.1
1910	58.1	8.6
1920	60.1	8.0
1930	58.3	8.0
1940	41.5	5.9
1950	41.6	7.6
1960	30.5	10.0
1970	25.8	9.1
1980	19.1	8.1
1990	16.3	7.4

Sources: U.S. Department of Commerce, *Historical Abstracts of the United States, Colonial Times to 1970;* U.S. Bureau of the Census, *Statistical Abstracts of the United States* (1987).

By 1984, retirees under the age of 70 were allowed to earn $6,000 before losing benefits. Furthermore, changes to the Social Security Act that year required some retirees to pay taxes on their benefits. Earnings up to $32,000 for a couple and $25,000 for an individual were exempt from taxes. After this, one-half of the social security benefit is taxable.

Because of this, since 1950 we have experienced a decrease in employment among male retirees since 1950. Currently, 16% are working. Women of retirement age, on the other hand, had relatively low participation rates throughout this century.

Lower labor force participation rates for the elderly do not seem to place the average retiree at risk financially. Radner (1989) reports that, if income were used as the single indicator of economic status, the elderly would appear to be at risk relative to other age groups. The economic status of the aged relative to other age groups is better than most other age groups, however, when income *and wealth* are combined into a single indicator.

In another study, Radner (1990) analyzed two other measures, (1) net worth, and (2) financial assets, once again to compare relative economic status of the aged. As can be seen in Table 7.9, the average elderly person, even the average older elderly, has a net worth greater than all the average persons in the other age groups with the exception of those who are between 55 and 64 years of age. When we examine their position relative to others in

Table 7.9.   Net Worth and Financial Assets (%)
of Age Groups in 1984[a]

Age group	Net worth	Financial assets
Under 25	2,160	350
25–34	8,100	800
35–44	35,500	2,160
45–54	56,500	4,150
55–64	72,460	10,000
65–75	62,060	11,900
Over 75	54,620	10,100
Total	32,600	2,600

[a] Net worth includes such nonliquid assets as housing
equity and automobiles. Financial assets include such
liquid assets as savings, stocks, bonds, and other investments.
Source: Adapted from Radner (1990: 3).

terms of liquid financial assets, the average elderly person's position is superior to all other age groups.

While this reflects medical, environmental, and social advances and to
some degree might be viewed as an indicator of overall improvement in
standards of living in a developed nation, it has brought with it the need to
develop a new social infrastructure to maintain the quality of life of these
persons. Reductions in mortality and increased longevity are inevitably accompanied by higher rates of morbidity, chronic illness, and disability. Thus
social-welfare mechanisms over time have come to include policies on
income maintenance, housing, residential care, specialized medical care,
and various social support services.

Policies and Programs: An Issue of Emphasis

Earlier in this chapter, we suggested that we have reached a point in the
evolution of our welfare state where the status of the elderly has improved
significantly compared to other age groups. Twenty-nine percent of all
federal expenditures and about one-half of all domestic spending targets the
elderly—a population group making up 12% of the total population. Furthermore, during the three-year period 1981–83, a period of high inflation
and budgetary shortfalls, expenditures not only grew but also exceeded
increases in the CPI by considerable margins. While the average annual rate
of inflation was 4.8% during this period, outlays increased by almost 13%
from 1981 to 1982 and by over 7% from 1982 to 1983.

Wilensky (1975) has suggested that this phenomenon is not unique to this country but has occurred in most mature industrial nations and is a major factor in understanding the overall growth of the welfare state (in expenditures) and the proportion of that growth going to the elderly. This section will identify and discuss the types of policies and programs that have been implemented.

Federal outlays for the elderly over the recent past have been distributed over nine major program areas (see Table 7.10). Ninety percent of these outlays can be classified as *social-insurance* expenditures and 10% as *social-assistance* expenditures. (As will be discussed later in this chapter, some aspects of the Older Americans Act would fall under the social-insurance model.) As discussed in greater detail in Chapter 2, social insurance—the *institutional approach*—incorporates such concepts as universal provision, entitlement, and needs-based benefits, which recipients receive as a matter of right and citizenship. Two of these programs are income maintenance programs (OASDI and other retirement/disability programs such as the Railroad Retirement Program and the Military Retirement Program) and one is a health insurance program (Medicare).

Social assistance—the *residual approach*—is built on a different set of assumptions, i.e., selective provision to the really needy as determined by their ability to pass a means test. Benefits are not provided as entitlements, although once individuals or families successfully complete the eligibility process, they are entitled to receive "available" benefits.

Table 7.10.   Percentage of Federal Outlays Benefiting
the Elderly

	1981	1982	1983
OASDI	56.0	56.2	57.8
Medicare	20.6	21.4	22.4
Other retirement/ disability	13.2	12.6	10.6
Medicaid	3.4	3.3	3.0
Housing	2.1	2.1	2.1
SSI	1.5	1.4	1.5
OAA	0.6	0.5	0.4
Food stamps	0.4	0.5	0.3
Title 20	0.3	0.3	0.3
Other [a]	1.9	1.7	1.6
Total	100.0	100.0	100.0
Total ($ millions)	$173,345	$195,150	$209,585

[a] Other includes such categories as ACTION, National Institutes on
  Aging, and Other Federal Health Care.
Source: Adapted from Estes and Newcomer (1983: 30).

It needs to be emphasized that 70% of all expenditures went to income maintenance programs, an additional 25% to medical-care services, and approximately 5% to housing, social services, community support services, food stamps, planning, and research. This distribution can best be understood by returning to our earlier discussion in Chapter 1 of appropriate roles of government.

Our capitalist system is built on the assumption that competitive markets will produce socially optimal results, i.e., when there is a demand for a specific service or good, someone will produce it. Furthermore, a competitive market will be characterized as one in which there will be a reasonable balance between consumers and producers (demand and supply), and products of different value and quality will be available for consumers with differing ability to pay.

The passage of the Social Security Act of 1935 was a clear reaffirmation of this belief. By providing cash grants to beneficiaries, the federal government underscored the importance of its laissez-faire role in the marketplace. Individual recipients could spend the money however they wished, and it was assumed that they would be able to meet their basic needs. *Implicit in this formulation was the belief that the major problem being experienced by the elderly was financial.*

The giving of pensions was also consistent with another of our strongly held beliefs. In the early years of the depression, it cost, on the average, $28 per month to maintain an individual in one of the thousands of county homes or poorhouses (this amount covered only operating costs). At the same time, the average state pension was only $14 per month. Pensions were cheaper and thus cost effective. It was fortunate for the needy aged that a more humane treatment was also more economical (Rimlinger 1971).

While income maintenance programs represent the major expenditures for the elderly (we have dealt extensively with those programs in Chapter 3), we will restrict our analysis in this chapter to other policy areas affecting the elderly.

Medical Care: Early Developments

The development of boarding homes in the first part of the twentieth century had a major impact on health care for the elderly. With increasing industrialization, urbanization, and their correlates (e.g., increased mobility and a growing cash economy), the living arrangements of many older persons were significantly altered. Boarding homes were part of the response to these changes. They were generally not large and had a noninstitutional character. When residents moved into these homes they were likely to be in reasonably good health. However, as they grew older their health declined, and mounting problems of physical functioning required attention. Rather than lose their income and evict long-term residents, many boarding homes began to provide nursing services, eventually evolving into convalescent or nursing homes. Thus many early nursing homes came into existence as facilities that were originally designed for residential purposes. These facilities were privately owned and not supported by public funds.

The passage of the Social Security Act made these boarding homes available to more aged. For the first time in this country's history, an economic floor was established and aged persons could expect financial assistance on a continuing basis. Many no longer were forced to suffer deprivation in their own homes or go to county infirmaries or homes for the aged. Given the means to make a choice, the elderly turned to nursing homes and boarding homes. In fact, by law the grants were not available to retired persons residing in county homes or almshouses.

Beginning in 1950, the federal government modified its policy of providing only cash payments to recipients and made available funds to those states willing to provide medical services to recipients of Old Age Assistance (OAA). States, in turn, would match these federal funds, establishing and administering a vendor system to reimburse providers. This policy was developed because experience indicated that regular cash payments did not cover medical expenses for all the elderly.

Prior to 1960, the maximum average monthly payment for OAA in which the federal government would participate was $65. This amount included both care payments and vendor payments for medical care. If they wished, states could pay more, but such additional payments were not matched by federal funds. Most, however, did not.

The passage in 1960 of Medical Assistance for the Aged (MAA), known more popularly as the Kerr-Mills Bill, substantially increased federal sharing in medical-care vendor payments. Under this legislation (P.L. 86-778) the federal government would share in all state expenditures without any limit (i.e., the $65 maximum mentioned above) under a federal matching percentage that ranged from a low of 50% in the wealthier states to a high of 80% in the poorer states. If a state chose to participate in the program, it was required to expand its medical-care coverage to aged who were poor and unable to purchase needed medical care even if they were ineligible for OAA. Finally, to encourage states to emphasize preventive services and to support elderly persons who wanted to remain in their own homes, the legislation required a state to provide both institutional and noninstitutional services. Despite fierce opposition from the American Medical Association, which charged that legislation such as this would open the door to socialized medicine, the Eisenhower administration was successful in effecting its passage.

Two far-reaching principles were established in this legislation. The first was that medical-care policies were to be seen as extensions of income maintenance (retirement) policies, "protecting elderly persons against the cost of episodic illness on the rationale that such costs are unbudgetable and cannot be reasonably be met by a regular monthly pension" (Ball 1971:21). Second, the role of government would continue to be nonintrusive. The medical-care market would not be interfered with other than by government paying for the care provided to the elderly by the private sector. This principle would be strengthened by the decision that the program would pay "usual and customary fees" as determined, not by government, but by the provider.

The passage of the Kerr-Mills Bill was the first major initiative on the part of the federal government in paying for medical-care services. In 1950, the total federal outlay for medical care under the OAA program was $36 million. Ten years later, these expenditures amounted to $280 million, an absolute increase of $244 million and an average annual increase of $24 million. One year after the passage of the MAA program, expenditures increased by 145% over the previous year, or $408 million (see Table 7.11).

By 1965, federal outlays had reached $800 million, an absolute increase of $523 million since 1960 and an average annual increase of $100 million. While the program was clearly developed within the *residual model* of social welfare, i.e., the program was means tested, selective in coverage (only the elderly who were poor were eligible), and initially viewed as serving only a relatively small number, it quickly became a major source of funding for a large number of recipients. The role of the federal government had increased considerably over a relatively short period of time; and however reluctant the federal government had been in the past to become involved in this particular market, there was no turning back.

Medicare and Medicaid

Arguably, the most significant piece of social legislation to be passed since the original Social Security Act of 1935 was the Medicare and Medicaid bill 1965 P.L. 89-77. Operationally, medical care was recognized as a right and government assumed a direct responsibility in assuring that right. As with other programs, the role of government was to be nonintrusive: government would finance medical care but would not interfere with the way that medical-care services were organized and delivered, i.e., it would support the existing free-market system. The two programs, one a health insurance program and the other a welfare program, though differing in administration and purpose, had one goal in common: to meet the medical needs of high-risk groups. Again, government chose to work within the present delivery system. Both were primarily vendor programs and reinforced the assumption

Table 7.11. Federal Payments for Medical
Care ($ millions)

Year	OAA	MAA	Total
1950	36	—	36
1960	280	—	280
1961	316	372	688
1965	421	382	803

Source: U.S. Department of Health, Education
and Welfare, *Trends*. Washington, D.C.:
U.S. Government Printing Office (1965).

that the removal of a financial barrier would improve the health status of people.

The legislation, at least in part, received widespread support because of the sudden jump in the cost of medical care (see Table 7.12). Throughout the 1940s and the 1950s, prices for medical services and hospital care were actually lower than the prices for other goods and services. From 1960 to 1965, however, increases in medical and hospital prices began to outstrip increases in the CPI. This proved disastrous to the elderly, most of whom were living on fixed incomes that did not rise as prices rose (OASDI and OAA became inflationary proof only in 1974). Moreover, only 47% of the aged had health insurance, and even these numbers had been declining (U.S. Department of Health, Education and Welfare 1968).

In addition, one in two elderly nursing home patients was receiving some form of public assistance, usually OAA and MAA, and 88 percent of all nursing home patients were elderly.

Table 7.12. Medical Care Prices,
1946–1965 [a]

Year	CPI	Medical prices	Hospital prices
1946	68.0	60.7	37.0
1950	75.2	73.4	57.8
1960	103.1	108.1	112.7
1965	109.9	122.3	153.3

[a] 1957–59 = 100.
Source: U.S. Department of Health, Education and
Welfare, "Medical Care Prices Fact Sheet,
1966–69," *Research Statistics Notes*, no. 2
(February 23, 1970).

The 1965 amendments reflected the major principles introduced in the original act. Just as there were two major initiatives in the income mainte- nance programs, i.e., a social-insurance program that provided benefits as entitlements (OASDI and UI) and a social-assistance program that provided benefits to those who could demonstrate eligibility by passing a means test (OAA, AB, APTD, and AFDC), so also there were two emphases in this health care legislation. The following discussion is not offered as a compre- hensive analysis of the legislation (such would require an additional chapter) but rather to demonstrate the importance of the legislation for the elderly.

As mentioned above, the federal government spent $800 million on medi- cal-care services in 1965. As significant as this amount was relative to previous expenditures, it paled in comparison to future years. In the two years after the passage of Medicare, the federal government had spent $3.4 billion on hospital and nursing home care alone. Twenty-five years after the passage of the legislation, these Medicare and Medicaid expenditures had reached the staggering total of $135 billion per year. Of this, the federal share was $110 billion; the remainder was the Medicaid share paid by states. Furthermore, the elderly have been and continue to be the major beneficiaries of these programs (see Table 7.13).

Title 18 (Medicare) falls into the social-insurance category in that it pro- vides a range of services to OASDI recipients (later, certain groups of handi- capped persons regardless of age were added) as an entitlement. Like OASDI, eligibility is not a function of passing a means test, but is strictly a matter of having participated in the Social Security System while working. The program has two major components.

Part A (also referred to as Hospital Insurance) is mandatory for all OASDI recipients and pays for hospital care and, to a less extent, skilled nursing care and home health services. The program is financed almost entirely through the Social Security tax and entitlement is earned while the indi- vidual is still working and not yet retired. The specific amount for health insurance has risen over the years; by 1990, of the 7.65% FICA tax, 1.75%

Table 7.13. Government Expenditures on
Medical Care, 1988

Program	Expenditures ($ billions)	Recipients (millions)
Medicare		
Part A	52.4	32.4
Part B	34.0	31.6
Medicaid	48.7	22.9

Source: *Social Security Bulletin,* Annual Statistical
Supplement, Table 7.F, pp. 304–305 (1989).

was set aside for Medicare payments. Over 90% of all expenditures are paid for from the trust fund and the rest from general revenues.

Part B (referred to as SMI, Supplemental Medical Insurance) pays for physician services, hospital outpatient services, home health care, and a variety of laboratory and other diagnostic services. All individuals receiving Part A are eligible for Part B, but unlike the former, participation is not mandatory. Furthermore, while the recipient of Part A has contributed to the program while working, Part B is financed in part from monthly premiums paid by the retiree (the premiums pay for approximately 25% of costs), with the remainder coming from general revenues.

Over the years, the federal government, concerned with rising prices, has introduced a number of cost containment measures. The two most notable of these are (1) the deductible, and (2) the coinsurance payment. In terms of deductibles—also known as first dollars—as of 1990, Medicare patients paid the first $592 of inpatient care (Part A) and the first $75 for services received under Part B per spell of illness.

Above these deductibles, the patient is also required to share the costs for covered services. The coinsurance for Part A in 1990 was $148 for each inpatient day from the sixty-first through the ninetieth day and $296 for each day of the 60-day lifetime reserve used in that spell of illness. A patient in a skilled nursing home pays $74 a day from the twentieth through the one-hundredth day per spell of illness. For services received under Part B, a patient is responsible for 20% of costs after the deductible has been paid.

Medicaid (Title 19), also established is 1965, is a residual program and falls in the social-assistance category. The program was an extension of the earlier programs discussed above that were established to pay for the medical-care needs of low income elderly. The new program paid for medical care for all needy persons who could meet the program's criteria. As with the other social-assistance programs operating at the time (OAA, AB, APTD, and AFDC), Medicaid utilized matching grants and strict means tests to determine eligibility.

States were allowed to set these criteria and choose the services to be covered under the program. The federal government established parameters and basic criteria, but gave the states considerable control. For whatever services the state chooses to provide, the federal government provides matching funds ranging from 50 to 83% of total costs. Specific matching formulas were those developed in the Kerr-Mills legislation of 1960. Allowable services include hospital care, nursing homes, physician services, outpatient services, diagnostic services, and prescription drugs.

While Medicaid is a social-assistance program for all age groups and not just people over 62 years of age, the program has become a major source of support for the elderly (see Table 7.14). Each year, over three million elderly receive services under the Medicaid program. While the number of eligible

Table 7.14.   Medicaid Recipients (Thousands)

Year	Total number of recipients	Number of recipients over 62
1972	17,606	3,318
1975	22,007	3,615
1980	21,605	3,440
1985	21,814	3,061
1988	22,907	3,159

Source: Social Security Bullétin, Annual Statistical Supplement,
Table 7.E, pp. 302–303 (1989).

individuals over the age of 62 has decreased over the past 15 years (a rate of decrease that mirrors the steady decline in this group's poverty rates), approximately 15% of Medicaid recipients are elderly. Moreover, this minority group accounts for 37% of all Medicaid costs and 75% of total nursing home costs (Lammers 1983).

Long-Term Care

While the overall rate of institutionalization among the elderly is between 5 and 6%, as many as 25% of the elderly will spend some time in a long-term care facility—usually a nursing home. Furthermore, 18% of those 85 years of age and older were institutionalized compared to 2% of the population between 65 and 74.

Given demographic shifts toward a more elderly population (e.g., the frail elderly) it is conservatively estimated that institutionalization for men will increase by 53% and for women 67% by the year 2000. To compound this problem, nursing home costs are rising about 10% per year. Average length of stay is 465 days and costs run $20,000 to $30,000 per year (Moon and Smeeding 1989).

During the decade of the 1980s, the cost to the nation for nursing home care increased from $27.2 billion in 1982 to $32 billion in 1986. Moreover, health economists predict that these costs will reach $129 billion by the year 2000.

Medicaid is the major source of public funding for long-term care and an increasing proportion of Medicaid funds are spent on long-term care. In 1981, Medicaid cost a total of $31.3 billion in federal and state funds and provided benefits for 22.5 million recipients. This single program paid over 40% of all nursing home costs, while Medicare and private insurance paid less than 3%. The rest were out-of-pocket expenditures (Health Care Financing Administration 1987).

Catastrophic Illness

The latter part of the 1980s witnessed an unexpected turn in policies for the elderly. Both Congress and the administration agreed that one piece remained to be put in place if the country were to establish a comprehensive set of health care policies.

On July 1, 1988 President Reagan signed the 1988 Medicare Catastrophic Coverage Act into law. This new addition to the Social Security Act was designed to protect elderly and disabled OASDI beneficiaries who incur catastrophic medical expenses due to illness or injury. The legislation reflected three basic objectives. It would:

*   cap beneficiary out-of-pocket expenses;
*   be self-financing; and
*   be affordable.

The basic purpose of the legislation was to assure every elderly person against financial ruin because of illness or a disabling condition. The benefits therefore did not provide assistance for early costs associated with an illness but emphasized services *after* the original Medicare benefits were exhausted (see Table 7.15). The number of days of coverage for skilled

Table 7.15. Comparisons between Medicare and Catastrophic Illness

	Medicare	Catastrophic Illness
Part A		
Deductible	$592	$504
Copayment	$140 for each day as an inpatient from day 61 to day 90; in addition, $296 for each day of lifetime reserve used	No copayment after deductible paid
	$74 for each day from day 21 to day 100 in a skilled nursing facility	Copayment of 20% of first eight days
	Ceiling of 100 days per spell of illness	Ceiling of 150 days per spell of illness
Part B		
Deductible	$75	$75
Copayment	20% of costs after deductible	20% of costs after deductible to a maximum of $1,370
Prescription drugs	None	$600 deductible and 50% copayment

nursing homes were increased and ceiling were lifted from hospice care and inpatient acute hospital care. Copayments were either removed (Part A for inpatient hospital care) or ceilings were established (Part B). Moreover, services not covered under the existing Medicare program were added, e.g., prescription drugs.

The new program was to have been funded through an across-the-board increase in the amount of premiums paid by each recipient. All would pay an additional $4 per month. A smaller group would pay still additional premiums based on their incomes and the amount of federal taxes they paid. Individual recipients would pay $22.50 for each $150 paid in taxes up to a maximum of $800 in a single year.

One year after passage, the catastrophic illness legislation was repealed. The reasons for this and its impact on a large number of elderly will be discussed in a later section.

The Older Americans Act

The year 1965 was a watershed year not only because of the enactment of Medicare and Medicaid, but also for the passage of the Older Americans Act. While this legislation never came close to matching the financial commitment Congress and the administration made in the medical-care field, it did have a broad impact on state and local services for the elderly. The purpose of the act was

> to provide assistance in the development of new or improved programs to help older persons through grants to the states for community planning and services . . . and to establish within the Department of Health, Education and Welfare an operating agency to be designated as the Administration on Aging. (U.S. Department of Health, Education and Welfare 1974:1)

Initial efforts under the legislation had two primary emphases: (1) the development of state planning capabilities, and (2) the provision of nutritional services to undernourished and malnourished frail elderly. States were required to establish State Units on Aging (SUAs), which were to be responsible for developing a comprehensive statewide plan to meet the needs of the elderly; to establish a participatory and open process that would determine priorities within that plan; to coordinate the existing service delivery system; and to stimulate the development of new services and the expansion of existing services. (The 1973 amendments added another planning layer with the establishment of local planning and coordinating agencies know as Area Aging Agencies, AAAs.) The 1965 act, appropriating $7.5 million, funded these activities from existing social-service grants and research funds.

For the remainder of the 1960s, the program's budget stayed relatively small. Planning systems were established and specialized service delivery systems evolved. Early priorities were on establishing programs that would address problems of fragmentation in the human service delivery system. Given this, communities were encouraged to develop (1) information and referral services, (2) outreach, and (3) transportation services.

The 1972 amendments established a national nutritional program for the elderly and provided funds for the development of centrally located and physically accessible centers responsible for providing hot, nutritional meals at least five days each week. These programs had multiple purposes. The obvious one was to improve the nutritional status of the elderly. Other objectives were concerned with the problem of social isolation many elderly were experiencing and the need to identify and deal with the array of social, physical, and emotional problems in their early stages rather than waiting until they became serious. The center was viewed as an ideal vehicle to achieve these objectives. A considerable amount of the social services were funded first through Title 20 (passed in 1974), and later through the Social Services Block Grant (passed in 1981).

By 1974, approximately 26% of all funds were used for planning and the provision of social services, 36% for nutritional services, and 29% for community service employment programs. Under the legislation, the following services were required:

- home health/homemaker
- information and referral
- nutrition
- outreach
- transportation
- home repairs/renovation

and the following services encouraged:

- education
- employment
- energy
- financial assistance
- housing
- mental health
- rehabilitation
- senior centers

Two of these are particularly important when analyzing services to the elderly: (1) housing, and (2) transportation. While we devoted an entire chapter to housing policies, it is important to point out that low-income elderly persons are major beneficiaries of these means-tested programs. It is

Table 7.16. Expenditures under the Older
Americans' Act

Fiscal year	Expenditures ($ millions)
1965	7.5
1974	104.0
1975	150.0
1976	200.0
1977	250.0
1984	758.0
1990	1339.0

reassuring to see that 60% of the elderly own their own homes and that an additional 10% live in private homes. Still, approximately 4% of the elderly receive housing benefits. Forty percent of all public housing units (over 500,000) are lived in by retirees, 357,774 elderly are receiving rent subsidies under the Section 8 program (this represents 50% of the total), and over 45,000 units for the elderly were built under the Mortgage and Construction Assistance Program (Section 202). The Urban Mass Transit Act (UMTA) provides funds for various transportation services for the elderly and handicapped. These programs, found in most communities, include services such as specially designed vans and buses that pick individuals up at their home and drive them to community agencies and other providers of human services.

While the initial appropriations under the Older Americans Act were small, they were to grow steadily (see Table 7.16). By the end of the 1980s, programs funded under the Older Americans Act had grown significantly, and over $1.3 billion was appropriated to four major program areas.

Approximately $722 million was spent on the provision of social services to the elderly under the Social Services Block Grant in 1990. In that same year, $117 million was appropriated to the Older American Volunteer's Program—a program in which 27,300 elderly persons functioned as foster grandparents to 73,400 children, and 12,700 elderly individuals provided companionship, respite care, and assistance in household management to homebound and frail elderly persons. $143 million was appropriated to nutritional programs; $357 million was spent on programs that provided part-time employment to over 400,000 retired persons; finally, $35 million was expended on specialized transportation services.

Haves and Have-Nots among the Elderly

Despite these advances for the average elderly person, not all the elderly are enjoying their retirement years. The problems in dealing with averages is that while statistics are useful in providing a single measure of the financial status of the elderly, they can lull us into a sense of complacency. By focusing on the average elderly person, we lose sight of the fact that all retirees are not average. Of those currently living in retirement, only 34% of men and 14% of women are receiving income from private pensions (see Table 7.17).

In terms of pensions, most women find themselves at a disadvantage when they join the retirement population. Many have never worked and are dependent upon their husband for retirement income. If their husband has participated in a pension plan they are more fortunate than those whose husbands did not, but for many women the benefits cease upon their husband's death, or run out after so many years. They outlive the benefits.

Others have worked, but given the historical practice of labor market segregation (see Chapter 8 for a more detailed discussion of this issue) found themselves in secondary labor market jobs that provided few benefits, let alone pensions. The only group of women who had higher rates of coverage than their male counterparts were never-married women (43%). These were the women who were likely to have been career employees and professionals.

Still, while men may have been better off than women, two of every three male retirees did not have pensions, a percentage that changed only slightly, depending on marital status. A large percentage of retirees, male and female, was dependent on a more limited number of resources.

Table 7.18 identifies the sources of income retirees draw from. In her analysis, Grad provides data on three groups: (1) all retirees, (2) the elderly in the top twentieth percentile (of income), and (3) those in the lowest quintile. The average retiree depends upon Social Security (OASDI) for 40% of his or her total income; on property income and earnings for another 40%, and on other sources of income, including private pensions and annuities, for another 20%. Upper-income retirees are less dependent upon Social Security (24%) than the average retiree, while poorer retirees are dependent on the government for most of their income (over 90% if we

Table 7.17. Percentage of Retirees with Private Pensions

Marital Status	Women	Men
Married	11	29
Widowed	14	38
Divorced	19	35
Never married	43	29
Total	14	34

Source: Woods (1988: 5).

Table 7.18.   Source of All Income for Retirees by Highest
              and Lowest Quintiles

	Retired worker (%)	Spouse (%)
All retirees		
OASDI	40	40
Property income	21	23
Earnings	20	18
SSI	1	1
Other	19	18
Highest quintile		
OASDI	24	22
Property income	29	33
Earnings	27	26
SSI	0	0
Other	21	19
Lowest quintile		
OASDI	85	78
Property income	<0.5	5
Earnings	3	4
SSI	8	11
Other	4	2

Source: Grad (1989).

combine both OASDI and SSI). Again, if we reexamine the data in Chapter 3, we see that while Social Security is the most generous of the income maintenance programs, the average benefit will raise the retiree just above the poverty level.

In the previous section, we discussed the major programs available to the elderly and concluded that, compared to other target groups, the elderly were more fortunate. However, favored treatment compared to other groups does not mean that all of the elderly benefit from these policies. In 1985, 21% of the elderly did not have private supplementary health insurance nor were they eligible for Medicaid. Of those with incomes under $5,000, 29% had neither supplementary insurance nor medicaid eligibility. Furthermore, only about 50% of the elderly who were eligible for SSI actually received it—an important finding since eligibility for Medicaid is tied to the elderly person's eligibility for SSI. Tragically, only about one-third of the elderly poor get Medicaid benefits (Meyer 1989).

Another tragedy is the Catastrophic Illness Insurance Program, which was enacted in 1988 with the wholehearted endorsement of the American Association of Retired Persons (AARP) and repealed only one year later. In great part the bill was repealed because of the intense lobbying activities of a vocal minority group of the aged who were angry that they, the elderly, would have to pay for the benefits (as in Part B) rather than receive them as an extension of Part A, which are financed by current workers. Their position was unequivocal: they argued that they were entitled to the benefits because they were retirees but that they should not have to pay for them.

We use the term *vocal minority* in the sense that a small group convinced the larger group of OASDI recipients that they would have to pay higher "taxes" for these questionable benefits. The reality was that 58% of the elderly would not have had to pay the surcharge—their total cost would have been the additional $4 monthly premium—and an additional 12% would have paid less than $100 beyond the $4 monthly charge. This meant that 7 out of 10 OASDI recipients would have had significant increases in benefits at minimal costs. Only about 6% of Medicare recipients would have had to pay the maximum surcharge. It was this group—the more affluent elderly, those with high incomes *and* retirement plans that already included most of the benefits to be covered under catastrophic illness—that initiated the pressure to repeal the program. Less than two million retirees who already had coverage did not feel it fair that they should be required to support the remaining 31 million Medicare recipients.

Crystal (1982) has argued that the gap among the elderly is, in fact, widening. While the data in Table 7.9 document the relative financial worth of the average elderly person and the data in Table 7.10 identify the considerable effort on the part of the federal government to support this population, the distribution of income among the elderly is highly slanted in favor of the upper-income elderly, who receive a disproportionate share of total income, including government benefits:

> [O]ne world is inhabited by those who are poor, sick and incapacitated; the other by those who are economically and physically well off. Much of aging policy subsidizes the latter at the expense of the former. (Crystal 1982:30)

Unresolved Issues

Our analysis of policies for the elderly brings us to an interesting juncture. We see that the federal government has made a significant and lasting commitment to ensuring a reasonable quality of life for individuals over the age of 62. A relatively small percentage of the population receives a disproportionate amount of available resources, a share that is likely to grow still higher.

This commitment is not only greater than that given to any other age group, but it differs in two other dimensions. First, most of the benefits are provided from a social-insurance perspective. Major programs such as OASDI and Medicare, and smaller but extremely important programs such as various transportation, nutritional, and socialization services, are available to all elderly persons (universal provision), are not means tested, and are entitlement programs. These programs are the clearest statement we have that a "total" population group is potentially at risk and therefore should be supported.

Second, most of the benefits and services are not only available to all elderly, but the package itself is the closest we have to a comprehensive service delivery system. The foundation was laid in 1935 with the passage of the Social Security Act, which guaranteed a source of income for virtually all retired persons. Later blocks, such as Medicare and the services provided or stimulated by the Older Americans Act of 1965, completed the structure. Elderly persons are provided income maintenance, medical care, services in the community, and institutional care when necessary. No other age group has such an infrastructure available to it; no other group has the equivalent of the "Elderly Bill of Rights" expressed in Title I of the Older Americans Act of 1965.

This same commitment, however, may have created a series of problems we will need to face over the next two to three decades. Currently, 12% of the population are allocated 29% of the federal budget and 48% of all domestic expenditures. Is this reasonable? Is it too much? Should it be more? As the aging population increases [by the year 2020, it is projected that the population over 65 will reach 15.5% (Bureau of the Census 1977)] should this ratio be maintained? By the turn of the century, almost 45% of the elderly population will be over 75 years of age and 11% will be 85 years of age or older.

It is this last group, the older elderly, the frail elderly, that causes us to pause. Not only is it the fastest growing age group, it is the age group that is more likely to be handicapped, more likely to need institutional care, and therefore more likely to need still more resources. Will we accept the reality that the ratio of expenditures will need to be increased?

How will priorities be established? What criteria will be used to determine the distribution of resources among age groups? Who will be involved in setting those criteria? What are the opportunity costs involved? Should the ability to keep people alive longer than ever before in our history be balanced with the issue of the quality of that life?

In 1988, the federal government expended over $330 billion on the elderly in five programs: Old Age Insurance of OASDI ($214 billion), Old Age Assistance of SSI ($14 billion), Medicare ($86 billion), elderly recipients under Medicaid (approximately $15 billion), and $1.3 billion for the service programs discussed earlier in this chapter. And we are still experiencing serious shortfalls in this area: 29% of elderly persons with incomes under $5,000 (the official 1988 poverty level for an individual was $5,980) have no insurance and are not eligible for Medicaid; 50% of all elderly persons eligible for SSI were actually receiving benefits. In the housing field, while 4% of all elderly are receiving benefits, as many as 20% need housing services. Given the federal deficit of $210 billion, how much more can we afford to spend?

The juncture we have reached is critical. To protect a cracking infrastructure (the effects of the Reagan administration's cutbacks in the service area will be felt for many years) and to ensure that the elderly in the greatest need will have their income, health, housing, and service needs met, we are likely to see a greater consensus among the nonelderly to transfer more and more of the benefits and services to the residual model—to introduce the means test as the major criterion for eligibility. Such a solution is appealing to many in that its purpose is to target those in the greatest need. Such a solution, however, would have considerable long-term effects on the shape of our social-welfare system and the human qualities of our society. These issues will be addressed in the final chapter.

CHAPTER 8

THE POOR AND THE PERMANENT UNDERCLASS

The past 10 years have seen the publication of a number of books and articles that have helped fuel a growing and often bitter debate about the welfare state. These publications, some with more fanfare than others, have been used by proponents and opponents of welfare expenditures to "prove" their point—that governmental intervention has or has not been effective in promoting individual self-sufficiency and social well-being. This debate revolves around the general issue of poverty and the more specific question of whether efforts over the past 50 years have assisted people to become independent or whether they have created a permanent underclass.

At one end of the continuum are the analyses of Murray (1984) and Gilder (1981). Charles Murray has argued that as social-welfare expenditures grew, the incidence and prevalence of poverty and related phenomena such as out-of-wedlock births have increased dramatically. Based on the analysis of secondary data, he concludes categorically that if AFDC were eliminated, poverty, especially as it relates to female-headed households, would disappear. In more general terms, he argues that poverty increases when benefit levels rise, and conversely, that poverty decreases when benefit levels contract.

Gilder's conclusion is similar to Murray's. Based on a number of "case studies" he argues that anyone who wants to work can, and if they are willing to make sacrifices like the earlier immigrants did, they can succeed in our capitalist economy. Welfare, on the other hand, erodes the work ethic without which people will always be dependent.

Walter Williams, a noted black economist/columnist has been arguing for years that minorities are in a worse position today than they were before the social programs of the 1960s were initiated, unleashing billions of dollars for ill-advised efforts to increase self-sufficiency. His position is simple and closely mirrors the New Right's position on the family (see Chapter 6). If high levels of expenditures had not been so readily available, minorities would have sought and found jobs, participated in the nation's economic growth, and developed their skills as entrepreneurs. Instead, they are even more dependent on the public sector and even further removed from the American mainstream than they were 25 years ago.

At the other end of the continuum are the works of Kahn (1984) and Schwartz (1983), who offer an entirely different view of that same system. In *America's Hidden Success,* Schwartz documents major improvements in the lives of many Americans as the direct result of existing social-welfare measures. Specifically, he points to the diminishing levels of hunger and malnourishment among the nation's children, declining levels of poverty among the elderly, and an overall reduction in the general population's morbidity and mortality rates.

Between these two positions are the studies of researchers who have been systematically grappling with these issues for a long time. Based on their analysis of a panel study of 5000 families, Duncan and his colleagues (1984) have concluded that poverty is a dynamic and not a static condition. Poverty was a temporary state for most people and only 2.6% of the total population were continuously poor between 1971 and 1978. However, equally reputable scholars such as Garfinkle (1985) and Bane and Ellwood (1983), using the same data, argue that such conclusions are misleading in that 60% of those who were poor in 1971 were still poor in 1978.

For decades policymakers have been debating the merits of the AFDC program. Critics of the program argue that the system creates intergenerational dependency, while proponents point out that the average length of stay in the program is approximately two years. Friedman and Hausman (1975), however, demonstrate that while the statistical norm might be two years, a significant number of families find themselves leaving and reentering the AFDC program.

We find these same issues emerging in the popular press and on television. In 1986 Bill Moyers presented a documentary on black families living in New Jersey, a documentary that seems to affirm the Murray and Gilder position. Based on a number of interviews with young adults, the viewer is forced to conclude that liberal public-welfare provisions were highly correlated with the young person's unwillingness to seek employment and were the "causes" of increased teenaged out-of-wedlock pregnancies. At the same time, the author of an article published in the *Atlantic Monthly,* using anecdotal material, argues that families can rise above poverty if they want to (Lemann 1986). Similar to Gilder, he offers examples of families who have succeeded and examples of those who have failed. The key, he argues, is that successful families believe in the work ethic and failures do not. At the heart of his argument is a reaffirmation of the culture of poverty theory.

One has to conclude that all of these seemingly contradictory positions and findings are, in fact, reflections of reality. It all depends on the data used by the individual author. On the one hand, AFDC rolls have increased over the past 25 years, but on the other hand, there has been significant fluidity and mobility within the recipient population. The average stay on AFDC may be two years, but many families find themselves moving in and out of the system. The likelihood today is that most elderly are not living in poverty as they were in the 1960s, but poverty rates for other groups have increased since 1980 after a significant reduction in the 1970s.

The problem with these arguments and debates, however, is that some of the authors are attempting to explain a complex issue with simple linear causality models. In doing so, they divert attention from more fundamental issues—one of which is the possible existence of a permanent underclass in this society. This chapter will explore a number of issues key to this phenomenon including:

- the relationship between poverty, social welfare, and dependency;
- whether a permanent underclass actually exists as defined by persistent poverty; and
- the success of general antipoverty strategies.

Social Welfare and Dependency

All welfare states, whether they have evolved during the various poor law eras or the twentieth century, have been criticized on the ground that they create dependency, i.e., that social-welfare provisions have not assisted people in becoming independent but rather have fostered dependency and eroded our traditional sense of the work ethic.

Over the past 30 years, this criticism has focused on our AFDC program. Beginning with the Kennedy administration and ending with the Carter presidency, the concern was for welfare reform with its objective of strengthening families and assisting them in reaching and then maintaining their self-sufficiency. None of these efforts, however, proposed a radical transformation of the existing welfare state. Policy and programmatic responses emphasized either the provision of social services (e.g., the 1962 Social Security amendments provided counseling services to AFDC mothers), employment opportunities (e.g., the 1967 amendments joining workfare requirements with a variety of social services), and income maintenance programs (e.g., the aborted Family Assistance proposal of 1970) or some combination of all (e.g., the Better Jobs and Income Initiative of 1977). What is common to all

of these administrations, Democrats and Republicans alike, was an acceptance of the need for social welfare programs in general and a belief that
once the right equation (social services, employment training, and income
maintenance) was found and implemented, the problem of long-term dependency would be resolved.

The Reagan administration, however, proposed a radical change in our
approach to social welfare and dependency: it seriously questioned for the
first time since the 1930s the need for a welfare state. The rhetoric of that
administration (the term rhetoric is used purposely in that during this administration many of the earlier proposed reforms were actually passed, i.e., the
1988 Social Security amendments affecting the AFDC program), supported
by the New Right and neoconservatives, held that government efforts in
general and those of the federal government in particular, to improve the
quality of life of individuals and families were both undesirable and harmful
in that they will always make people dependent.

The welfare state itself is the problem—it can never be a solution—and
efforts to modify its structure were misguided. President Reagan's solution to
the welfare problem was to have government (preferably state or local)
continue to meet the needs of the elderly and handicapped but to turn
responsibility for all others back to the family, to local communities, to the
private sector. Reagan's positions are ideologically in tune with those of
President Hoover, who declared unconstitutional all federal assistance to
state income maintenance. In 1931, at the height of the Depression, Hoover
announced:

> Between October 19 and November 25, America will feel the thrill of a great
> spiritual experience. In those few weeks, millions of dollars will be raised in
> cities and towns throughout the land (by Community Chests), and the fear of
> cold and hunger will be banished from the hearts of thousands. (cited in Piven
> and Cloward 1971:52)

Economic Policy and Social Welfare: The Theory

What is important to note is that both positions (pro– and anti–welfare
state) ignore or reject the possibility that long term dependency is a function
of the economic system. In fact, both agree that the major concern for this
government is to support and strengthen the existing economic system. As
discussed in Chapter 1, this position is grounded in the belief that our
competitive market system is, and will continue to be, an efficient and just
allocator of resources. Economic growth will create new jobs and, in time,
double the standard of living for everyone. Poverty will disappear.

Those who argue for welfare reform believe that, given market imperfections and the tendency of the market system to experience natural and

unavoidable contractions, government has some responsibility to intervene, when necessary, to protect the well-being of those whose quality of life is threatened. Social policies are important in that they humanize the potentially harmful consequences of economic policies. Short-term unemployment is a fact of life in this society, but its effects can be mitigated by such mechanisms as temporary unemployment insurance and (re)training programs for adults as well as social insurance for those who are unable to work, i.e., the aged and the disabled. This is the position held by the Progressives at the turn of this century and of theorists such as Marshall, Briggs, Titmuss, and Keynes, whose ideas were introduced in earlier chapters.

Those who argue for massive government retrenchment, on the other hand, while agreeing that continuous economic growth is the key to eradicating poverty, believe that government intervention, especially through social-welfare measures, inhibits economic growth, destroys the incentive to work, creates greater dependency, and eventually will drastically reduce the quality of life for all people. This is the position held by the leading theorists of the nineteenth century, such as Bentham, Pareto, Malthus, and Spencer.

Most conservatives and some liberals in this country assume that trickle-down has been successful in the past and will continue to be successful in the future. In a previous chapter we discussed trickle-down in the housing market. In that market, it is assumed that as some people are able to afford more costly housing, the houses that they sell become available to those in a lower income bracket and so on down the chain, until even the poor have housing available to them.

When we introduce the term in the context of poverty, we use it in a different way. In general, we assume that as the economy grows, people are able to purchase more goods, and thus more jobs are created to produce those goods. This argument has taken a number of forms over the years.

Keynes (1973), for example, offered this basic strategy as a way out of the world depression of the 1930s. As we pointed out in Chapter 3, he argued that excessive savings and low levels of investment would decrease the demand for goods and services, which in turn would increase unemployment. Instead, he proposed that government should increase its spending levels, even if this were to result in deficit spending, and should lower its taxes on consumers so that their purchasing power would be increased. The net effect would be the creation of new jobs.

The Townsend Movement, in the 1930s, offered a similar though somewhat unique formulation of the trickle-down theory. Francis Townsend, a charismatic California physician, proposed that all elderly persons be given an outright monthly grant with the simple provision that they spend it during that month. The assumption in this case was that those people who were too old to be actively involved in the work force could have an effect on the unemployment rate by creating a demand for products, which would generate new jobs for those who wanted to work.

The most recent version of the trickle-down theory is quite different in form but still draws on the same assumptions. Rejecting the Keynesian notion of deficit spending and the idea of giving one group an out and out grant of money, the decade of the 1980s introduced the idea of supply-side economics. Supply-side economics proposes that if taxes are lowered, most people will be in a position to purchase more goods and services. Furthermore, most will also have an incentive to save money, thus generating a pool of additional monies that will be invested in industry, which in turn will, in producing those goods and services, be required to hire more people. Given this, the unemployment rate will decrease and dependency on social-welfare programs will become even more of a residual approach as initially intended.

The reality is that while the theory is attractive there is little evidence that many of the poor have benefited. To put it another way, some groups may have benefited, but many other groups have not. To address this, let us examine the experience of the past 30 years.

Poverty first became a national policy issue in the 1960s. This does not mean that the prevalence of poverty was not of concern to the federal government before that decade. There was a concern for the poor in earlier periods, usually during the ever recurring depressions during the latter half of the eighteenth century and first third of this century. What was different during the 1960s was not only the interest on the part of government and those human service agencies dealing with poverty, but also the growing interest on the part of social and behavioral scientists, who found poverty— its nature, causes, and solutions—to be an acceptable area of academic inquiry.

Economic Policy and the Discovery of Poverty

Poverty existed before the 1960s, but it was never discussed, analyzed, or "treated" to the same extent. Moreover, poverty had become a media event. Just as the Viet Nam war entered family life through nightly news programs in the latter part of the decade, depicting the extent and ravages of poverty was commonplace in the first part of the 1960s. We were exposed to the conditions of coal miners, and elderly, sharecroppers, and children living in slums. Phenomena that were hidden in the past could not be swept away in the emerging telecommunication era, and documentaries such as "Harvest of Shame" narrated by Edward R. Murrow were singled out for honors. Poverty had become an industry.

One of the first tasks in the early 1960s was to measure poverty. How many people in the country were poor? Whereas President Roosevelt might have been comfortable in using Edith Wood's finding that one-third of the nation was poor (see Chapter 4) policymakers in the early days of the Kennedy administration demanded more accurate data on the incidence and prevalence of poverty and more information on the characteristics of the poor.

Initial efforts by the Council of Economic Advisors (1964) using the figure $3,000 for a family and $1,500 for an individual living alone as the poverty line, estimated that between 33 and 35 million people were poor in 1962, of whom 11 million were children. This represented 20% of the total population. The council also provided information on the incidence of poverty and argued that some groups were at greater risk than others. For example,

- 44% of minorities were poor;
- 17% of whites were poor;
- 45% of farm families were poor;
- 84% of farm families headed by a minority person were poor;
- 18% of non–farm families were poor;
- 74% of families headed by a domestic worker were poor; and
- 37% of families headed by a person with less than an eighth-grade education were poor.

In 1963, the definition of poverty moved from a somewhat crude single figure (i.e., $3,000 for a family) to a more flexible poverty line—one that made allowances for different needs of families with varying numbers of children and adults. Building on a study carried out by the Department of Agriculture in 1955 that identified the amount of food required by adults and children to maintain their health and the costs of that food, DHEW developed an "economy budget" that became the basis for determining whether a specific family's income was above or below the amount needed to meet basic needs. While the agency eventually provided estimates for 124 different kinds of families, the common denominator was the rationale that low-income families spent one-third of their posttax income on food (Orshansky 1965a, 1966c).

In 1964, for example, DHEW estimated that each family member needed to spend $0.70 per day per family member for food. By 1988, because of inflation this amount had grown to $3.07 per person per day.

Using this method of counting the poor, DHEW estimated that approximately 35 million people were poor in 1963, of whom 15 million were children. Further, with these refined measures, more accurate estimates were possible. While the earlier risk estimates of the Council of Economic Advisors were supported by the new analysis, the new analysis added the aged (25% were poor) and families headed by a female (48% were living under the poverty line). Based on the most recent update of the census, Orshansky also reported that of children:

- over 20% of all children were poor;
- 38% of poor children were minorities;
- 60% of minority children were poor;
- 43% of the poor were children;
- 40% lived in households in which the head of household worked full time; and
- 67% of all children living in a female-headed household were poor.

Of the aged:

- 25% of the aged were poor; and
- the aged made up 25 percent of the poor.

Of adults:

- 20% of poor adults worked full time;
- 40% of poor adults worked part time; and
- 15% of the poor were disabled.

The emerging profile of the poor in the early 1960s suggested that they were likely to be old, disabled, or children (83 percent of all poor persons). Furthermore, individuals were more likely to be poor if they were minorities, living in the South, or members of a farm family or a female-headed household. And finally, as Moreau et. al., (1962) pointed out, the poor were likely to be uneducated or poorly educated—that they had failed to improve their status relative to previous generations and had fallen behind relative to the current generation.

The Council of Economic Advisors (1964) argued that if we were to begin dealing with the problem of poverty we would need to implement a three-pronged strategy:

1. *An economic strategy:*
   - accelerate economic growth;
   - fight discrimination;
   - improve regional economies;
   - rehabilitate urban and rural communities; and
   - improve labor markets.
2. *An employment strategy*
   - expand educational opportunities;
   - enlarge job opportunities for youth;
   - improve the nation's health; and
   - promote adult education and training.
3. *Income maintenance strategy:*
   - assist aged and disabled.

It is interesting to note that these prescriptions are a sharp departure from the theory discussed earlier in this chapter—that economic growth alone will successfully deal with the problem of poverty. As a general strategy, the council assumes, as a given, the appropriateness of direct and active state intervention in the economy. The first set of recommendations targets policies to strengthen the economic system (the creation of jobs), while the second set of recommendations is concerned with improving the qualifications of those in the work force (the fit between jobs and workers). This goes far beyond the classic human capital approach, which argues that the reason people are unemployed is that they lack the skills, motivation, or personal habits necessary to obtain and hold jobs. Finally, the council recognized that some people, specifically the old and the disabled, were not likely to be affected by these strategies and would need more direct assistance.

Anderson and Locke (1964), however, provided us with some insights into who would more likely benefit from which of these three basic strategies. From an historical perspective they argued that different strategies are needed and that these strategies depend upon the nature of poverty in a society at a particular time. When a society has a large number of people who are poor, few individuals find their way out of poverty regardless of economic growth. This happens because a few people control or have access to most of the society's wealth. As a society becomes more egalitarian and as a significant portion of the population begins to increase its skills and/or gain political power, a large number of people move out of poverty quite fast. Finally, they describe a third phase in which only a residual remain in poverty. In this phase, as the masses become more affluent, fewer and fewer of the poor are able to leave poverty.

Following this, they divided the unemployed/poor population into three groups:

Group 1: white, non—farm families headed by a male under the age of 65. This group, they suggested, responds quickly to economic growth.

Group 2: nonwhite, non—farm family headed by a male under the age of 65. This group responds to economic growth but not as quickly as group 1.

Group 3: predominantly farm families, female-headed families, people over 65. These people are isolated from economic growth and income does not trickle down.

Based on their analysis of the 1959 census, they concluded that 65 percent of the poor were in the second phase and that steady economic growth would move most of them out of poverty. In fact, they predicted that for every 2.5% increase in the GNP, we would experience a corresponding 1 percent decrease in the poverty population. Their analysis would suggest that the first set of recommendations (the economic strategy) would probably assist groups 1 and 2 and the third strategy (income maintenance) would benefit the aged but that the remainder in group 3 clearly needed services identified under the second strategy (the human capital strategy).

Economic Policy: Thirty Years of Growth

The theory discussed in the previous sections not only supports most of our theoretical assumptions of a free-market economy, i.e., capitalism, it has been the foundation of most of our antipoverty efforts. Furthermore, it is so much a part of our individual and collective belief system, that we rarely ask for empirical evidence that demonstrates its efficacy. We assume that it must work because we believe that it works.

Table 8.1 offers 28 years of data on 5 critical variables: (1) each year's GNP in constant dollars (this reflects "real growth" controlling for inflation), (2) the annual percentage change in GNP, (3) the annual percentage change in the number of new jobs, (4) the annual unemployment rate, and (5) the annual poverty rate.

With all of its limitations, the GNP is the single best statistic to measure a nation's economic growth. The major methodological and conceptual problems arise when we attempt cross-national comparisons (Myrdal 1972). Given the theory we have discussed in this chapter, we would expect to see an increase in the number of new jobs, a decrease in the unemployment rate, and a decrease in the poverty rate as the GNP increases, and a corresponding decrease in the number of new jobs and an increase in unemployment and poverty when the GNP decreases.

Over the 28 years from 1960 to 1987, the GNP increased 131% in constant dollars and the poverty rate decreased by 39% (from 22.2 to 13.5). The average annual increase in the GNP over this period was 3.3%, the annual increase in new jobs was 1.98%, and the average unemployment rate was 6.13%. Did the theory hold up?

From Figure 8.1 we see that the poverty rate decreased sharply during the 1960s, leveled off during the 1970s, and increased during the 1980s. To what extent do the predictor variables explain this pattern?

The three trends shown in Figure 8.2 offer little evidence that the theory is working. First, since we see a U-shaped poverty curve, we would expect more of an *inverted* U-shaped curve depicting changes in the GNP and the increase in new jobs and a U-shaped curve *similar* to the poverty curve for unemployment.

While the average increase in the GNP shows considerable fluctuation, with the possible exception of the 1960s, the percentage of new jobs created stayed within a relatively narrow range. It was in the 1960s that we see a steady decline in the poverty rate without a comparable increase of the same magnitude in the number of new jobs created. In the 1960s, the average

Table 8.1. Economic Growth and Poverty

Year	GNP (Constant $)	Change from pre-preceding year (%)	Increase in jobs (%)	Unemployment rate (%)	Poverty rate (%)
1960	1,665.3	1.3	1.0	5.5	22.2
1961	1,708.7	2.6	1.2	6.7	21.9
1962	1,798.4	5.3	0.2	5.5	21.0
1963	1,873.3	4.1	1.7	5.7	19.0
1964	1,973.3	5.3	1.7	5.2	18.0
1965	2,087.6	5.8	1.9	4.5	16.6
1966	2,208.3	5.5	1.7	3.8	15.4
1967	2,271.4	2.8	2.1	3.8	14.7
1968	2,365.6	4.1	1.8	3.6	12.8
1969	2,423.3	2.4	2.5	3.5	12.1
1970	2,416.2	0.3	2.5	4.9	12.6
1971	2,484.8	2.8	1.9	5.9	12.5
1972	2,608.5	5.0	3.1	5.6	11.9
1973	2,744.1	5.2	2.7	4.9	11.1
1974	2,729.3	0.5	2.8	5.6	11.6
1975	2,695.0	−1.2	2.0	8.5	12.3
1976	2,826.7	4.9	2.5	7.7	11.8
1977	2,958.6	4.7	3.0	7.1	11.6
1978	3,115.2	5.3	3.3	6.1	11.4
1979	3,192.4	2.5	2.6	5.8	11.6
1980	3,187.1	−0.2	1.9	7.1	13.0
1981	3,284.8	3.1	1.6	7.6	14.0
1982	3,166.0	−3.6	1.4	9.7	15.0
1983	3,279.1	3.6	1.2	9.6	15.2
1984	3,501.4	6.8	1.8	7.5	14.4
1985	3,618.7	3.3	1.7	7.2	14.0
1986	3,721.7	2.8	2.0	7.0	13.6
1987	3,847.0	3.4	1.7	6.2	13.5

Sources: For data on GNP, Report of the President: Annual Report of the Council of Economic Advisors (1989); for employment data, U.S. Department of Commerce, Statistical Abstracts of the United States (1989); for data on poverty, Social Security Bulletin, Annual Statistical Supplements, 1962–89.

annual increase was 1.58% (range of 0.2 to 2.5%); in the 1970s, 2.64% (range of 1.9 to 3.3%); and in the 1980s, 1.67 % (range of 1.2 to 2.0%). Changes in the unemployment rate correspond as hypothesized in the 1960s (i.e., as poverty rates decreased, so also did unemployment). However, unemployment rates showed increases in the 1970s while the poverty rates stabilized. Although poverty did not seem to be related to unemployment,

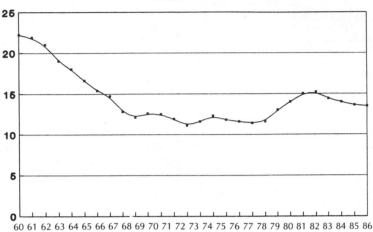

Note: These Data are from Table 8.1

Figure 8.1

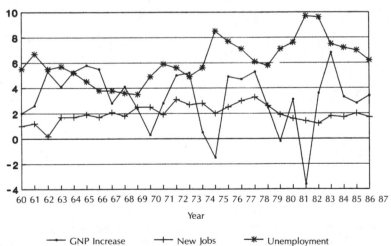

Note: These Data are from Table 8.1

Figure 8.2

Table 8.2.   Changes in Poverty Rates (%)

1960–65	−25
1965–70	−24
1970–75	−2
1975–80	+1
1980–85	+7
1985–87	−3
1960–87	−39

unemployment did increase in those years when there were sharp down swings in the GNP, e.g., 1970, 1975, 1980, and 1982.

As mentioned earlier, the poverty rate decreased by almost 9 percentage points (from 22.5% in 1960 to 13.5% in 1987). This represents an overall decrease of 39%. However, this figure is somewhat misleading in that most of the decrease occurred in the 1960s (see Table 8.2).

While there are any number of possible explanations for these unexpected trends, our purpose here is only to examine the hypothesis that economic growth is the most important factor in solving the problem of poverty in our society. One could argue, for example, that the poverty rate has dropped from 22 percent to 13 percent; another might argue that the number of poor was still 32.5 million persons in 1987—close to the estimated 34 million of 1963. What is clear, however, is that we do not see the predicted correspondence between increases in the GNP and decreases in poverty. The improvements we have experienced occurred in the decade of the 1960s, and since then we have attempted, with mixed success, to maintain that level.

Earlier we discussed the characteristics of the 35 million people who were poor in the early 1960s. What are the characteristics of the almost 33 million who were poor in the late 1980s? Based on the studies of Joe and Rogers (1985) and Ellwood (1987) we find that there have been some shifts in the distribution of poverty.

The percentage of persons and families living below the poverty line was reduced significantly, but the probability of escaping was not one of random chance, nor were the odds equal for all families. Families headed by white males (and a growing number of minority families headed by males who are graduates of high school) who have been temporarily displaced because of market disturbances continue to find employment when the economy turns up. These are Anderson and Locke's group's 1 and 2—the transitional poor.

Rural families, female-headed families (especially minority families) the elderly, and the disabled, on the other hand, did not find themselves affected by economic growth over the past 30 years. As discussed in Chapter 3, advances in the social-insurance programs have dramatically helped the

elderly (whereas 25% of the elderly were living in poverty in the early
1960s, approximately 12% had incomes below the poverty line in the late
1980s) and the disabled. The others, however, have remained in poverty.

In 1963, 20% of all children were living in poverty. In 1983, 20% of all
American children were still living in poverty. The statistical likelihood of a
specific child being in poverty was, however, related to the type of family he
or she was living in. In 1963, 66% of all children in families headed by a
female were poor—a percentage four times higher than for children living in
a male-headed household (Orshansky 1965a,b). Twenty years later, the disparity still held for white children growing up in a household headed by a
mother, and nonwhite children growing up in families headed by a female
had higher rates than those in 1963 (see Table 8.3).

Finally, while these statistics are informative, they are primarily a static
description of a population at one point in time and, as such, tell only part of
the story. Ellwood's recent panel study (1987) fills a much needed gap in our
understanding. After following a cohort of 3.5 million children born in an
average year in the early 1970s, he concluded that 8 of every 10 children
raised in a two-parent family, 2 of every 3 children raised part of the time in a
single-parent family, and less than 1 of every 10 children raised entirely by a
single parent escape poverty.

Conversely, while 2 of every 3 children raised entirely in a single-parent
family experience long-term poverty, 12% of children raised part of the time
in a single-parent family and only 2% of children raised in a two-parent
family experience long-term poverty. Furthermore, almost half of all the
children living in poverty were raised entirely by a single parent.

Ellwood then concludes that while 20% of all children may be poor at any
one time (the census data), 7.6% of all children experience 50% of the
poverty years (the panel data). Here he makes the point that we need to
distinguish between one child living in poverty for ten years (long-term
poverty) and ten children living in poverty for one year (short-term poverty)
(see Table 8.4).

Table 8.3. Poverty Rates (%) among Children, 1984

	White	Black	Hispanic
In female-headed families	48	69	71
Mother never married	71	77	86
Separated or divorced	47	67	70
In male-headed families	12	24	27

Source: Congressional Research Series and Congressional Budget Office, *Children in Poverty,* Washington, D.C.: U.S. Government
Printing Office (1985).

Table 8.4.   Poverty Rate (%) for Children in Different
             Family Types [a]

	Two-parent	Part-time two-parent	Single-parent
Never poor	80	67	7
Temporarily poor	18	21	31
Long-term poverty	2	12	62

[a] Temporarily poor is defined as 1–6 years; long-term poverty is defined as 7–10 years. Two-parent family is defined as growing up with two parents present for the entire period; part-time two-parent is defined as being raised partly in a single-parent family and partly in a two-parent family; single-parent is defined as being raised entirely in a single-parent family.
Source: Adapted from Ellwood (1987).

Poverty, the Work Ethic, and Dependency

The notion of the work ethic has been so ingrained in people that it has assumed the aura of natural law—a principle that has transcended time and is believed by most people always to have been a part of human existence. We need to be reminded, however, that the work ethic is the product of the early nineteenth century. As discussed earlier (see chapter 3) the emerging economic system needed a mobile supply of labor and the ability to convert large numbers of agricultural workers into disciplined factory workers. To accomplish this, the state developed a number of social policies such as the principle of less eligibility and created institutions such as the poorhouse or "house of industry." Finally, the work ethic assumed not just moral and theological dimensions, it became an intrinsic part of the total human being.

Christopher Lasch (1977) in his provocative work *Haven in a Heartless World,* however, has argued rather convincingly that the work ethic, to be successfully implemented, had to go beyond employment issues:

> Ever since Max Weber showed the connections between Protestantism and capitalism, and demonstrated, moreover, that the connections lay at the level not of formal religious doctrine but of "psychological sanctions," it has been clear that modern civilization requires among other things, a profound transformation of personality. The Protestant concept of the calling not only dignified worldly life, insisted on the moral value of work . . . it also upheld the spiritual dignity of marriage and domesticity. (1977:4)

As the nineteenth century evolved, the "ideal" family type to meet the needs of the prevailing economic system was systematically redefined. This new concept of the family held that the father had to be the head of the house, that the mother was responsible for the care of the house and the children, and that, in return, the children owed their parents honor and obedience. Parents had the responsibility to produce authority-oriented children—children who would meet the requirements of the labor market.

Donzelot (1979), a French social scientist and colleague of Michael Foucault, is penetrating in disclosing what he terms the latent functions served by societal institutions. Writing within the same general perspective as Lasch, he argues that human service professionals should be more appropriately labeled "social pathologists"—a cadre of professionals who have undermined the family through social control mechanisms. In *The Policing of Families,* he writes of the "colonization of the family" by the helping professions, of their "full penetration into family life," of their "ceaseless technocratic interventionism," of the "continuous surveillance they exercise over domestic life," and of "the transfer of sovereignty to the corrective system that never stops swelling."

The term policing used in the title of his book comes from Foucault's emphasis on the biopolitical dimensions of society. Policing, he suggests, is not to be understood in the limiting repressive sense we give the term today, but it has a much broader meaning that encompasses all the methods for developing the "quality of the populations and the strength of the nation." Not trusting the family to carry out these necessary functions—the shaping of values and behavior required to meet the needs of the industrial revolution—extrafamilial organizations assumed responsibility.

By the second half of the twentieth century, however, fewer workers (especially those who were unskilled) were required by the labor market. The work ethic, so important a century ago, has become less important. This is the crux of the current dilemma. Individuals are still being socialized to believe that they can achieve personal satisfaction only through their attachment to the work force and then are systematically denied the possibility of finding a job. They are also socialized to believe that a two-parent, father-headed family is superior to other forms.

One of the more significant and controversial reformulations of this thesis is found in the Moynihan Report published in 1965:

> Deterioration of the Negro family is the fundamental source of weakness of the Negro Community in the present time. The Negro family in the urban ghettoes is crumbling . . . Poverty has forced the ghetto into a matriarchal and highly unstable pattern of family life which perpetuates itself over the generations, gave rise to a complicated tangle of pathology. (cited in Rainwater and Yancey 1967:39 ff.)

Moyinhan's insistence on the pathology of the matriarchal family (intended or not) left the impression that the problem resided in the family and was not to be found in structural factors. Moyinhan's thesis can lead and has led to one of two conclusions: (1) Because poor families are not like the ideal family they are not governed by the work ethic. (2) Because they lack the work ethic they have experienced family deterioration. Both conclusions, however, are built on the assumption that either the individual or family is at fault and is exhibiting pathology. The publication of the report brought an intense attack from various groups who either (1) denied the importance of the family and defined the problem of poverty solely in structural terms (e.g., economic or discriminatory factors) or (2) defended the matrifocal household as a healthy adaptation to ghetto life.

Lasch rejects these conclusions:

> Blacks living in the ghetto also subscribe to the work ethic, to a middle class norm of marriage in which the husband works and the wife stays home with the children, but they find it impossible to sustain the ideal in the face of poverty. The male, unable to find steady work, often leaves the family. Even when he stays at home, he hesitates to make an emotional investment in relations in which he is certain to fail. (1977:160)

In fact, Lasch has turned the argument around and suggests that it is because the black male believes in the work ethic and not in its absence that he is forced to desert his family. Adult blacks are not different from whites in their acceptance of the work ethic, and because of this they also believe that their identity and worth are tied to their success in the labor market. Given this, the only alternative is to walk out.

The ability of single parents to educate their children and instill in them the habits of persistence and hard word has been undermined by the parent's own frustrations and economic deprivation. The children, raised in such an environment, learn how to survive but pay a great price in doing so. As the youth goes through this process, he or she becomes disabled for life in other surroundings, especially in school and the workplace. Piven and Cloward (1971) pointed out almost 20 years ago that poverty, family deterioration, and loss of control over the young is usually accompanied by the spread of certain types of behavior, including failure in school, crime, addiction, and increased out-of-wedlock pregnancies.

Furthermore, the numbers of these families are likely to increase significantly over the next few decades. Previously (see Chapter 6), we pointed out that the overall birth rate has been steadily dropping each decade. However, the birth rate for minority women, although dropping also, is significantly higher than the general rates (see Table 8.5).

While the trend among families is to have fewer children than previous generations, more and more families are deciding not to have children. Although we see this occurring in all families, it is most pronounced in white families, where one-half do not have any children compared to 41% of black families and 35% of Hispanic families.

Table 8.5. Family Size by Race

	1970	1975	1980	1985	1987
Families with no children (%)					
White	44.8	47.2	49.3	51.8	52.0
Black	38.9	36.8	38.2	42.6	41.0
Hispanic	29.8	29.4	31.2	33.9	35.1
Average family size					
White	3.52	3.36	3.23	3.16	3.13
Black	4.63	3.90	3.67	3.60	3.52
Hispanic	NA	NA	3.90	3.88	3.83

Source: U.S. Bureau of the Census, *Statistical Abstract of the U.S., 1989,* p. 50, Washington, D.C.: U.S. Government Printing Office.

When we couple this with the fact that increases in the birth rates are found among younger women (10 to 19; see Table 8.6), and that these increases in the number of children are likely to be found in single, never-married female-headed households, we are faced with the reality of a growing underclass.

Today, more than one million teenagers become pregnant each year, and half of these choose to deliver and keep their children. A disproportionate number of these mothers are from minority groups, and most are from poor families. Finally, two of every three teen mothers will not graduate from high school. We are faced with the prospect that the chronically poor will produce a significant percentage of the future's adults who is turn will be poor also.

Table 8.6. Birth Rates by Age [a]

Age	1960	1970	1980	1987
10–14	0.8	1.2	1.1	1.3
15–19	89.1	68.3	52.7	50.6
20–24	258.1	167.8	115.1	108.2
25–29	197.4	145.1	112.9	109.2
30–34	112.7	73.3	61.9	69.3

[a] Rates are per thousand live births.
Source: U.S. Bureau of the Census, *Statistical Abstracts of the United States, 1989,* pp. 61–62, Washington, D.C.: U.S. Government Printing Office.

What possibly distinguishes the current generation of the chronically poor (especially the youth and young adults) from their parents and grandparents is a rejection of the work ethic. The work ethic makes no sense whatsoever when there are no jobs available or if the only jobs available are in the secondary labor market, paying marginal wages, with no hope of advancement, and characterized by continuous fluctuations that result in a revolving-door experience with the welfare system. As Merton (1957) pointed out, if traditional channels are closed, some youth will find alternative pathways to success. While society may label these behaviors as deviant and irrational, for the youth they are the only meaningful avenues open, since the work ethic has little meaning. This sense of hopelessness is the major difference between the temporary and permanent underclass. This is, and will continue to be, a major stumbling block for future policy initiatives.

The Permanent Underclass

Whereas in the 1930s there was *mass* unemployment, in the postwar period we have been experiencing *class* unemployment. In 1947, 32% of all families were poor. By 1956 there had been a reasonable economic recovery and this percentage had dropped sharply to 23%. Over the next six years, the percentage of families escaping poverty had slowed down, and by 1962, 20% of all families were still poor. Presently, almost 14% are living in poverty.

These advances, however, were not equally experienced by all. Special groups have been singled out by the workings of the economy to suffer, while all others have experienced increasingly improved standards of living. As Harrington argues:

> America for the first time in its history has a hereditary underclass. Most of the children of the poor have become the fathers and mothers of the poor. (1975: 111).

The weight of evidence would suggest that the existence of a permanent underclass—the permanently poor—was inevitable given our economic system. Over 50 years ago, in forecasting the economic and social order of the post depression era, Tugwell attempted to warn the country of the dangers of emerging industrial trends:

> We now know that there are millions of workers, formerly employed by industry, who cannot be reabsorbed by our present industrial system, assuming it to remain unchanged, even if the volume of physical production is brought back to the levels of the turbulent twenties. In 1932, I am told, industry could produce as much as in 1923 with one-third less labor . . . When new machines forced the workers out of jobs, they were expected to applaud the spirit

of progress and find other jobs if they could . . . the millions out of work were expected to resign themselves to industrial bad luck. (1934:36–37)

In time, and mainly because of the war, many eventually did rejoin the labor force and Tugwell's warning was muted. These new jobs, however, required much more education and higher order skills. Those without skills found themselves restricted to the economic underworld—to low-paying industries or industries requiring lower levels of skills.

Over the past 20–30 years, technological advances and automation were instrumental in enlarging the underclass, in so far as they destroyed tens of thousands of unskilled and semi-skilled jobs that had been the major source of employment for minorities. With few skills and poor educational background, they found themselves totally unprepared for this new environment with its highly sophisticated labor market requirements.

Stoesz (1985), in reviewing the experiences of the past 25 years, documents the extent to which these events have affected the prevalence of poverty. He cites the earlier study of Piven and Cloward (1971), who pointed out that between 1950 and 1969 one million farms were lost to mechanization; the works of Robbins (1983) and Benjamin (1983), who described the hardships experienced by coal miners and their families in West Virginia when the extractive industries mechanized; and the deep and enduring poverty of the inner cities experiencing economic displacement and creating an underclass of millions of workers who were left in regions without a need for their "skills" (Garreau 1981; Dorfman 1982).

Kuttner's recent study (1984) also offers support to Tugwell's prediction. While most argue that shifting from a manufacturing economy to a service economy is a sign of progress, Kuttner disagrees:

In theory . . . just as mechanization of agriculture freed human workers to do more industrial tasks, the automation of industry should free workers to do more highly refined jobs and enjoy leisure time. Unfortunately the workings of the market do not necessarily produce that happy outcome. (1984:169).

Kuttner points out, contrary to the theory, that an industrial economy employs a large number of relatively well paid production workers in industries such as manufacturing and construction, while a service or high technology economy may employ a small number of highly paid professionals at one extreme, but a large number of poorly paid workers at the other end. Furthermore, the number of high-paying jobs in previously high-paying industries have decreased over the past 20 years. He concludes that "technological advances are not translating into gains for the blue collar worker . . . the work is becoming more routinized and lower paid" (1984:174).

A growing number of people—referred to by some as the permanent underclass—have become a "surplus population" in that they are only marginally useful to the economy. Some people are unemployed because they lack the necessary skills, education, or experience; or because they are the wrong color or live in the wrong place, or because technological changes are making their skills obsolete.

Despite the evidence that members of the underclass are victims of an economic system that has little or no use for them, the historical response has been to turn the argument around and suggest that the reason lies not in the economy but in the permanent underclass itself. While the language may be different, the analysis is the same as that offered by Bentham in the nineteenth century: they have lost the work ethic (see Chapter 3). In the view of many, the task facing the country is similar to that facing the theorists of the early decades of the previous century—to offer explanations that are grounded in the ideology of the work ethic and to develop social programs that will rekindle the drive to work.

William Wilson, a widely recognized social scientist and spokesperson for this general position, has recently become embroiled in a public debate as intense as that experienced by Moynihan in the 1960s. In his 1987 work, he offered the following definition of the permanent underclass:

> people who live in neighborhoods populated almost exclusively by the most disadvantaged segments of the black urban community, that heterogeneous grouping of families and individuals who are outside the mainstream of the American occupational system. Included in this group are individuals who lack training and skills, and either experience long term unemployment or are not members of the labor force, individuals who are engaged in street crime and other forms of aberrant behavior, and families that experience long term spells of poverty and/or welfare dependency. (1987:8)

While he seems to define the concept in terms of poverty, unemployment, welfare dependency, and single parenthood—conditions that affect large groups of people from different ethnic groups—he emphasizes the "blackness of the underclass" and offers a dangerously distorted picture.

Wilson, in his analysis, seems to reject the notion that institutional racism played any part in the 1980s in either creating or solidifying the existence of this underclass. In fact, he discards the need for or importance of affirmative action and other civil-rights policies. Billingsley (1989) charges that Wilson not only denies the existence of institutional racism but also accepts the human capital argument. For Wilson, the reason that the underclass is the underclass is that it lacks skills, knowledge, and most importantly, motivation—the work ethic.

Dependency: A Critique of Social Welfare

Social-welfare programs in capitalist societies do not cause dependency, nor are they responsible for the existence of a permanent underclass any more than social-welfare measures caused cyclical downturns in the economy, obsolete capital in certain industries, automation, structural unemployment, or the decay of the inner cities. Despite this, the welfare system continues to be blamed for the persistence of seemingly intractable problems.

Social-welfare measures have been created to solve crises and problems created by a market economy with its inevitable hot and cold cycles, but the measures can only modify the system since they are only peripherally related to the causes. The overall social-welfare strategy attempts to identify an appropriate equation made up of three components: (1) income maintenance, (2) employment training, and (3) social services. This search for the solution has proven over time to be not so much elusive, but more a problem of adequacy given society's concern·to eradicate long-term dependency and to (re)instill the work ethic.

Income maintenance programs provide a family with subsistence level support and then penalize families if they are able to supplement this with even minimal employment opportunities. Employment training programs showed short-term results for some (usually white males) but for the permanent underclass, "success" was usually a short-term job with a high probability of returning to the welfare rolls. While there was significant movement from welfare to work, there was as much movement from work to welfare.

In areas with large-scale structural unemployment, welfare recipients were being trained for jobs that either did not exist or, if they did, paid less than the poor could obtain from welfare. Quite simply, the employment programs were powerless in that they could not create jobs. In fact, they have had the unintended effect of convincing many that the work ethic is an irrelevant concept.

As Ginzberg (1976) argued, every administration since the passage of the Full Employment Act of 1946 has refused to consider supporting a program that actually creates jobs, e.g., a public jobs program. There have been, of course, limited efforts to deal with the job side of the equation, e.g., tax breaks for private employers who hire the "hard to employ" and some emergency efforts through public-service strategies. Both of these have been viewed as temporary or emergency efforts dealing with cyclical unemployment and not with the permanent unemployment of the underclass. He concludes that "the country has yet to move up to the starting line" (1976:2) in implementing the promises of the 1946 act. Instead, our employment policies have been primarily focused on the training for and placement of the unemployed into the existing labor markets.

We see, then, that our government's overall approach in this area is similar to its response to the housing problem (see Chapter 4). It can be characterized as a supply-side strategy in that it assumes that economic growth by itself will create new jobs, which will in turn be filled by the currently unemployed. To understand this belief is to understand this society's approach to solving most social problems. It reinforces the dominant view that markets, whether these are the housing, employment, medical-care, or educational markets, work most efficiently if they are not interfered with by government.

The overriding assumption has been and continues to be that employment opportunities exist—the solution being one of identifying and removing barriers some people experience in finding appropriate jobs. In part, these barriers were assumed to be discriminatory practices on the part of employers and, in part, deficits on the part of the unemployed. Early efforts included the Civil Rights Act of 1964, which prohibited racial or gender discrimination in employment and the Elementary and Secondary Education Act of 1967, which established the Work Incentive Program (WIN). Other efforts included programs such as the Cooperative Area Manpower System (CAMPS) established in 1967, the Comprehensive Employment Training Act (CETA) of 1973, and the Jobs Training Partnership Act passed in 1981.

These initiatives are grounded in what is known as "human capital theory." If a dual labor market exists, it reflects differences in the skill and educational levels of the workers. This theory rejects the notion that sex or racial discrimination operate within the employment market. People are not able to obtain and hold meaningful jobs because they lack the skill necessary to hold these jobs—not because they are women, black, Hispanic, or Native American. Their jobs are marginal because they are marginal (at least in terms of employment skills). The problem is one of job training—not state involvement, whether this involvement is in the creation of jobs or in the establishment of quotas for certain groups of workers. In fact, those who espouse the human capital approach praise our society since it has created jobs for those who are ill trained and offer little to the work force. They seem to be saying that only in a capitalist society is it possible that marginal people are given the opportunity to find marginal jobs—for which they should be grateful. Furthermore, if they work hard and if they improve their skills, they might move up to the primary labor market.

While it is difficult to evaluate these efforts in their totality, it is clear that the permanent underclass was not being helped. Critics continue to point out that "creaming" has occurred, and with reduced funding levels, the existing employment programs are likely to exacerbate this practice.

On the other hand, the more recent "solutions" of the Reagan administration are equally faulty. Our competitive market system has not proven to be an efficient and just allocator of resources and "economic growth has not doubled the standard of living for everyone." Poverty remains with us and the numbers are growing.

Toward a Reformulation

It would seem that we are faced with a number of options. If we continue to separate social and economic policies and treat dependency only as a social and not an economic problem, and if we further look to a solution in traditional social services, employment training, and income maintenance programs, we will continue to treat the problem through historic poor-law provisions. The choice is between the more humane poor-law strategies of the twentieth century or the more orthodox and punitive nineteenth century poor laws. Neither course, however, will solve the problem of dependency nor will it (re)instill the work ethic into this population.

If we are convinced that the work ethic is still important for other than just economic reasons (our economy might not need all adults in the work force if production is the objective) and we are unwilling to provide a reasonable level of guaranteed income support to female-headed families, the unemployed, and the underemployed, then the only rational strategy is to create meaningful jobs.

The strongly held belief that government should be the employer of last resort does not mean that government should only take a reactive role in the employment sector. The federal government can and should create jobs in the public sector similar to those initiated in the New Deal and those created by programs of the 1960s such as the Appalachian Regional Commission ($4.5 billion), and the Economic Development Commission ($4.8 billion), through which funds were channeled to sagging local economies. If, as we have argued, the youth of the permanent underclass have rejected the work ethic (or at least the version of the work ethic that mainstream society accepts) because of a sense of hopelessness that has turned to anger, they need to be resocialized. It follows that if the private labor market continues to ignore these youth, a public labor market has to be created to provide opportunities for paid employment, combined with relevant education and vocational training for those who are not able to find work in the private sector.

As we reexamine our policies and look for new ways to solve seemingly intractable problems, we need to sift carefully through proposals that have already been offered but never acted on. A number of these were developed in the 1960s during that period when we seemed to make a national commitment to eradicate poverty. We do not argue that we should continue or expand the initiatives of that period. We are not even arguing that they were a success or a failure. What is important now is to seek solutions that can deal with present problems. A number of analysts during the 1960s did provide critiques and directions that, if acted upon, might have eased the situation.

The insights offered by Titmuss (1966) are as relevant today as they were 25 years ago. First, he argued that the theory that economic growth would solve the poverty problem was really an assumption that had not been tested. This theory, which he labeled "the optimistic automated model," assumed that (1) continuous economic growth would double the standard of living for everyone and that poverty, as measured by 1966 standards, would disappear, and (2) the competitive market is and will continue to be an efficient and just allocator of resources.

Titmuss contended, however, that the position that economic growth needs to precede social growth—that without economic growth we cannot afford social programs—is a simplistic solution to a complex problem.

He predicted that we were underestimating the extent and rate of obsolescence of much of our social capital, especially schools and housing. He suggested further that we were also underestimating the rate and effects of scientific, technological, and economic changes and were ignoring the impact they were having on the poor and the unskilled. We were underestimating the cumulative effects of discriminatory school systems and housing and labor markets. And finally, we were overestimating the potentialities of the poor and the permanent underclass to understand and participate fully in an increasingly complex society, and the will of all people to move toward a more equal society. Titmuss concluded his argument with the charge that we were exaggerating the capacity of private markets to resolve social problems.

In an earlier article, Titmuss (1963) suggested that we take our lead from Myrdal (1960), who offered a number of proposals in his *Beyond the Welfare State*. These included:

- aggressive economic development;
- full employment;
- equality of opportunity for youth;
- social security; and
- protected minimum standards of health, nutrition, housing, and education.

What is notable is Myrdal's insistence that while economic prosperity is essential to eradicating poverty and improving the standard of living for all, a deep and abiding political commitment to these goals is even more important.

Galbraith (1958) and Schorr (1963), two of the more prolific analysts of poverty during this period, severely criticized existing and proposed policy initiatives on the basis that, with the exception of the emerging civil-rights efforts, solutions to poverty assumed a case-by-case, family-by-family approach. While the programs of the 1960s were likely to have been more humane that those of the nineteenth century, they were similar in philosophy to institutions such as the earlier Charity Organization Societies—the poor were responsible for their poverty and they, the poor, had to change. For Galbraith and Schorr, this residual approach had to give way to a more institutional formulation if we as a nation were to be serious about dealing with poverty.

Finally, Miller and Rein (1964) are representative of a large group of analysts who maintained that poverty was not a condition that lent itself to short-term investments. They were critical of existing efforts (especially the expanding demonstration programs) as forms of "ad hoc tinkering" that would not be successful. Instead they argued for sustained and comprehensive long-range efforts.

Strategies for the 1990s and Beyond

The directions offered by the above critics found their way into much of the work of the Council of Economic Advisors in the 1960s. Earlier in this chapter we outlined their proposals as falling into three major categories (see p. 194).

Of the three general strategies the council identified, most of the effort to date has focused on the second and third—the employment and income maintenance strategies—with little real effort in the area of economic development. And yet, it is only in the first that a nation deals with the creation of jobs. The second attempts to prepare individuals for existing jobs and the third attempts, in theory, to provide the individual with income when he or she is no longer able to work.

Economic Development and Employment

These three interdependent strategies are basically concerned with two issues: full employment for those who can work and protection for those who cannot. It is only through full employment, moreover, that we can directly deal with the fundamental issue of dependency. The Council of Economic Advisors in its 1964 report was reiterating the promise of the Full Employment Act of 1945 and the earlier statement by Roosevelt, who introduced the concept in his 1944 State of the Union Address, his "Economic Bill of Rights." Even this was preceded by the president's assertion at the height of the Depression that Americans wanted jobs and not the dole.

Kuttner considers that Beveridge's (1944) report on employment "remains the definitive exposition on why full employment must be the centerpiece of social citizenship. Without it, the social fabric of the welfare state falls apart" (Kuttner 1984:32). In Chapter 3, we pointed out that Beveridge considered income maintenance to be one of the pillars of a caring society. For Beveridge, full employment is the foundation upon which all other social policies are built. Beveridge, like Roosevelt, saw unemployment in more than economic terms, and, in commenting on the potentially adverse affects on those who were not employed, both were unwilling to deal with the issue only as a macroeconomics issue (i.e., the balance between employment and inflation). Unemployment was a human and personal problem to be resolved by society:

Unemployment remains a personal catastrophe . . . even if an adequate income is provided by insurance or otherwise. Idleness, even on an income, corrupts; the feeling of not being wanted demoralizes . . . As long as there is long term unemployment not due to personal deficiency, anybody who loses his job fears that he may be one of the unlucky ones who will not get another job quickly. The short term unemployed do not know that they are short term unemployed until their unemployment is over. (Beveridge 1944:19)

Beveridge, like Roosevelt, believed in the work ethic, but went beyond the rhetoric that has mesmerized so many. To hold individuals to the work ethic without making it possible for them to get jobs was contrary to what Beveridge believed a modern society to be. In allowing unemployment, our society becomes more and more divided; that is, the employed are pitted against the unemployed, the haves against the have-nots.

Full employment will not solve the total poverty problem, but without full employment it will get even worse. First, the future stability of our economic system requires full employment. Second, a national commitment is built not on a society that is divided, but in Boulding's (1967) terms, a society that is integrated and, in Titmuss's formulation, an altruistic society that fosters a sense of community. Third, while we have presented data in this chapter that shows the risk of being poor to be higher among single-parent-headed families, among minorities, and among rural families; of the two-parent families who are living below the poverty level, 33% were headed by a male who could not find work. Even among single-parent families headed by a woman, 13% of the women worked and 22% tried to find work but could not. These are the individuals and families who would benefit from the reality of a full-employment society. Income maintenance programs are not the long-term solution to their problems. Still, even full employment must be put in perspective. One-half of the 17 million new jobs created in the 1980s paid a year-round full-time equivalent of less than $11,611, which is just about equal to the current (1990), officially defined poverty level. This is not the type of full employment proposed by Beveridge, Roosevelt, or the Council of Economic Advisors.

To deal with the growing problem of regional unemployment in this country, we might learn from the experiences of a number of European countries where national governments actively become involved in macroeconomic policies and employment sectors. Kuttner (1984) provides an interesting contrast to our economic policies and the role of government in his study of a number of other countries, including, Sweden, Austria, West Germany, Norway, and Japan.

All of these countries have a fairly large public sector (with the noted exception of Japan) and more direct government involvement than we do and yet have been able to strike a balance between relatively low unemployment rates, a more equal distribution of wages and income resulting in less of a need for redistribution, and an economy with significantly less inflation.

While the form of government involvement may differ across these countries, the level of involvement in each far outstrips that of our government. In Japan, for example, government takes an active role in planning and brokering with the private sector. Sweden and Austria, on the other hand, have centralized economic bargaining policies. All attempt to keep wage increases in line with real growth in their economies and thus hold down inflation.

Kuttner argues that it is not the specifics of the policies, nor the particular institutional arrangements that have evolved, that seem to explain the success these countries have had in maintaining full employment and in keeping wage increases in line with real economic growth, but the nature of the relationship between government, the unions, and industry that makes the difference. In each of these countries there appears to have been a conscious movement away from relationships previously driven by conflict and mistrust to one that recognizes that in achieving each party's best interests, the best interests of the other parties are also being achieved.

Underpinning each, Kuttner contends, is the notion of a social bargain through which a

> well organized and powerful labor movement exchanges overt class conflict and militant bargaining over wages for a high employment society with a generous social wage, a state policy commitment to greater equality, and substantial influence for organized workers. (1984:148)

While the labor movement in this country has lost much of its influence and many of its members, the labor movement in these European countries is as powerful as ever. The unions are not only strong, but they are united. When unions enter into collective bargaining, they bargain for all unions— equal pay for all workers doing the same kind of work regardless of the specific industry, and a narrowing of wage differences between low- and high-skill workers and between men and women.

Given this, they are in a position to keep inflation down by "subordinating short term wage demands to other labor goals, e.g., full employment, egalitarian wage distributions, retraining opportunities, work place enrichment and welfare objectives" (Kuttner 1984:142). Kuttner argues, moreover, that it is only when there are strong unions and a refined social bargaining machinery that parties will have mutual respect and be willing to look beyond narrowly defined self-interests.

Kuttner concludes that these experiments, whether they are called a social bargain model, a labor corporatism model, or simply collective bargaining, are grounded in refined and expanded Keynesian principles, which assume that the role of government is to pump resources into regions where there is a need for new jobs and/or for the retraining of workers. Moreover, these governments combine training with wage subsidies and job placement services for those workers who have been temporarily displaced.

It is clear from the above that Kuttner gives priority to the value of community in his analysis. In fact, he argues that without this belief in community, there would be no social bargain. Separate unions recognize that they exist in a community of unions, and jointly with government and industry they accept the reality that together they are a community—whether it is called a society or a nation. Furthermore, they reject the idea of zero sum gain since they believe that for each to benefit, they all must benefit.

Income Maintenance

In Chapter 3, we discussed this country's major income maintenance programs in some detail. In this section, we will discuss those aspects of those programs as they relate to the issues of dependency, poverty, and single-parent families. The Council of Economic Advisors assumed that effective job creation and job preparation policies would meet the income needs of most Americans. Those unable to participate in the labor force—the elderly and the disabled—would be supported through a reasonably generous income maintenance program.

The council's position was similar to those who drafted and implemented the Social Security Act of 1935. The Social Security program offered a two-pronged system: one for labor force participants and one for those who were unable to work. For the former group, a combination of employee benefits and government social insurance provides protection against illness, disability, and unemployment and funds for retirement. For the latter group (i.e., children, the permanently disabled, and the elderly) government provided a safety net. Congress and the administration believed that the social-insurance program would, in time, meet most people's needs and that only a small group—a residual population— would need social assistance. Unfortunately, both were only half right. The social-assistance programs have not dwindled and women heading families with children have not been able to achieve and maintain their economic independence.

As early as 1966, in their report to the secretary of DHEW the Advisory Council on Public Welfare pointed out:

> Public assistance payments are so low and so uneven that the Government is, by its own standards and definitions, a major source of the poverty on which it has declared unconditional war. (1966:5)

At any one time, only 50 percent of the poor receive welfare benefits and, as discussed in Chapter 3, even those who received social-assistance benefits (e.g., SSI and AFDC) did not receive enough to raise them above the poverty level.

In 1967, Congress amended the Social Security Act to allow AFDC recipients to retain some of the money they earned in outside employment. Previously, for every dollar the recipient earned, the benefit was reduced by a like amount. Arguing that the policy was a work disincentive and one that discouraged the work ethic, recipients were now allowed to keep the first $30 they earned and one-third of the remainder. In 1981, however, this was seriously modified. The Omnibus Budget Reconciliation Act (OBRA) lowered the amount of money that could be disregarded and limited the $30 plus one-third to four months. While our rhetoric remained the same—the work ethic was to be instilled in welfare dependents—our actions suggested that it was only that, rhetoric.

Since the early 1970s there has been an increase in the number of children in single-parent families but a corresponding decline in the number of families receiving AFDC. Furthermore, after adjusting for inflation, the combined value of the AFDC grant and food stamps has decreased by at least 25 percent over that past 15 years. Furthermore, as recently as 1987, one-half of the women who became single-parent heads of households did not receive court-ordered child support payments; and of those who did, only half received the full amount. Finally, the average annual child support award was $2,215, but even this average was lower for black families ($1,754) and Hispanic families ($2,011).

Females heading families for the past 30 years found themselves in a catch 22 position. Many wanted to work (Handler 1972) but found that the jobs available to them were in the secondary labor force. Pay was minimal, the likelihood of mobility and career advancement was nonexistent, and most important of all, these jobs did not provide benefits. Stigmatized by society because they were dependent and on welfare, they found that they could not take these jobs without seriously jeopardizing their children's well-being. Being on welfare meant being eligible for Medicaid, food stamps, housing benefits, and day-care. Working in a job that paid $5 an hour meant earning a gross income of slightly more than $10,000 a year—less than the poverty level. Not only would the family still be living in poverty, but now they would not have health insurance and other basic benefits.

The welfare reform measures of 1989 rectified many of the more glaring anomalies. First, all states are required to initiate the AFDC-UP program, which offers benefits to families with two parents. Before this amendment the program was permissive, and less than one-half of the states were participating. The intent of this program has been to support families before their problems become so severe that the father leaves. Second, training is available (and required) for single parents with children over three years of age and required for one of the parents in a two-parent household regardless of the age of the children. Third, recipients are able to retain a number of their AFDC-related benefits, including Medicaid, for one year after they begin working. Finally, a nationwide mandatory child support program was implemented.

However, the earlier Child Support Enforcement Program was not very successful over the period 1980–87, the years immediately preceding these amendments (see Table 8.7). Successful collections in AFDC cases never exceeded 11% in any single year and the amount recovered was approximately 7% of the AFDC monies spent in those cases. The success rate was significantly higher in non-AFDC cases but still amounted to only 30 percent of the cases.

Furthermore, these efforts at reducing dependency will fail if the federal government does not assume a more proactive and more aggressive role in the economy and in the employment sector. To train people for jobs that do not exist or are dead-ended is not a solution to the problem of dependency.

Ellwood (1987) argues that our income maintenance programs are built on a questionable set of assumptions, the most troublesome one being the implicit belief that the poor are a homogeneous population. He comes to this conclusion by pointing out that we have only one antipoverty program. The reality is, however, that we have a large number of families experiencing short-term poverty and a small number experiencing long-term poverty. Each requires different solutions. The three-pronged proposal from the Council of Economic Advisors 25 years ago is as valid today as it was then because it does differentiate and it links dependency to more structural issues that must be dealt with if the problem is to be ameliorated.

In conclusion, we are not suggesting that social services and employment training are irrelevant. While we have argued that they cannot solve the problem in the absence of more proactive economic policies, we would also argue that the latter will not produce the desired effect without the former.

Table 8.7. Child Support Enforcement Program

	Cases with collections (%)		
	AFDC cases	Non-AFDC cases	AFDC recovered
1980	11.0	28.7	5.2
1981	10.7	28.2	5.2
1982	10.8	30.3	6.8
1983	10.2	30.0	6.6
1984	10.5	29.4	7.0
1985	11.0	30.3	7.3
1986	10.1	31.4	8.6
1987	10.7	31.7	9.2

Source: U.S. Bureau of the Census, *Statistical Abstracts of the United States, 1989*, pp. 61–62. Washington, D.C.: U.S. Government Printing Office.

Whatever it is that is supposed to trickle down with economic growth, does not reach those on the bottom. Unskilled and semiskilled workers who had been able to find and hold jobs in the industrial sector do not have the skills required in a growing service economy. Social skills may not have been important on an assembly line, but they are essential in jobs requiring social interactions. As long as we refuse to reexamine the meaning and value of the work ethic, and as long as we define an individual's worth in terms of his or her employment, we have the responsibility to provide the individual with meaningful employment and the skill required for these jobs.

CHAPTER 9

THE POLITICAL ECONOMY OF SOCIAL WELFARE: PROMISES AND PROBLEMS

Policy Analysis and Critical Theory

The previous 6 chapters have analyzed a number of policy areas, three of which dealt with substantive issues and three others with populations who are the targets of policy initiatives. It should be clear by this point that Boulding's conclusion that "social policy looks like a sticky conglomeration of the ad hoc" (1967:8) is fairly accurate. Although we have developed a framework to provide, in Boulding's formulation, some common threads to unite all social policies and some common denominators to evaluate seemingly heterogeneous policies, (1) the disparity between rhetoric found in statements of specific policies and the actual policies that are implemented, and (2) the glaring contradictions found between and within policies make the policy analysis task extremely difficult.

Still, we believe that the framework offered in the first two chapters of this book is a reasonable attempt to meet Boulding's charge. We began with the argument that to understand this country's social policies is to understand this country's political economy; that all of our social policies are shaped by the needs of our economic system. We then expanded the framework by incorporating first principles such as freedom, equality, and community and the separate but related notion of citizenship.

It is this addition that makes this analysis somewhat different. Most analysts, operating within the positivist framework, offer descriptions and explanations of policies but stop short of providing an "understanding" of the policy. This, they argue, goes beyond the purview of the "detached scientist" and enters the realm of the policymaker in that it introduces "values" and preferences. To move beyond the traditional approach is to blend the empirical with the normative.

This latter is the position of Habermas and the current school of critical theory. "The intent of critical theory is to provide us with an accurate depth understanding of our historical situation" (Bernstein 1982:217) and to help us "grasp invariant irregularities of social action as such and when they express ideologically frozen relations of dependence that, in principle, can be transformed" (Habermas 1971:310). As discussed in Chapter 2, Habermas is a major critic of rational planning and rational decision theory. He argues that as each society evolved, some groups gained power and others lost power; that those with power developed mechanisms to maintain that power; and that over time patterns of discrimination and inequality have become so ingrained that they are rarely questioned or if questioned, are quickly displaced. Given this, he concludes that rational decisionmakers will only accept courses of action that maintain the status quo, that maintain the existing imbalances. To do otherwise would be "irrational." Rejecting this, Habermas suggests that the analyst has a responsibility to expose these patterns of inequalities and dependence:

> Critical theory aspires to bring the subjects themselves to full self-consciousness of the contradictions implicit in their material existence, to penetrate the ideological mystifications and forms of false consciousness that distort the meaning of existing social conditions . . . where the theoretical understanding of the contradictions inherent in existing society, when appropriated by those who are exploited, becomes constitutive of their very activity to transform society. (Bernstein 1982:182)

Perhaps the most widely recognized theorist and practitioner of this approach in the Americas is Paulo Freire, whose commitment to the idea that empowerment must begin with understanding and insight is captured in the titles of his books, e.g., *Pedagogy of the Oppressed* (1981), *Education for Critical Consciousness* (1982), and *Learning to Question* (1989).

Such is the theoretical background for the particular framework used in this analysis of existing social policies in this country. It is offered as one attempt, and only one attempt, to develop "common threads" and a "common denominator."

Social Policy and Social Action

Policy was described in Chapter 1 as an expression of values and preferences, and therefore policy analysis is as much a normative activity as it is an empirical activity. However, while a specific policy or set of policies may express a statement of "what should be done" and while these statements may have the power of law or statute, social policy cannot coerce changes in many behaviors or attitudes. It can, nevertheless, create an environment that is supportive to a change in those behaviors or attitudes. For example, Boulding (1967) argues that a major objective of any social policy is to "build community." It is clear that Boulding is concerned with creating environments in which human beings assume responsibilities for the well-being of others, where human exchanges go beyond the dominant rationale of quid pro quo, and where the rights of the individual do not take precedence over the rights of the community. No social policy, however, can coerce people to do these things, can force them to become integrated in a community, if they do not want to.

Titmuss (1971), however, offers an example of how a policy can support or stimulate a sense of community through his cross-national analysis of blood donors. In countries where individuals are not reimbursed for donating blood, he found virtually no cases of serum hepatitis and few instances in which the supply of blood ran out, compared to countries that allowed individuals to sell their blood or give blood only when they were guaranteed they would receive blood when they needed it. He characterized the former societies as those in which people gave out of a sense of altruism and community. They gave because others needed; they trusted that if they were in need, others, often strangers, would give. He characterized the latter societies as those in which individuals transacted with others primarily to "maximize" their self-interests. His argument was not that each system shaped the behavior or attitudes of people. Rather, each system was a reflection of dominant attitudes and behaviors and, in part, these reflected the ideology of the existing political economy. He concluded, however, that if a society wanted to change these attitudes, policies could support (not cause) the change.

A second example of how government attempts to affect attitudes and behavior is the parenthood insurance policy implemented by the Danish government in the 1970s. Recognizing that most parents found it necessary to work outside the home even when they had young children, the government provided each family a number of days of paid leave—days that were to be used when one of their children was sick and unable to go to school or for other forms of child care. The initial policy was carefully drafted so that both fathers and mothers would be encouraged to share the child care functions. In effect, the Danish government was stating through public policy that child rearing, unlike childbearing, was not dependent on the gender of the parent, that fathers had a role in caring for their children. After a few years the government found that in most instances the mother and not the father stayed home when their children were sick. The existing policy was then modified further to encourage fathers to share in these tasks. However, the new policy was more a carrot than a stick. It did not force fathers to ıate, e.g., by requiring the father to use a certain percentage of the ~~leave~~ ~~such~~ a policy could prove harmful to the children and the parents). Rather, it extended the number of covered days but allowed the mother to use only the original number. In this way, the state created an environment that encouraged fathers to share in the parenting of their children.

First Principles and Citizenship

In Chapter 2, we argued that while social policy is concerned with choosing among multiple, conflicting, and yet desirable goals, there are no scientific rules that help us make these choices. As Rein (1976) has suggested, values provide the criteria by which we judge the desirability of a course of action, each of which needs to be judged within the framework of its value assumptions. However, to be viable, these values need to be relevant; they have to reflect the values of a society, or at least, the values some groups in that society hold. This grounding in existing values serves not only as its strength and legitimacy, but also as the root of its problems. Values will always be controversial since very few values are universally agreed upon within a society.

In Chapter 2 we discussed three such basic values—(1) freedom, (2) equality, and (3) community—and suggested that while all three may be desirable organizing principles for social policy formulation since they are espoused by a large number of people in this society, they cannot be simultaneously maximized. The issue becomes one of determining which value is to be given primacy. If we begin with a communitarian first principle, absolute liberty is not possible, because social responsibilities take precedence over individual rights. The same happens, of course, if we begin with freedom, with its emphasis on individualism. Finally, while a concern for equality would require some redistribution (at the expense of some individuals' freedom), an egalitarian society is not necessarily one in which a sense of community is strong. We concluded the discussion with the argument that our existing political economy tends to give greater weight to the first principle of freedom with its emphasis on competitive markets, the importance of the individual, and an economic definition of the human person that assumes people interact with others through bilateral, impersonal transactions.

And yet, our emphasis throughout the book has been on the need to balance economic objectives with social objectives, to begin moving away from a system that defines the single purpose of social policies to function as instruments of economic policies, to one that gives greater weight to the first principle of community. Is such a calculation possible or is Friedman (1962) correct when he states that we must start with extending freedom and choice, that anything else is paternalistic and in the long run counterproductive to the economic and social well-being of a society?

Perhaps a way out of this apparent impasse can be found in Marshall's concept of citizenship as introduced in Chapter 3. Taking a historical perspective, Marshall suggests that rights, whether they are narrowly or broadly defined, were allocated on the basis of an individual's or group's ability to claim citizenship. Initially, these rights were limited to what Marshall terms *civil citizenship:* "the rights necessary for individual freedom, liberty of the person, freedom of speech, thought and action, the right to own property and to conclude valid contracts and the right to justice." (1965:71). Over the next hundred or so years, these rights were expanded to include the "right to participate in the exercise of political power, as a member of a body invested with political authority or as an elector of the members of such a body" (1965:72)—*political citizenship.* Finally, only in this century were these rights expanded to include "the whole range from the right to a modicum of economic welfare and security and the right to share to the full in the social heritage and to live the life of a civilized being according to the standards prevailing in that society. The institutions most closely connected with it are the educational system and the social services" (1965:72)—*social citizenship.*

The parallels between these two formulations are intriguing:

freedom ↔ civil citizenship
equality ↔ political citizenship
community ↔ social citizenship

The language of Milton Friedman when he discusses freedom and T. H. Marshall when he discusses civil citizenship is quite similar. The major difference is that Friedman, in arguing that freedom, equality, and community are incompatible or at least cannot be viewed as equally important, views freedom as the most important first principle. Marshall, on the other hand, suggests that each is important in its own right and that some are prerequisites to others. The three categories of rights evolved sequentially over the past three hundred years. Furthermore, in his view, civil rights (freedom) had to precede political rights (equality) and social rights (community) were only possible after the first two were established. Given this argument, we are not faced with either/or categories but with a continuum—the end point being community: "Citizenship is a status bestowed on those who are full members of a community" 1965:84). In Friedman's view we begin and end with the first principle of freedom; in Marshall's formulation, freedom is the first step in the journey to community.

Given this analysis, we would suggest that in this society we have reached a point somewhere between equality and community, between political and social citizenship. We touched on this in Chapter 6 when we discussed various rationales for government intervention into the lives of families. One rationale introduced was that of rights as opposed to other rationales such as need, compassion, or justice. Beginning with Rawls's position based in contract theory and moving on to Rothman's argument that our preoccupation with rights in this country grew out of a profound mistrust of government, we are forced to conclude that we live in an adversarial society, one in which people relate to other as competitors.

To humanize this society and to protect the rights of citizens, we have established a number of policies that emphasize *equality of opportunity*— that all people should have the same opportunity to achieve their potential, whether they are handicapped children (legislation to mainstream handicapped children in the public school system), minorities (civil-rights legislation dealing with school systems, housing, employment), or disabled (the Disability Act of 1990 states that handicapped persons have the same rights and privileges as nonhandicapped persons).

I suggested that we would probably locate this society someplace on the continuum between political rights and social rights, between equality and community, because, even though the emphasis in most policies seems to be on equality of opportunity rather than equality of outcome, we do have a number of programs that are expressions of social citizenship or community, e.g., OASDI, Medicare, and public education. The next issue to be dealt with is the extent to which it is possible to evolve even further on the continuum without diminishing our civil and political rights. Is it possible to achieve some balance between economic and social objectives?

Economic and Social Markets

In Chapter 1, we pointed out that in our particular form of political economy, we assume that an economic system characterized by perfectly competitive markets provides socially optimal results, i.e., products of the highest quality will be provided at reasonable prices when consumers want them. A corollary to this general proposition is that filtering occurs with economic growth, i.e., benefits will eventually accrue to everyone, even those with the lowest income. A second corollary is that when a particular market is found to be imperfect, government is expected to engage in corrective measures. Government intervention, however, is to be as nonintrusive as possible and should cease as soon as that market becomes competitive once again. Finally, the role of government is to support market theory and principles of free enterprise.

The evidence in the previous chapters would suggest that the theory has failed in a number of areas. We have experienced economic growth over the past 30 years, governments have become involved, and the nature of the involvement has been in support of the workings of those markets. Despite these efforts, significant numbers of people are still poor, unemployed, homeless or living in less than adequate housing, and unable to obtain the medical care they need. Furthermore, if an "invisible hand" does exist, it is both sexist and racist in that women and minorities experience an even higher incidence of these problems.

The housing market has failed to produce the quantity and quality of shelter at reasonable prices needed by millions of people in this country despite the investment of billions of public dollars in that market. The billions of dollars channeled to the medical market have neither produced improved health indicators nor have they controlled rising costs. Tax subsidies and human capital policies have not been able to stimulate the development of meaningful jobs at the level needed.

The issue is not whether a market economy works—it clearly does. A more fundamental issue is whether *all* goods and services should be delivered through these economic markets. Is it perhaps more fruitful to think of two separate markets: (1) economic markets and (2) social markets?

In defining the distinguishing characteristics of social services, Titmuss, Rein, and Kahn (see Chapter 5) question the assumption that social services (broadly defined) are the same as other goods and services. For Rein, social services are "collective interventions which are outside the market place to meet the needs of individuals as well as to serve the corporate interests of the wider community" (1970:43). Kahn makes the same point when he suggests "social services . . . consisting of programs made available by other than market criteria" (1969:179). Titmuss continued the discussion by arguing that while an acceptable objective of an economic market is to maximize profit (to do otherwise would be irrational), it is inconceivable in a caring society that one group is allowed to make a profit from the misery of others, whether that misery is physical illness, inadequate housing, or emotional problems, or to charge prices that are out of the reach of people who need the services. None of these theorists are calling for the abolition of the free-enterprise system and private markets. All are arguing, however, that in some instances, and with certain goods and services, social markets are preferable to the dynamics of economic markets.

One proposed solution would involve following the experiences of a number of European countries, especially those countries that have

1.   maintained a market economy,

2.   established a number of social markets such as health care and social services, and

3.   have accepted the notion that industry needs to establish social contracts with employees and government that produce a balance between reasonable profit margins and reasonable wage increases.

These efforts, discussed in the previous chapter, have been successful in keeping inflation within bounds and employment at very high levels. Finally, in these countries, industry has assumed a major responsibility for both the provision and financing of a wide range of health and welfare benefits as part of the costs of doing business. It is not a choice between capitalism and socialism. A robust set of social policies requires a healthy market economy, a free-enterprise system tempered or modified by social concerns. Further-more, the evidence would seem to suggest that in these countries there is a strong conviction that concerns for the quality of life of all citizens are related to economic growth. As Kuttner argues, competition has been tem-pered with a sense of community, and community includes industry, unions, and the government.

This would suggest that if we are able to differentiate between economic and social markets, and if we are able to move away from the deeply held notion that competition is the only way to achieve growth and that to sup-port the dependent is contraindicated in a capitalist society since it invari-ably retards economic growth, we might begin to move from a society that favors individualism to one that encourages community and a sense of shared responsibility.

Barriers to Achieving Community Issues

A major barrier that needs to be addressed is the issue of "interest group politics" (Lowi 1969) and its effect in moving us closer to a "new class war" (Piven and Cloward 1982). We touched on the latter in the chapter on the elderly. As measured by the amount of resources allocated to them, the status of the elderly, relative to other age groups is superior. And yet:

> Despite the general improvement and the increasing reliance on public pro-grams, the distribution of income among the elderly population remains highly skewed, with the bottom group getting a small share not only of total income but of government benefits. (Crystal 1982:30)

The elderly are not a homogeneous group. There are wealthy and middle-class elderly, low-income and poor elderly. This class war became apparent in the passage and repeal of the catastrophic illness legislation. As discussed in Chapter 7, a small group of the wealthier elderly was able to mobilize large numbers of elderly to pressure Congress to repeal this legislation, with the argument that the elderly were being unfairly taxed. The reality was that these more affluent elderly (approximately two million people) would have had to pay a surcharge to finance part of the costs while the remaining 31 million elderly would have had to pay nothing or a small amount on a monthly basis. This small number already had equivalent coverage through their retirement plans and did not want to pay for duplicate coverage. In countless letters to the editor across the nation, wealthy or upper-middle-class retirees argued that it was not fair that they be required to support elderly persons who had not made provision for such coverage while they worked. They were being penalized for working hard and achieving success.

The above is a clear example of the absence of a sense of community among the elderly. As long as one group did not benefit more than the other, there was an appearance of community and common need. However, once one segment believed that another group was benefiting *at its expense,* community gave way to individual interests. It did not seem to matter that they had more than other elderly persons or that some elderly had greater need. They argued that it was only fair if all elderly were treated the same despite Titmuss's conclusion that such an approach is grossly unfair if some people have greater need. For him, a just system is one that positively discriminates, that gives more to those who need more and less to those who need less.

A second issue is the apparent unwillingness of the elderly to become less parochial (in the sense that they seem to be concerned only with issues affecting the elderly) and to become concerned with the well-being of others. Single-interest politics on the part of the elderly was not only successful in the past but was probably necessary to highlight their needs and acquire resources. There is growing evidence, however, that unless the elderly and their advocates show some interest for broader social concerns, concerns that do not directly deal with aging problems, their future will be shaped by advocates for these other groups. Furthermore, there is a high probability that these other groups will reject the claims of the elderly, who are beginning to be perceived as selfish and unconcerned about other groups.

We see this in communities throughout the nation where elderly citizens aggressively fight against raising property taxes needed to maintain or improve the quality of the local educational system. A 1983 Gallop poll of public attitudes toward the public schools found that 62% of the elderly opposed higher school taxes (Preston 1984). Their reasoning seems to be that since they no longer have children in school, they should not be expected to pay for the education of those families who do. Again, we see the absence of a sense of community—a sense that children are important to all and not just to their families—that the total community has a responsibility for their upbringing.

The class war, then, is not just among the elderly, but between the elderly and other groups. These divisions are critical if we are to resolve the issue of fairness as it relates to the distribution of available social-welfare resources. Are resource distribution issues always a win-lose situation with some groups being penalized because the elderly are benefiting? As discussed in

Chapter 7, the welfare of the elderly has improved significantly in almost every area of social policy since the early 1960s. However, over this same period, the well-being of children has deteriorated. The two poverty lines in Figure 9.1 are almost mirror images. As the poverty rate for the elderly has decreased, the rate for children has increased. In 1970, 16% of those under the age of 14 lived in poverty compared to 24% of those 65 years of age and older. By 1982, the situation had been reversed: 23% of children lived in poverty compared to 15% of the elderly. If the cash value of services is factored in (much of it Medicare and Medicaid payments), the percentage of elderly persons living in poverty drops to 4% while the percentage of children drops only to 17% (Preston 1984).

Preston also attempted to determine the amount of public expenditures each group received. He notes that Bane's finding that average government expenditures for the elderly in 1960 were three times the expenditures for each child stayed the same through 1979. He also estimates that the allocations for the elderly were six times higher that those for children in 1984, and given the larger number of children compared to elderly, per capita expenditures for the elderly were ten times higher than those for children.

What, if any, is a reasonable rationale for these differences? Do the elderly need more benefits? The data in Chapters 6 and 8 suggest otherwise. The next section will explore a major issue that needs to be dealt with if we are to move beyond these divisive dynamics.

Universal Services and Community

In Chapter 2, we discussed the positions of Richard Titmuss and Milton Friedman, articulate advocates for universal and selective provision of social services, respectively. Each of these theorists argues that his position is the right course of action given the needs of modern society.

Titmuss reaches his conclusion by applying an analytical framework that gives emphasis to the importance of community, while Friedman concludes the opposite given his emphasis on the first principle of freedom. The issue, as stated, is clearly that of choosing one over the other.

The historical argument for universal services is basically an argument for community. The underlying assumptions of this approach include:

- A recognition that many of the stresses facing families and individuals are beyond their control. They are victims of broader social and economic forces rather than the cause of their own problems.
- A belief that *all people* are at risk due to external stress and pressure caused by industrialization and urbanization.
- A recognition that because all people experience these risks, we need to respond to these collectively.

Poverty

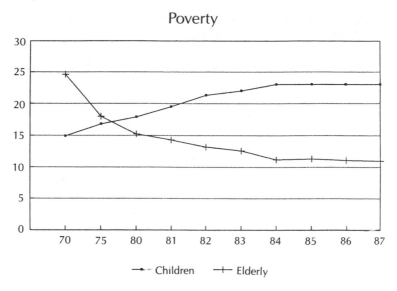

--•-- Children   --+-- Elderly

Percentages

Figure 9.1

- In responding collectively, we believe in notions of common need and shared responsibility.
- Therefore, all people with specific common need should be supported by the larger community and that support should be provided through a single system, i.e., they should be treated the same.
- Services could be viewed as entitlements and citizenship should be the primary criterion for eligibility.
- Whereas needs testing builds community, means testing is divisive and stigmatizing.
- When people believe they have a right to services, they are more likely to use them when needed; when people are made to feel they do not have a right to services, they often go without needed services.
- To respond to needs by providing different levels, types, and amounts of services, and by developing separate systems for different groups of people with common needs, is to reject belief in community.

The traditional argument for selective services is grounded in a different set of assumptions, all of which are concerned with the rights of the individual:

- Families should be viewed the same way we view economic markets, i.e., they are to be accepted as functioning optimally until proven otherwise.

- Since most of today's families and individuals can meet their own needs, to become involved in their lives would interfere with their right to privacy.
- If we were to become involved in the lives of these families, we would be, in effect, telling them that they are not capable of meeting their own needs without outside help.
- Such a patronizing approach would lead to further weakening of the family, leading inevitably to family deterioration and increased levels of dependency.
- Just as it is appropriate for the state to become involved in markets only when there is clear evidence that a market is imperfect, the state should only become involved with families when there is clear evidence of family pathology or family breakdown.
- When the state becomes involved with imperfect markets, it does so as nonintrusively as possible and for as short a period as possible. To do otherwise would permanently distort that market. So also with families. Assistance to families should be temporary and families should be encouraged to become self-sufficient and independent.
- It is important, then, to distinguish between those who need public help and those who do not.
- The most philosophically acceptable and administratively feasible way to make these distinctions is through a means test.
- While a means test may stigmatize the recipient, it guarantees that only those with need actually receive services.
- To provide services to those who do not need those services or to provide benefits or services to those who could purchase them on their own is inefficient and therefore irrational and inappropriate.

The traditional arguments outlined above force us to think in either/or terms. We choose policies that support interdependence and community or those that support independence and individualism. The problem with this formulation, however, is that as with most dichotomies, both have inherent problems. Whereas universal provision of services clearly supports notions of a more egalitarian society, it is costly. Since the world recession beginning in the early 1970s, a number of European countries with a tradition of universal services have introduced means testing for some of their benefits. A more relevant question today is not whether we should have universal or selective provision of benefits but whether it is possible to achieve the goals associated with universal services in such a way that the efficiency concerns are also addressed.

First, it is critical that the universal vs. selective argument be put into a historical context. Proponents of universal provision were primarily concerned with the dismantling of the poor law with its emphasis on providing assistance only to those who had failed. While pressure in Europe for change in the welfare state began to build in the early years of the twentieth century, it took the trauma of a world depression and a world war actually to achieve it. Unlike this country with its rhetoric of a class-free society, a society in which individuals through hard work could improve their social class, most European societies were still experiencing century-old rigid class distinctions. Furthermore, not only was an individual likely to remain a member of a particular class throughout his or her life, there was little communication between the classes. Middle and upper classes had little understanding of the widespread poverty experienced by large number of families.

World War II changed this. First, most of the military were from the working and poorer classes, and most of the domestic hardships associated with the war were felt by their children and families. The allied countries, one by one, presented their people with a vision of a new order (as Beveridge called it, a blueprint for the future), a more equal order, a fairer society, and a society with fewer class distinctions.

Some of these governments (such as the United Kingdom) were concerned with the morale of the military during the early days of defeat, in part in recognition that working and poor families were bearing the brunt of the war effort and in part because more and more middle-class and more affluent families for the first time became aware of the living conditions of the majority of people. Given this, the war-time government promised the British a broad range of entitlement progress in the area of health, housing, employment, and income maintenance. Other countries, especially those that were occupied, made similar commitments for the postoccupation era. The war created communities where previously there had been divisions. People suffered in common; they expected to share the future in common. When peace finally did come, society after society in Europe began to tear down the existing poor laws and replace them with systems providing universal services. It was a clear expression of the promises made during the war for more egalitarian societies.

However, almost 50 years have passed and many of those who vividly remembered the workhouses and other poor-law institutions that were operating through the 1930s are now elderly or dead. The majority of the population in most countries was born *after* World War II. Memories, like attitudes, do change over time. What has to be done is to separate the problems universal provision of services were to correct from the specific structures and mechanisms that were implemented.

The overall problem to be resolved was the alienation and mistrust experienced by most people living in a divided society. The desired end state was the development of a sense of community and shared responsibility. Specific problems were (1) the impact of stigmatization of the recipient under systems characterized as selective (impacts that were both psychological and behavioral and affected utilization negatively); (2) the existence of dual systems—one for the poor and another for the nonpoor; (3) an apparent aversion to offer services that would, when possible, prevent problems from occurring (e.g., retraining workers with obsolete skills) or, when that was not possible, buffer the consequences of those events (e.g., pensions for those unable to work, health insurance for those who are ill); and (4) financing mechanisms, especially fee for service, which resulted in many people not receiving services.

Kahn, as early as 1973 and later with his colleague, Kamerman (1976, 1987), offered us perhaps the most systematic and thoughtful critique of this issue. Almost 20 years ago he pointed out that even those advocates for selective provision support the need for universal services in some areas of social life, e.g., public health and public education. These areas of public social utilities, in Kahn's terminology, would probably fall under the public interest—externality rationales. For those who identify themselves as selectivists, the task is to limit these to only a minimum number of high-priority areas. Kahn, at that time, argued against the notion of a dichotomy, i.e., either universal or selective, and suggested it was more a matter of context, emphasis, and the specific policy.

In his later works with Kamerman, the issue was recast "to reflect a far more complex, subtle and sophisticated elaboration of the options" (1987: 277). They accept the need to be more efficient (at least in terms of public expenditures) but they neither discard the concept of universal services nor do they apparently argue for more selective service provision. First, they cite the work of Garfinkle (1982), who found that means testing did not produce more efficiency (the argument of the selectivists). Given this, they conclude that universal services would be preferable if the financing problem could be resolved.

Next, they explore the issue of making universal benefits taxable. There is precedence for this not only in this country with our taxing of Social Security benefits for the more affluent elderly population but in a number of other countries, especially in the area of pensions and children or family allowances. Every individual or family is treated the same at the point when they qualify for the benefit. Benefits are universal, there is no means testing, and therefore, in theory, no stigmatization. Every individual or family experiences the same tax process, i.e., all are required to submit data to the Internal Revenue Service or its equivalent. Finally, depending on total family income (which includes the dollar value of the benefit, the tax bracket, and the existing tax rates), some families will have much if not all of the benefit taken back through income taxes, others will have some of the benefit taxed, and still others will keep the total amount.

Not only would this apply to income transfers, but to any benefit, including nongovernmental in-kind benefits such as private health insurance. For example, government could conceivably pay the health insurance premiums for the unemployed and poor from revenues generated by taxing employee benefits. That portion of benefits paid for by the employer is treated as taxable.

Finally, Kahn and Kamerman extend the analysis by comparing and contrasting means testing and income testing as viable policy instruments. They conclude that means testing will always tend to stigmatize since, by definition, it involves an assessment of the total worth of the individual. Not just income is examined, but all of the individual's or family's assets must be verified. Income testing, on the other hand, would be restricted to just that—income—and would be verified through tax returns or wage statements.

This distinction is an interesting parallel to the one made in the nineteenth century between poverty and pauperism (discussed in Chapter 3). Means testing is compatible with notions of pauperism in that both evaluate the person's eligibility for services or benefits by examining every aspect of that person's life, while income testing restricts the eligibility to one area of the person's life—the amount of income he or she is able to generate:

> A policy package can be designed to permit income testing without stigma if one can build on a foundation of strong universalism and moves relatively far into the income distribution and to continue universal benefits but control costs by including such benefits as taxable income. (Kamerman and Kahn 1987:280)

This would seem to be as reasonable a way out of the dilemma as possible without radically changing our system of political economy. Government would not provide services but would guarantee to all that these services will be available. Stigma is minimized and, in the context of community, all people have equal access to a single system with each paying according to ability.

The Final Issue: The Importance of Work

The most important single criterion that shapes our system of social welfare has been and continues to be employment. Accepting the political philosophy of Bismarck, we have devised two social-welfare approaches over the past 60 years. The first ties benefits to the recipient's work history and tends to be relatively generous. The second provides a basic level of benefits to those who do not have this attachment and are still considered able to work. These benefits are relatively miserly.

It is clear that while we have, in theory, rejected the earlier poor laws, we have retained a number of their key aspects. Social welfare still plays a social-control function—a function that includes a concern for maintaining a stable, reliable, and motivated labor force and one that inculcates the need to accept authority. As it has evolved over the past two centuries, this system contains elements that reward those who meet these criteria and punish those who do not.

Given this, people in need are still placed in one of two categories. The first group, those who have retired because of age or disability, are rewarded because they have a history of working and they have contributed to the economy. In the language of the poor law, they are the "worthy poor." The second group, those who are not working and are not disabled or elderly, those who have sporadic employment histories, those who seemingly have no legitimate reason not to work, are punished. They are the "unworthy poor" and their presence is a distinct threat to the economy. By treating them harshly, by giving them less that they need to meet their needs, we are both encouraging them to become a part of the labor force and discouraging those who are working to stop.

Toward the end of Chapter 2, we introduced Friedman's discussion of this country's two basic approaches to social welfare: (1) the social-insurance model and (2) the pure-welfare model. The components of these models were excerpted in Table 2.1. In Table 9.1, we have modified Table 2.1 to incorporate some of the other key concepts used throughout this analysis.

The two basic models that are found in most Western societies include some aspects of both the institutional and residual models. As discussed earlier, social policies divide people into one of two groups: those who are experiencing problems through no fault of their own (institutional) and those who are to blame for their own situation (residual).

In those instances where the condition, problem, need, etc., is not perceived to be the fault of the individual, benefits tend to be restitutionary. Furthermore, under the institutional approach, recipients are viewed as having a right to those benefits as long as they meet the legal definition of a beneficiary. In part, these benefits are provided as a right because the beneficiary has "paid" for them while working; he or she has earned them.

Underlying the residual approach is the view that the individual who experiences problems does so by choice; he or she is not blameless. With this as a beginning point, people should not be allowed to feel too comfortable by receiving more than subsistence. Therefore, benefits cannot be restitutionary but only for maintenance at a minimum level. Recipients are not entitled to receive benefits, and means testing, rather than needs testing, is the preferred policy. Whereas programs tend to be universal when benefits are defined as rights, in means-tested programs they are selective in provision. Finally, unearned benefits carry a stigma and the process of determining eligibility and monitoring the status of these individuals and families is basically one that keeps them from receiving the benefits.

Table 9.1. Models of Social Welfare

Model	Institutional	Residual
Approach	Universal	Selective
Principle	Social insurance	Social assistance
Beneficiaries	Worthy	Unworthy
Purpose	Prevention	Curative
Objective	Restoration	Minimum standards
Employment	Earned benefits	Unearned benefits
Eligibility	Entitlement	Charity

Only by applying these concepts can we fully understand why we deal in such different ways with groups who have the same needs. In Chapter 7, we suggested that the state has made a commitment to the elderly that it has made to no other group (with the possible exception of veterans, though this is experiencing some erosion). Why was Congress willing to pass the Older Americans Act and not the Young Children Act, the Single Parent Act, the Full Employment for Young Adults Act, and so on? Are the objectives found in Title 1 of the act only appropriate to the elderly? What if we were to leave out any reference to the elderly?

- An adequate income . . . in accordance with the American standard of living.
- The best possible physical and mental health which science can make available without regard to economic status.
- Suitable housing, independently selected, designed and located with reference to special needs and available at costs . . . can afford.
- Full restorative services for those who require institutional care.
- Opportunity for employment with no discriminatory personnel practices.
- Pursuit of meaningful activity within the widest range of civic, cultural and recreational activities.
- Efficient community services including access to low cost transportation, which provides social assistance in coordinated manner and which are readily available when needed.
- Immediate benefit from proven research knowledge which can sustain and improve health and happiness.
- Freedom, independence and free exercise of individual initiative in planning and managing their own lives. (Health, Education and Welfare 1974:2-3)

It would be difficult to argue that these objectives do not apply to the nonelderly, e.g., to children, to parents (single or otherwise), to young adults, to the disabled. If these are appropriate objectives (or as it has called, a Bill of Rights for the elderly), why not extend these same objectives and rights to all by virtue of need and citizenship? These objectives are an embodiment of the principles one would find in an institutional model as described in Table 9.1. and yet only the elderly, as a group, are provided benefits within this approach. Other groups, as much in need, receive benefits that tend to be provided within the assumptions of the residual model. Why? The one difference between the elderly and the other groups is the notion that the former have earned these benefits and the others have not. While nine objectives have been listed above, we purposely left out the sixth objective:

- Retirement in health, honor, dignity, after years of contributions to the economy.

This is the one statement that is specific to the elderly. In reality, it is not an objective, but a rationale for the other objectives. The elderly are provided these benefits because they worked hard and contributed to the economy. The language is interesting. It does not say that the benefits are provided because they were paid for while working; it states that the benefits are provided because of contributions to the economy while working. The earned-rights criterion takes a subtle but important meaning, best understood within a framework of political economy. The elderly earned these benefits because they were good citizens who were willing to live within acceptable boundaries of what constituted good behavior. Unlike other groups, they were productive.

But who actually pays for these benefits? The OASDI system is a "pay as you earn" system, but each generation of retirees is actually supported by then current workers. Moreover, as discussed in Chapter 3, current beneficiaries are likely to receive significantly more than they contributed. A retiree who began paying into the system from its inception and retired in 1980, would have contributed only $14,371, assuming his or her contributions were at the maximum level. If this were doubled to reflect the employer's contributions, the retiree would have a grand total of less than $29,000. How many months did it take for the retiree to receive more than he or she paid into the system? An annuity this size would produce monthly benefits of less than $200 at 8%. In 1988, the average monthly benefit for a retired worker was over $500 and the maximum was close to $1,000. The current deduction rates are now so high that in the six years from 1981 to 1986, individuals paying the maximum were required to pay approximately $14,500. In those six years that is as much as anyone paid in the 44 years from 1937 to 1980. The benefits that retirees receive are being paid for by people who are now working.

Another example of who pays for the benefits the elderly receive is in the area of health insurance. While the percentage of general revenue (collected in the form of income taxes) used to support Part A, hospital insurance, is relatively small (approximately 10%), 75% of the funds used for Part B, physician services, comes from general revenues. In practice this has meant that taxpayers, primarily those in the labor force, are providing an average annual subsidy of $2,400 for each Medicare recipient. What complicates this is the fact that working-age adults are nearly four times as likely as the elderly to be unable to obtain medical care and more than three times as likely to have major financial difficulties because of illness.

Arguments such as the above are often misunderstood. In no way is it offered as an argument to cut back on the type and amount of benefits for the elderly. Rather, it is offered as an argument to treat the nonelderly the same as the elderly. If there is a guaranteed income policy for the elderly, there should be one for all people, whether it takes the form of a children's allowance or a negative income tax. If there is value in offering national health insurance for the elderly, there is value in offering the same coverage for the rest of the population. We base this conclusion on Watson's argument of comparative justice as discussed in Chapter 6. People with similar needs should be treated the same way.

Is this possible, given the size of the national debt and the federal deficit? Yes and no. No, if we expect government alone to provide these benefits. Yes, if we look for more realistic partnerships between industry, government, and citizens. As many European countries have demonstrated, social benefits are a part of the costs of business and therefore should be provided through industry-based mechanisms, whether these take the form of providing pensions, paying for health insurance, or providing services such as daycare. We need to deal with the problem of financing retirement benefits not after people retire but while they are working. Too many people who are working, disproportionately women and minorities, are in jobs that either have no benefits or extremely limited benefits. To wait until they retire and then to supplement minimum Social Security benefits with SSI is not the long-range solution. Moreover, strategies that involve the use of taxing benefits or introducing user fees are not, in theory, antithetical to the provision of universal services. However, individuals and families must recognize that they live in a community of people with responsibilities for each other, including as Titmuss argues, strangers. No one is totally independent.

Finally, if recipient groups are to be provided with the level of benefits needed for a reasonable quality of life, divisive strategies will have to be minimized and people will have to recognize that their individual welfare is dependent on everyone's welfare.

Perhaps Shylock's admonition was Shakespeare's attempt to offer a universal warning to societies that pit one group against another, whatever the cause. If we take some liberties with his argument and replace the words *Jew* and *Christian* with the name of any other group (e.g., children, disabled, single mothers, unemployed, homeless) we end with a disturbing scenario:

Hath not a . . . eyes? Hath not a . . . hands, organs, dimensions, senses, affections, passions? Fed with the same food, hurt with the same weapons, subject to the same diseases, healed by the same means, warmed and cooled by the same winter and summer as a . . . ? If you prick us, do we not bleed? if you tickle us, do we not laugh? If you poison us, do we not die? And if you wrong us, shall we not revenge? If we are like you in the rest, we will resemble you in that. If a . . . wrong a . . . what is his humility? Revenge. If a . . . wrong a . . . what should his sufferance be by . . . example? Why, revenge. The villainy you teach me I will execute, and it shall go hard but I will better the instruction. (*The Merchant of Venice,* Act III, Scene 1, 61–76)

If we deny mothers and children today, what guarantee do we have that they will not deny the aged tomorrow? If elderly persons argue that they have no responsibility for children, what argument do they have if the children reject any responsibility for them? If we deny support to the unemployed and homeless, what claim for support do we have if we experience unemployment and lose our homes? All of our transfer programs are built on the principle of trust, as they should be.

REFERENCES

Aaron, H. 1972. *Shelters and Subsidies*. Washington, D.C.: Urban Institute.

Advisory Council on Public Welfare. 1966. *Having the Power, We Have the Duty*. Report to the Secretary of the Department of Health, Education and Welfare. Washington, D.C.: U.S. Government Printing Office.

Anderson, M. 1971. *Family Structure in Nineteenth Century Lancashire*. Cambridge: Cambridge University Press, 1951.

Anderson, W. and Locke, H. 1964 "Trickling Down: The Relationship between Economic Growth and the Extent of Poverty among American Families." *Quarterly Journal of Economics* 78 (11): 511–24.

Arrow, K. 1951. *Social Choice and Individual Values*. New York: Wiley.

Baldwin, S. 1985. *The Costs of Caring*. London: Routledge and Kegan Paul.

Ball, R. 1971. "United States Policy toward the Elderly." Pp. 1–21 in *Care of the Elderly*, edited by A. Exton-Smith, J. Evan, and J. Grimely. New York: Academic Press.

Ball, R. 1981. "Employment Created by Construction Expenditures." *Monthly Labor Review* 12:38–44.

Bane, M. and D. Ellwood. 1983. "Slipping into and out of Poverty: The Dynamics of Spells and the Dynamics of Dependence: The Routes to Self Sufficiency." Mimeo, Harvard University, Cambridge, MA.

Banfield, E. 1955. "Notes on a Conceptual Scheme." Pp. 303–329 in *Politics, Planning and the Public Interest*, edited by M. Myerson and E. Banfield. New York: Free Press.

Banfield, E. and J. Q. Wilson. 1963. *City Politics*. Cambridge, MA: Harvard University Press.

Barber, G., S. Slavin, and S. Barnett. 1983. "Impact of Reagan Economics on Social Services in the Private Sector." *Urban and Social Change Review* 16:27–32.

239

Baumheimer, E. and A. Schorr. 1977. "Social Policy." Pp. 1453–1562 in *Encyclopedia of Social Work,* 17th edition. Washington, D.C.: National Association of Social Workers.

Benjamin, R. 1983. "In West Virginia, Recession Is a Mild Word." *Baltimore Sun,* January 30.

Berger, P. and H. Kellner. 1970. "Marriage and the Construction of Reality." Pp. 33–41 in *Recent Sociology,* edited by H. Dreitzel. London: Macmillan.

Berger, P. and J. Neuhaus. 1977. *To Empower People: The Role of Mediating Structures in Public Policy.* Washington, D.C.: American Enterprise Institute.

Bernstein, R. 1982. *The Restructuring of Social and Political Thought.* Philadelphia, PA: University of Pennsylvania Press.

Beveridge, W. 1942. *Social Insurance and Allied Services.* London: HMSO, Cmd 9663, and New York: Macmillan.

Beveridge, W. 1943. *The Pillars of Security.* New York: Macmillan.

Beveridge, W. 1944. *Full Employment in a Free Society.* London: Allen and Unwin.

Billingsley, A. "The Sociology of Knowledge of William J. Wilson: Socio-historical Context." *Journal of Sociology and Social Welfare* 16 (4):7–39.

Bolan, R. 1980. "The Practitioner as Theorist." *Journal of the American Planning Association* 46:264–74.

Bott, E. 1955. "Urban Families: Conjugal Roles and Social Networks." *Human Relations* 15:346–57.

Boulding, K. 1967. "The Boundaries of Social Policy." *Social Work* 12:3–11.

Briggs, A. 1967. "Welfare State in Historical Perspective." Pp. 25–45 in *The Welfare State,* edited by C. Schottland. New York: Harper Torchbooks.

Brim, O. 1968. "Socialization through the Life Cycle." Pp. 333–349 in *Sourcebook in Marriage and the Family,* edited by M. Sussman. New York: Houghton Mifflin.

Bronfenbrenner, U. 1974. "Developmental Research, Public Policy and the Ecology of Childhood." *Child Development* 45:1–5.

Bulmer, M. 1981. "The British Tradition of Social Administration: Moral Concerns at the Expense of Scientific Rigor." *Hasting Center Report,* pp. 35–42.

Carisse, C. 1972. "Family Values of Innovative Women: Perspectives for the Future." Pp. 35–51 in *Cross National Family Research,* edited by M. Sussman and B. Cogswell. London: E. J. Brill.

Carroll, J. 1973. "The Inevitability of the Nuclear Family." *Humbolt Journal of Social Relations* 5(2):60–66.

Coll, B. 1970. *Perspectives in Public Welfare: A History.* Washington, D.C.: U.S. Department of Health, Education and Welfare, U.S. Government Printing Office.

Council of Economic Advisors. 1964. "Poverty in America." *Monthly Labor Review* 87:285–91.

Crosland, C. 1970. *The Future of Socialism.* New York: Schocken Books.

Crystal, S. 1982. *America's Old Age Crisis.* New York: Basic Books.

Dahrendorf, P. 1976. *Inequality, Hope and Progress.* Liverpool: Liverpool University Press.

deLeeuw, F. and N. Ekanem. 1971. "The Supply of Rental Housing." *American Economic Review* 12:214–26.

deLeeuw, F. and R. Struyk. 1975. *The Web of Urban Housing: Analyzing Policy with a Market Simulation Model*. Washington, D.C.: Urban Institute.

Demos, J. 1983. "Family Home Care: Historical Notes and Reflections." Pp. 161–175 in *Family Home Care: Critical Issues for Services and Policies*, edited by R. Perlman. New York: Haworth Press.

Department of Housing and Urban Development. 1974. *Housing in the Seventies*. Washington, D.C.: U.S. Government Printing Office.

Derthick, M. 1975. *Uncontrollable Spending for the Social Services*. Washington, D.C.: Brookings Institute.

Derthick, M. 1979. *Policymaking for Social Security*. Washington, D.C.: Brookings Institute.

Dewey, J. 1939. *Theory of Valuation*. Chicago: University of Chicago Press.

DiNitto, D. and T. Dye. 1987. *Social Welfare: Politics and Public Welfare*. Englewood Cliffs, NJ: Prentice Hall.

Dokecki, P., H. Able, et al. 1986. "Scholars and Ethics: Towards an Ethically Relevant Agenda for Scholarly Inquiry into Mental Retardation." Pp. 17–37 in *Ethics of Dealing with Persons with Severe Handicaps*, edited by P. Dokecki and R. Zaner. Baltimore: Paul Brookes.

Donnison, D. 1976. "An Approach to Social Policy." *Australian Journal of Social Issues* 11(1): Supplement.

Donzelot, J. 1979. *The Policing of Families*. New York: Pantheon.

Dorfman, D. 1982. "Costs Are Dictating Business Migration from Big Cities." *Washington Post*, September 27.

Dror, Y. 1967. "The Planning Process: A Facet Design." Pp. 93–116 in *Planning–Programming–Budgeting*, edited by F. Lyden and E. Miller. Chicago: Markham.

Dror, Y. 1970. "Prolegomenon to Policy Sciences." *Policy Sciences* 1:135–50.

Dror, Y. 1971. *Design for Policy Sciences*. New York: American Elsevier.

Drucker, P. 1968. *The Age of Discontinuity*. New York: Harper and Row.

Dyckman, J. 1969. "The Practical Uses of Planning Theory." *Journal of the American Institute of Planners* 35:298–301.

Ellwood, D. 1987. *Divide and Conquer*. Occasional paper #1, Ford Foundation Project on Social Welfare and the American Future, New York.

Estes, C. and R. Newcomer, eds. 1983. *Fiscal Austerity and Aging*. Beverly Hills, CA: Sage.

Fish, G. 1978. "Housing Policy during the Great Depression." Pp. 129–142 in *The Story of Housing*, edited by G. Fish. New York: Macmillan.

Folsom, J. 1943. *The Family and Democratic Society*. New York: Wiley.

Freidmann, J. and B. Hudson. 1974. "Knowledge and Action: A Guide to Planning Theory." *Journal of the American Institute of Planners* 40:2–14.

Freire, P. 1981. *Pedagogy of the Oppressed*. New York: Continuum.

Freire, P. 1982. *Education for Critical Consciousness*. New York: Continuum.

Freire, P. 1989. *Learning to Question*. New York: Continuum.

Friedman, B. and L. Hausman. 1975. *Work and Welfare Patterns in Low Income Families*. Waltham, MA: Brandeis University Press.

Friedman, M. 1962. *Capitalism and Freedom*. Chicago: University of Chicago Press.

Friedman, R. 1968. "Models of Social Welfare." Discussion paper, Institute for Research on Poverty, University of Wisconsin, Madison.

Galbraith, J. 1958. *The Affluent Society.* New York: Penguin.

Garbarino, J. 1987. "Family Support and the Prevention of Child Abuse." Pp. 91–114 in *America's Family Support Programs,* edited by S. Kagan et al. New Haven, CT: Yale University Press.

Garfinkle, I., ed. 1982. *Income Tested Transfer Programs: The Case For and Against.* New York: Academic Press.

Garfinkle, I. 1985. "Years of Poverty, Years of Plenty: An Essay Review." *Social Service Review* 59:283–94.

Garreau, J. 1981. *The Nine Nations of North America.* Boston: Houghton Mifflin.

Gil, D. 1973. *Unravelling Social Policy.* Cambridge, MA: Schenkman.

Gilbert, N. and H. Specht. 1981. *Handbook of the Social Services.* Englewood Cliffs, NJ: Prentice Hall.

Gilder, G. 1981. *Wealth and Poverty.* New York: Basic Books.

Ginzberg, E. 1976. *The Purposes of an Economy: Jobs for Americans.* Englewood Cliffs, NJ: Prentice Hall.

Glazer, N. 1983. *Ethnic Pluralism and Public Policy.* Lexington, MA: Lexington Books.

Glick, P. 1979. "Children of Divorced Parents in Demographic Perspective." *Journal of Social Issues* 35:170–82.

Goffman, E. 1961. *Asylums.* Garden City, NY: Anchor.

Goode, W. 1975. *World Revolution and Family Patterns.* Glencoe, IL: Free Press.

Gordon, M. 1973. *The Nuclear Family in Crisis.* New York: Harper and Row.

Grabill, W. 1976. "Premarital Fertility." *Current Population, Special Series* 23(63). Washington, D.C.: Bureau of the Census.

Grad, S. 1989. "Income and Assets of Social Security Beneficiaries by Type of Benefit." *Social Security Bulletin* 52(3):4–8.

Gries, J. and J. Ford. 1932. *Housing Objectives and Programs.* Washington, D.C.: National Capitol Press.

Habermas, J. 1971. *Knowledge and the Human Interest.* Boston: Beacon Press.

Habermas, J. 1973. *Theory and Practice.* Boston: Beacon Press.

Habermas, J. 1975. *Legitimation Crisis.* Boston: Beacon Press.

Hall, M. P. 1952. *The Social Services of Modern England.* London: Routledge and Kegan Paul.

Handler, J. 1972. *Reforming the Poor: Welfare Policy, Federalism and Morality.* New York: Basic Books.

Handler, J. 1973. *The Coercive Social Worker.* Chicago: Rand McNally.

Harney, K. 1989. "Nation's Housing." *Washington Post,* January 22.

Harrington, M. 1975. *The Other America.* Baltimore: Penguin.

Harris, A. 1971. *Handicapped and Impaired in Great Britain.* OPCS, Social Survey Division. London: HMS.

Harris and Associates. 1981. *Aging in the 1980s: Americans in Transition.* Washington, D.C.: NCOA.

Hart Research Associates, Inc. 1979. *A Nationwide Survey of Attitudes toward Social Security.*

Hauser, P. 1976. "Aging and Worldwide Population Change." Pp. 58–86 in *Aging and the Social Sciences,* edited by R. Binstock and E. Shanas, New York: Von Nostrand Reinhold.

Health Care Financing Administration. 1987. "National Health Expenditures, 1986–2000." *Health Care Financing Review,* Summer: 1–35.

Health Insurance for the Aged and Medical Assistance. P.L, 89–77. 1966. Vol. 79. U.S. Statutes at Large. Washington, D.C.: U.S. Government Printing Office, pp. 286–423.

Heatherington, E., M. Cox, and R. Cox. 1977. "The Development of Children in Mother Headed Families." Paper presented at the Families in Contemporary America Conference, George Washington University, Washington, D.C., June 11.

Heller, W. 1967. *New Dimensions of Political Economy.* New York: Norton.

Helvering v. Davis, 301 U.S. 619, 641, 57, Sup. Ct. 904, 908, 81 L. Ed. 1307 (1937).

Hobbs, N., P. Dokecki, K. Dempsey, and R. Moroney. 1984. *Strengthening Families.* San Francisco: Jossey Bass.

Horton, J. 1964. "The Dehumanization of Anomie and Alienation: A Problem in the Ideology of Sociology." *British Journal of Sociology* 15:280–91.

Housing Act of 1937. P.L. 75–412. 1938. Vol. 49. U.S. Statutes at Large. Washington, D.C.: U.S. Government Printing Office, pp. 314–356.

Housing Act of 1949. P.L. 81–171. 1950. Vol. 63, U.S. Statutes at Large. Part 1. Washington, D.C.: U.S. Government Printing Office, pp. 413–444.

Housing Act of 1968. P.L. 90–448. 1969. Vol. 82. U.S. Statutes at Large. Washington, D.C.: U.S. Government Printing Office, pp. 476–611.

Humphrey, H. 1977. Cited in the *Washington Post.* May 13, p. 8.

Joe, T. and C. Rogers. 1985. *By the Few, for the Few.* Lexington, KY: Lexington Books.

Johnson, L. 1952. "The Housing Act of 1949." Pp. 194–209 in *Two Thirds of a Nation: A Housing Program,* edited by N. Strauss. New York: Knopf.

Joseph, K. 1974. "Britain: A Decadent Utopia." *The Guardian,* October 21.

Kahn, A. 1969. *Theory and Practice of Social Planning.* New York: Russell Sage Foundation.

Kahn, A. 1984. "Why a Modern Society Needs Strong and Sensitive Government." Paper presented at conference, *Measuring the Impact of Interventions: New Perspectives on Social Work Practice,* School of Social Work, Arizona State University, Tempe, May 15.

Kahn, A. and S. Kamerman. 1975. *Not for the Poor Alone: European Social Services.* New York: Harper and Row.

Kamerman, S. and A. Kahn. 1976. *Social Services in the United States.* Philadelphia: Temple University Press.

Kamerman, S., and A. Kahn. 1987. "Universalism and Income Testing in Family Policy: New Perspectives on an Old Debate." *Social Work* 32:277–80.

Kanter, R. 1978. "Work in America." *Daedalus* 107:47–48.

Keith, N. 1973. *Politics and the Housing Crisis Since 1930.* New York: Universe.

Keynes, J. 1931. *Essays in Persuasion.* New York: Harcourt Brace.

Keynes, J. 1973. *General Theory of Employment, Interest and Money.* New York: Macmillan.

Kohlberg, L. and R. Mayer. 1972. "Stages of Moral Development." *Harvard Educational Review.* 42:5–20.

Kristol, I. 1978. *Two Cheers for Capitalism*. New York: Basic Books.

Kristol, I. 1983. *Reflections of a Conservative*. New York: Basic Books.

Kuttner, R. 1984. *The Economic Ellusion*. Boston: Houghton Mifflin.

Kuznets, S. 1953. *Share of Upper Income Groups in Income and Savings*. New York: National Bureau of Economic Research.

Lammers, W. 1983. *Public Policy and the Aging*. Washington, D.C.: CQ Press.

Lampman, R. 1984. *Social Welfare Spending: Accounting for Changes from 1950 to 1978*. Orlando, FL: Academic Press.

Lasch, C. 1975. "The Family in History." *The New York Review of Books* 22: 35–38.

Lasch, C. 1977. *Haven in a Heartless World: The Family Besieged*. New York: Basic Books.

Laslett, P. 1965. *The World We Have Lost*. London: Methuen.

Laswell, H. 1951. "The Policy Orientation." Pp. 1–12 in *The Policy Sciences: Recent Developments in Scope and Methods,* edited by D. Lerner and H. Laswell. Stanford: Stanford University Press.

Laswell, H. 1970. "The Emerging Conception of the Policy Sciences." *Policy Sciences* 1:3–14.

Lemann, N. 1986. "The Origins of the Underclass." *Atlantic* 257:31–55.

Levy, M. 1966. *Modernization and the Structure of Societies*. New Brunswick, NJ: Princeton University Press.

Lewin, M. and S. Sullivan, eds. 1989a. *The Care of Tomorrow's Elderly*. Washington, D.C.: American Enterprise Institute for Public Policy Research.

Lewin, M. and S. Sullivan. 1989b. "Overview." Pp. 1–10 in *The Care of Tomorrow's Elderly,* edited by M. Lewin and S. Sullivan. Washington, D.C.: American Enterprise Institute for Public Policy Research.

Lindblom, C. and D. Cohen. 1979. *Usable Knowledge*. New Haven, CT: Yale University Press.

Lowi, T. 1969. *The End of Liberalism: Ideology, Policy and the Crisis of Public Authority*. New York: Norton.

Macbeath, A. 1957. *Can Social Policies Be Rationally Tested?* London: Oxford University Press.

MacIntyre, A. 1981. *After Virtue*. Notre Dame, IN: Notre Dame University Press.

Mannheim, K. 1940. *Man and Society in an Age of Reconstruction*. New York: Harcourt, Brace and World.

Marcus, S. 1978. "Their Brother's Keepers: An Episode from English History." Pp. 41–66 in *Doing Good: The Limits of Benevolence,* edited by W. Gaylin, I. Glasser, S. Marcus, and D. Rothman. New York: Pantheon.

Marsh, D. 1970. *The Welfare State*. London: Longman.

Marshall, D. 1969. *The English Poor in the Eighteenth Century*. New York: Kelley.

Marshall, T. 1965. *Class, Citizenship and Social Development*. New York: Anchor Books.

Marshall, T. 1972. *Social Policy*. London: Hutchinson.

Marshner, C. 1981. "The Pro-Family Movement and Traditional Values." Pp. 148–66 in *What Is Pro Family Policy?* edited by L. Kagan. New Haven: Yale University Press.

Mayer, R., R. Moroney, and R. Morris. 1974. *Centrally Planned Change.* Urbana: University of Illinois Press.

Mercer, C. 1967. "Interrelations among Family Stability, Family Composition, Residence and Race." *Journal of Marriage and the Family* 29:456–60.

Merton, R. 1957. *Social Theory and Social Structure.* Boston: Houghton Mifflin.

Meyer, J. 1989. "Retirement and Changing Demographics." Pp. 123–136 in *The Care of Tomorrow's Elderly,* edited by M. Lewin and S. Sullivan. Washington, D.C.: American Enterprise Institute for Public Policy Research.

Meyerson, M. 1956. "Building the Middle Range Bridge for Comprehensive Planning." *Journal of the American Institute of Planners* 22:58–64.

Meyerson, M. and E. Banfield. 1955. *Politics, Planning and the Public Interest.* New York: Free Press.

Miller, S. and M. Rein. 1964. "Poverty and Social Change." *American Child* 50:10–15.

Moon, M. and T. Smeeding. 1989. "Can the Elderly Afford Long-Term Care?" Pp. 137–160 in *The Care of Tomorrow's Elderly,* edited by M. Lewin and S. Sullivan. Washington, D.C.: American Enterprise Institute for Public Policy Research.

Moreau, J., M. David, W. Cohen, and H. Brager. 1962. *Income and Welfare in the United States.* New York: McGraw-Hill.

Moroney, R. 1976. *The Family and the State: Considerations for Social Policy.* New York: Longmans.

Moroney, R. 1980. *Families, Social Services and Social Policy.* Washington, D.C.: U.S. Government Printing Office.

Moroney, R. 1981. "Policy Analysis within a Value Theoretical Framework." Pp. 78–102 in *Models for Analysis of Social Policy,* edited by R. Haskins and J. Gallagher. Norwood, NJ: Ablex.

Moroney, R. 1986a. *Shared Responsibility: Families and Social Policy.* New York: Aldine.

Moroney, R. 1986b. "Family Care: Towards a More Responsive Society." Pp. 139–165 in *Ethics of Dealing with Persons with Severe Handicaps,* edited by P. Dokecki and R. Zaner. Baltimore: Paul Brookes.

Morris, R. 1986. *Rethinking Social Welfare: Why Care for Strangers?* New York: Longmans.

Morris, R., I. Leschier, and A. Withorn. 1978. *Analysis of Federally Supported Social Services: Options and Directions.* Waltham, MA: Florence Heller School, Brandeis University.

Mott, P. 1976. *Meeting Human Needs: The Social and Political History of Title XX.* Columbus, Ohio. National Conference on Social Welfare.

Moynihan, D. 1986. *Family and Nation.* San Diego: Harcourt Brace Jovanovich.

Moynihan, D. 1988. *Came the Revolution.* San Diego: Harcourt Brace Jovanovich.

Murray, C. 1984. *The Future of Social Welfare.* New York: Basic Books.

Myrdal, G. 1940. *Population: A Problem for Democracy.* Godkin Lecture, 1938. Cambridge: Harvard University Press.

Myrdal, G. 1966. *Beyond the Welfare State.* N.H.: Yale University Press.

Nagel, E. 1956. *Logic without Metaphysics.* New York: Oxford University Press.

National Association of Home Builders. *Housing America: The Challenges Ahead.* Washington, D.C.: NAHB. 1985.

Nisbet, R. 1967. *The Sociological Tradition.* New York: Basic Books.

Norton, A. and P. Glick. 1976. "Marital Instability: Past, Present and Future." *Journal of Social Issues* 32:8–12.

Novak, M. 1989. "The Enemy 'R' Us." Pp. 177–84 in *The Care of Tomorrow's Elderly,* edited by M. Lewin and S. Sullivan. Washington, D.C.: American Enterprise Institute for Public Policy Research.

O'Neill, D. 1967. "Unfinished Business of the Welfare State." Pp. 70–78 in *The Welfare State,* edited by C. Schottland. New York: Harper Torchbooks.

Orshansky, M. 1965a. "Measuring Poverty." *The Social Welfare Forum.* New York: Columbia University Press.

Orshansky, M. 1965b. "Who's Who among the Poor: A Demographic View of Poverty." *Social Security Bulletin* 28:3–32.

Orshansky, M. 1966. "More about the Poor in 1964." *Social Security Bulletin* 29:3–38.

Ozawa, M. 1982. *Income Maintenance and Work: Incentives towards a Synthesis.* New York: Praeger.

Parsons, T. 1951. "Illness and the Role of the Physician: A Sociological Perspective." *American Journal of Orthopsychiatry* 21:452–60.

Parsons, T. and R. Bales. 1955. *Family, Socialization and Interaction Process.* Glencoe: Free Press.

Phillips, A. 1958. "The Relation between Unemployment and the Rate of Change of Money Wages." *Economica* 25:283–300.

Pinker, R. 1973. *Social Theory and Social Policy.* London: Heinemann.

Piven, F. and R. Cloward. 1971. *Regulating the Poor: The Functions of Public Welfare.* New York: Vintage.

Piven, F. and R. Cloward. 1982. *The New Class War.* New York: Pantheon.

Plotnick, R. 1987. "Income Distribution." Pp. 880–888 in *Encyclopedia of Social Work,* 18th edition, edited by A. Minahan. Silver spring, MD: NASW.

Political and Economic Planning (PEP). 1937. *The British Social Services.* London: Allen and Unwin.

Poloma, M. 1970. "The Myth of the Egalitarian Family: Familial Roles and the Professionally Employed Wife." Paper presented at the Sixty-Fifth Annual Meeting of the Americal Sociological Association, Washington, D.C.

Ponsioen, J. 1962. *The Analysis of Social Change Reconsidered: A Sociological Study.* The Hague: s'Gravenhage, Mouton.

Popper, K. 1968. *The Logic of Scientific Discovery.* New York: Basic Books.

Poynter, J. 1969. *Society and Pauperism.* London: Routledge and Kegan Paul.

Preston, S. 1984. "Children and the Elderly in the U.S." *Scientific American* 251:44–48.

Pruger, R. 1973. "Social Policy: Unilateral Transfer or Reciprocal Exchange." *Journal of Social Policy* 2:283–301.

Public Welfare Amendments of 1967. P.L. 90–248. 1968. U.S. Statutes at Large. Washington, D.C.: U.S. Government Printing Office, pp. 871–921.

Radner, D. 1989. "Net Worth and Financial Assets of Age Groups in 1984." *Social Security Bulletin* 52:9–14.

Radner, D. 1990. "Assessing the Economic Status of the Aged and Non-Aged Using Alternative Income-Wealth Measures." *Social Security Bulletin* 53:2–14.

Rainwater, L. and W. Yancey. 1967. *The Moynihan Report and the Politics of Controversy.* Cambridge, MA: Harvard University Press.

Ranney, D. 1969. *Planning and Politics in the Metropolis.* Columbus, OH: Charles E. Merrill.

Rawls, J. 1971. *A Theory of Justice.* Cambridge, MA: Harvard University Press.

Rein, M. 1970. *Social Policy: Issues of Choice and Change.* New York: Random House.

Rein, M. 1976. *Social and Public Policy.* New York: Penguin.

Report of the Poor Law Commission of 1832. 1905. Cd. 2728. London: HMSO.

Report of the Royal Commission on the Poor Laws and the Relief of Distress. 1909. Cd. 4499, Vol. 3. London: HMSO.

Rice, M. 1978. "Housing in the 1960s." Pp. 348–62 in *The Story of Housing,* edited by G. Fish. New York: Macmillan.

Ridley, J. 1968. "Demographic Change and the Role and Status of Women." *Annals of the American Academy of Political and Social Sciences* 375:15–23.

Rimlinger, G. 1971. *Welfare Policy and Industrialization in Europe, America and Russia.* New York: John Wiley.

Robbins, W. 1983. "90% Jobless Rate Grinds West Virginia Coal Town." *The New York Times,* April 10.

Robinson, I. 1972. *Decision-Making in Urban Planning.* Beverly Hills, CA: Sage.

Roosevelt, J. 1988. "Don't Touch Social Security." *USA Today,* September 28.

Roper and Associates. 1976. *American Families: Changing Attitudes.*

Rothman, D. 1979. "The State as Parent." Pp. 69–96 in *Doing Good: The Limits of Benevolence,* edited by W. Gaylin. New York: Pantheon.

Rowan, P., T. Randleman, and D. Smith. 1982. "An Overview Profile of EAP's in the U.S. in 1982." *Labor-Management Journal on Alcoholism* 12:23–31.

Schnare, A. 1977. *Residential Segregation by Race in U.S. Metropolitan Areas.* Washington, D.C.: Urban Institute.

Schorr, A. 1963. *Slums and Social Insecurity.* Washington, D.C.: U.S. Department of Health, Education and Welfare.

Shorr, A. and P. Moen. 1977. "Single Parents: Public and Private Image." Paper prepared for the Task Force on Mental Health and the Family, President's Commission on Mental Health.

Schottland, C. 1963. *The Social Security Program in the United States.* New York: Appleton-Century-Crofts.

Schottland, C. 1967. *The Welfare State.* New York: Harper Torchbooks.

Schussheim, M. 1974. "Toward a New Housing Policy: The Legacy of the Sixties." CED Paper #29, Washington, D.C.

Schwartz, D., R. Ferlauto, and D. Hoffman. 1988. *A New Housing Policy for America.* Philadelphia: Temple University Press.

Schwartz, J. 1983. *America's Hidden Success.* New York: Norton.

Segre, S. 1975. "Family, Stability, Social Classes and Values in Traditional and Industrial Societies." *Journal of Marriage and the Family* 37:431–36.

Sherman, S. 1989. "Public Attitudes toward Social Security." *Social Security Bulletin* 52(12):2–16.

Silverman, A. 1971. *User Needs and Social Services.* Report prepared for the House of Representatives, Subcommittee on Housing, Committee on Banking and Currency. Washington, D.C.: U.S. Government Printing Office.

Sorokin, P. 1941. *The Crisis of Our Age.* New York: Dutton.

Stack, C. and H. Semmel. 1974. "Social Insecurity: Breaking up Poor Families." *Welfare in America: Controlling the Dangerous Classes.* Englewood Cliffs, N.J.: Prentice Hall, pp. 89–105.

Stegman, M. 1970. "The New Mythology of Housing." *Trans-action* 7:55–62.

Steiner, G. 1971. *The State of Welfare.* Washington, D.C.: Brookings Institute.

Steiner, G. 1976. *The Children's Cause.* Washington, D.C.: Brookings Institute.

Steiner, G. 1981. *The Futility of Family Policy.* Washington, D.C.: Brookings Institute.

Stoesz, D. 1985. "The Case for Community Enterprise Zones." *Urban and Social Change Review* 18:20–23.

Strauss, N. 1944. *The Seven Myths of Housing.* New York: Knopf.

Subcommittee on Executive Reorganization, House of Representatives. 1966. Pt. 9, p. 2030; pt. 11, p. 2837. Washington, D.C.: U.S. Government Printing Office.

Subcommittee on Housing and Community Development. 1975. *Evolution of the Role of the Federal Government in Housing and Community Development.* Committee on Banking and Currency, House of Representatives, 94th Congress, First Session. Washington, D.C.: U.S. Government Printing Office.

Tawney, R. 1961. *The Acquisitive Society.* London: Fontana.

Tawney, R. 1964. *Equality.* London: Allen and Unwin.

Titmuss, R. 1950. *Problems of Social Policy.* London: HMSO and Longmans.

Titmuss, R. 1958. *Essays on the Welfare State.* London: Allen and Unwin.

Titmuss, R. 1966. "Social Policy and Economic Progress." *The Social Welfare Forum.* New York: Columbia University Press.

Titmuss, R. 1968. *Commitment to Welfare.* London: Allen and Unwin.

Titmuss, R. 1971. *The Gift Relationship.* London: Allen and Unwin.

Trattner, W. 1974. *From Poor Law to Welfare State.* New York: Free Press.

Tugwell, R. 1934. "Relief and Reconstruction." *Proceedings of the National Conference of Social Work.* Chicago: University of Chicago Press.

U.S. Bureau of the Census. 1977. "Projections on the Population of the United States, 1977 to 2050." *Current Population Reports.* Washington, D.C.: U.S. Government Printing Office.

U.S. Bureau of the Census. 1984. *Money, Income and Poverty: Status of Families and Persons in the U.S. Current Population Reports,* Consumer Income Series, P-60, No. 145. Washington, D.C.: U.S. Government Printing Office.

U.S. Bureau of the Census. 1988. *Statistical Abstract of the United States.* Washington, D.C.: U.S. Government Printing Office.

U.S. Department of Health, Education and Welfare. 1968. "Health Expenditures Fiscal Years 1929–69 and Calendar Years 1928–68." *Research and Statistics Notes,* No. 18. Washington, D.C.: U.S. Government Printing Office.

U.S. Department of Health, Education and Welfare. 1974. *Older Americans Act of 1965, as Amended and Related Acts.* Washington, D.C.: U.S. Government Printing Office.

U.S. Department of Housing and Urban Development. 1974. *Housing in the Seven-*

ties: A Report of the National Housing Policy Review. HUD Publication no. HUD-PDR-64. Washington, D.C.: U.S. Government Printing Office.

Veiller, L. 1910. *Housing Reform: A Handbook for Practical Use in American Cities.* New York: Russell Sage.

Veiller, L. 1914. *A Model Housing Law.* New York: Survey Associates.

Vickers, G. 1968. *Value Systems and Social Processes.* New York: Basic Books.

Vincent, C. 1967. "Mental Health and the Family." *Journal of Marriage and the Family* 29:18–39.

Watson, D. 1980. *Caring for Strangers: A Practical Philosophy for Students of Social Administration.* London: Routledge and Kegan Paul.

Wicksell, K. 1958. *Selected Papers on Economic Theory.* London: Macmillan.

Wilensky, H. 1975. *The Welfare State and Equality.* Berkeley: University of California Press.

Wilensky, H. and C. Lebeaux. 1965. *Industrial Society and Social Welfare.* New York: Free Press.

Wilson, W. 1987. *The Truly Disadvantaged: The Inner City, the Underclass and Public Policy.* Chicago: The University of Chicago Press.

Wood, E. 1919. *The Housing of the Unskilled Worker: America's Next Problem.* New York: Macmillan.

Wood, E. 1939. "The Development of Legislation." Pp. 98–113 in *Public Housing in America,* edited by M. Schnapper. New York: H.H. Wilson.

Woods, J. 1979. "Race and Housing." Pp. 213–235 in *The Story of Housing,* edited by G. Fish. New York: Macmillan.

Woods, J. 1988. "Retirement Age Women and Pensions: Findings from the New Beneficiary Survey." *Social Security Bulletin* 51(5):3–9.

Yankelovich, Skelly and White. 1977. *Raising Children in a Changing Society.* Minneapolis: The General Mills American Family Report.

Yankelovich, Skelly and White. 1985. *A Fifty Year Report Card on the Social Security System: The Attitudes of the American Public.* Washington, D.C.: NOAC.

Young, M. and R. Wilmott. 1973. *The Symmetrical Family.* London: Routledge and Kegan Paul.

Zimmerman, C. 1974. "Family Influence upon Religion." *Journal of Comparative Family Studies* 5(2):1–16.

AUTHOR INDEX

251

SUBJECT INDEX

255

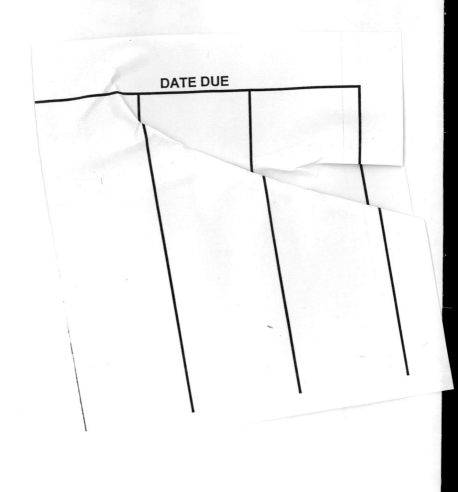

DATE DUE